Cars, Automobility and Development in Asia

T0341125

As the gravity of the world economy shifts east, many Asian countries are experiencing rapid economic and social transformations. The private automobile is a core driver of many such transformations through strategies of industrialisation; but also, crucially, as one of the ultimate individual consumer products acting as a powerful agent in restructuring social practices and urban spaces.

Cars, Automobility and Development in Asia explores the nexus between automobility and development in a pan-Asian comparative perspective. The book seeks to integrate the policies, production forms, consumption preferences and symbolism implicated in emerging Asian automobilities. Using empirically rich and grounded analyses of both comparative and single-country case studies, the authors chart new approaches to studying automobility and development in emerging Asia.

Cars, Automobility and Development in Asia is a valuable resource for academics, professionals and researchers working on automobility, cars, industrial development and development more broadly in Asia. It is also of interest to sociologists, political scientists, development researchers, urban planners and economists working on similar questions and challenges in other world regions.

Arve Hansen is Research Fellow at the Centre for Development and the Environment, University of Oslo, Norway.

Kenneth Bo Nielsen is Postdoctoral Research Fellow at the Department of Sociology, University of Bergen, Norway.

Routledge Studies in Transport, Environment and Development

Cars, Automobility and Development in Asia

Wheels of change

Edited by Arve Hansen and
Kenneth Bo Nielsen

LONDON AND NEW YORK

First published 2017 by Routledge

2 Park Square, Milton Park, Abingdon, Oxfordshire OX14 4RN
711 Third Avenue, New York, NY 10017

Routledge is an imprint of the Taylor & Francis Group, an informa business

First issued in paperback 2018

British Library Cataloguing-in-Publication Data
A catalogue record for this book is available from the British Library

Library of Congress Cataloging-in-Publication Data
Names: Hansen, Arve, editor. | Nielsen, Kenneth Bo, editor.
Title: Cars, automobility and development in Asia : wheels of change /
edited by Arve Hansen and Kenneth Bo Nielsen.
Description: Abingdon, Oxon ; New York, NY : Routledge, 2017. |
Series: Routledge studies in transport, environment and development
Identifiers: LCCN 2016011428 | ISBN 9781138930704 (hb) |
ISBN 9781315680286 (ebook)
Subjects: LCSH: Automobiles–Social aspects–Asia. | Automobile
industry and trade–Social aspects–Asia. | Economic development–Social
aspects–Asia.
Classification: LCC HE5688.A6 C37 2017 | DDC 303.48/32095–dc23
LC record available at https://lccn.loc.gov/2016011428

ISBN: 978-1-138-93070-4 (hbk)
ISBN: 978-0-367-02707-0 (pbk)

Typeset in Goudy
by Wearset Ltd, Boldon, Tyne and Wear

Contents

PART III
Contested car cultures: consuming automobility

Illustrations

Figure

Tables

Contributors

Editors

Arve Hansen is Research Fellow at the Centre for Development and the Environment, University of Oslo, Norway.

Kenneth Bo Nielsen is Postdoctoral Research Fellow at the Department of Sociology, University of Bergen, Norway.

Contributing authors

Daniel Fleming is Associate Professor Emeritus at the Department of Social Sciences and Business, Roskilde University, Denmark.

Kaoru Natsuda is Associate Professor of Development Economics at the College of International Management, Ritsumeikan Asia Pacific University, Japan, and Visiting Scholar at the Institute of East Asian Studies, Charles University, Czech Republic.

Beth E. Notar is Associate Professor of Anthropology at Trinity College, Hartford, USA.

Joshua Hotaka Roth is Professor of Anthropology and Asian Studies at Mount Holyoke College, USA.

Henrik Søborg is Associate Professor at the Department of Social Sciences and Business, Roskilde University, Denmark.

Rolando Talampas is Associate Professor at the Asian Center, University of the Philippines Diliman.

Stefan Tetzlaff is Postdoctoral Fellow based at the Centre for South Asian Studies (CEIAS), School for Advanced Studies in the Social Sciences/ National Centre for Scientific Research (EHESS-CNRS) in Paris, France.

John Thoburn is Emeritus Reader in Economics in the School of International Development, University of East Anglia, UK, and Visiting Professor at Ritsumeikan Asia Pacific University, Japan.

Peter Wad is Associate Professor at the Copenhagen Business School, Denmark.

Harold Wilhite is Professor of Anthropology and Research Director at the Centre for Development and the Environment, University of Oslo, Norway.

Acknowledgements

The idea for this book has been slowly germinating ever since we, in 2012, sat down to co-author a short, comparative article on car use and transportation in Vietnam and India for *Tvergastein*, the outstanding students' journal of the University of Oslo's Centre for Development and the Environment. At the time, co-editor Nielsen had, over a decade and a half, been observing how an ever growing array of new car models were increasingly displacing the once-iconic Ambassador car from India's roads, while co-editor Hansen had closely observed how cars had begun to squeeze out the equally iconic Honda motorbike from Vietnam's urban traffic. Clearly, a growing number of cars on Asian roads were indicative of not just a newfound economic confidence and capacity, and changing consumer aspirations, among important social strata; they were also effecting important changes in how people move around, where and how far they go, and creating new avenues for the expression of social identity and difference. From these stray observations a shared interest (and eventually this book) emerged in exploring how the car is changing Asian societies, economies and forms of politics in a context in which 'the Asian century' is upon us.

First and foremost we would like to thank our contributors, who responded so positively to our invitation to join the project. Thanks especially to Roli, who joined us late in the process and who worked overtime to meet our increasingly inflexible deadlines, and to Kaoru Natsuda for his input to the sections on Japan and Korea in the opening chapter titled 'Wheels of change'. We also extend our gratitude to the University of Oslo's Centre for Development and the Environment for hosting us while we worked on this book. A warm thanks to the entire team at Routledge for responding so munificently to our initial book proposal, and for taking a keen interest in the progress of the project over the last 18 months.

The chapter by Kenneth Bo Nielsen and Harold Wilhite titled 'The rise and fall of the "people's car": middle-class aspirations, status and mobile symbolism in "New India"' was originally published in *Contemporary South Asia* in 2015 (see www.tandfonline.com/loi/ccsa20#.VrteYfl97IU). We are grateful to Taylor and Francis for their kind permission to include it in this book.

Part I
Introduction

1 Wheels of change

Cars, automobility and development in Asia

Arve Hansen and Kenneth Bo Nielsen

The private car is one of the most powerful commodities to emerge from the technological progress of the last centuries. The relative freedom, comfort and convenience associated with owning a car have become central to expectations of development and modernity worldwide. The private car is, perhaps, the closest we get to a truly global 'blueprint of modernity', and increases in car ownership ratios are among the most predictable changes in consumption patterns resulting from economic growth and increasing affluence (see Medlock and Soligo 2002). The automobile industry has, in turn, played a central role in the history of both capitalism and (albeit to a lesser extent) socialism, and is a defining part of the regionalising and globalising production processes of contemporary capitalism.

After decades of rapid economic growth in the Asian region, the car is entering Asia at full speed, rapidly displacing or replacing other modes of transportation, most notably in the large urban conglomerations. While a few East Asian countries – particularly Japan and South Korea – are long-established leading players on the global car scene, new Asian countries are joining the race for a piece of what Drucker (1946) famously labelled 'the industry of industries'. The growing number of cars on Asian roads simultaneously indexes a newfound economic confidence, altered modes of industrial-technological production and capacity, new forms of urbanisation, and rapidly changing consumer aspirations and practices among important social strata, first and foremost the emerging middle classes. Yet in spite of these visible trends – and barring the several studies of the emergence and consolidation of the auto industry in key Asian economies (for example Doner 1991; Gallagher 2006; Wad 2009; Shimokawa 2013; Natsuda *et al.* 2015) – the role of the car in contemporary 'emerging' Asia has received little academic attention. *Cars, Automobility and Development in Asia* is an attempt to give the car the attention we think it deserves in Asian development, in a context in which Asia is not just home to half the global population, but also to some of the world's largest, and fastest growing, economies. The chapters in this book, individually and collectively, seek to chart new ways in the study of automobility and development in emerging Asia through an integrated perspective that incorporates the policies, production forms, labour regimes, consumer aspirations and symbolism that are implicated in Asian automobilities. The questions we examine are: What role does the car play in different Asian economies? How does the car industry figure in Asian economic development? Why are cars so popular, why do people buy them, and how do they drive them? What potential and actual consumer aspirations and identities do they tap into, and how do they impinge on the everyday lives of Asians in different contexts? We address these, and related, questions through a combination of comparative multi-country and in-depth single-country case studies covering India, China, South Korea, Thailand, Malaysia, Indonesia, the Philippines, Vietnam and Japan, thereby engaging with both the already mature capitalist countries, as well as some of the most rapidly growing Asian economies. What these countries all have in common is that they, although to very different degrees (see Table 1.1), produce cars within their national borders.

The chapters that follow take the reader through the dense traffic of Manila and Hanoi; onto the shared Japanese road; inside the Indian Tata Nano; and to Chinese auto expos and drag racing; and they analyse the car industry as a site for policy making, labour organising, industrial evolution, and nationalist aspirations. In the remainder of this introduction we contextualise these overarching questions and cases, before we present a brief overview of the book's contents.

Cars: yesterday, today and tomorrow

Although a wide range of innovative horseless carriages predated it – from Cugnot's three-wheeled *fardier à vapour* in 1769 to the rather explosive early British steam cars – the modern motor car as we know it is broadly considered an invention by Karl Benz and Gottlieb Daimler in Germany towards the end of the nineteenth century. The 'age of the car' properly started when sales 'soared' and Benz, in 1894, sold a full 136 vehicles (Parissien 2013). Later, France became the global centre of car production, with Armand Peugeot as one of the early pioneers producing bicycles, tricycles and, eventually, automobiles. In the early twentieth century Peugeot produced over 10,000 vehicles per year, with strong competition from other pioneers, such as the Renault brothers. But it was Henry Ford's assembly lines that paved the way for modern mass production. His Model T Ford became the first 'global car' and the first car that cost less than the average annual wage (Parissien 2013).

Adolf Hitler was inspired by Henry Ford when setting things in place for the production of the German 'people's car', the Volkswagen. But it would nevertheless take a long time before Europe would catch up with the US again, even if European countries remained important automobile producing countries throughout the twentieth century. In 1960 the largest shares globally of the automobile industry were represented by the US (with more than 50 per cent of total production), followed by Germany, the UK, France, Italy and Canada (Dicken 2011). Since then, the gravity of the world economy has been shifting eastwards and so has automobile production, even if that development seemed very unlikely around 1960. Just as there was a time when no one expected that the US would emerge as the leading car manufacturer in the world (Parissien

2013), certainly no one expected Japan to later do the same. As Ha-Joon Chang (2008) writes, when Toyota – originally a manufacturer of textile machinery – in the late 1950s tried to sell its 'Toyopet' cars in the US, it was a major failure and had to be withdrawn from the market. Producing cars was at the time largely seen as something that should be left to the already developed countries, with little room for new actors.

Yet a few East Asian countries were to prove these predictions wrong. The automobile industry played a central role in the successful industrialisation of Japan and South Korea in particular, the early forerunners in Asian car production. Toyota and Nissan were both established in the early 1930s, and even if World War II delivered a serious blow to the Japanese car industry, the role played by Japan as an emergency supplier for the US Army after the outbreak of the Korean War in 1950 facilitated a quick recovery (see for example Flink 1988). In the decades that followed, protective industrial policies provided fertile ground for the Japanese car industry to expand, both at home and abroad. Today, Toyota, Nissan, Honda and Suzuki all figure in the top ten of the world's largest producers of passenger cars (see Table 1.2) and are well-known car brands the world over.

South Korea joined the league of leading car nations later, following the implementation of the country's first automotive industrial policy in the 1960s. In the 1970s Korean companies such as Hyundai and Daewoo successfully linked up with leading multinational producers, and in 1976 the first Korean-designed vehicle was manufactured (Auty 1994). Again, while no one could have predicted that the small Hyundai auto repair shop would later evolve into a leading auto producer (Chang 2008), South Korea had in fact been producing trucks and cars for 20 years before it started exporting them (Amsden 2001). Hyundai is today the world's third largest manufacturer of passenger cars.

Asia now accounts for more than half the total manufactures of cars globally. As is to be expected, the growth has been most spectacular in China, where 23.5 million new cars hit the road in 2014 alone (OICA 2015a), a number that is expected to climb to more than 30 million within the next few years. This corresponds roughly to every adult citizen of a large European country acquiring a new car every year, a number that is truly staggering in both relative and absolute terms. In fact, Chinese car production alone represented approximately a quarter of the total global production in 2014 (OICA 2015b). But, as Table 1.1 shows, a range of other Asian countries are also emerging as car producers – particularly India, Indonesia and Thailand, but also Malaysia, the Philippines and Vietnam. And, as Table 1.2 illustrates, we find a full 16 Asian motor vehicle manufacturers in the global top 25.

Car manufacturing plays a central role in the economic development aspirations of Asia's late-industrialisers, but the significance and impact of cars extend far beyond the spheres of industrial production and policy. Millions of new cars are registered every year all across Asia and, in a region otherwise known for its diverse streetscapes of motorised and non-motorised vehicles on two, three or four wheels, the private car is rapidly taking the driver's seat in the fields of

Table 1.1 Production, sales and motorisation rates in South, East and Southeast Asian car producing countries

Country	Automobile production (2014)	Total new vehicle sales (2014)	Cars per 1,000 inhabitants (2013)
China	23,722,890	23,491,893	91
Japan	9,774,665	5,562,887	603
South Korea	4,524,932	1,661,868	394
India	3,840,160*	3,176,763	20
Thailand	1,880,007	881,832	208
Indonesia	1,298,523	1,208,019	77
Malaysia	596,600**	666,465	397
Taiwan	379,223	282,130	312
Pakistan	146,130**	146,882	15
Philippines	77,628	269,492	35
Vietnam	48,871	133,588	21
Bangladesh	536	51,900**	4

Source: compiled by authors based on OICA statistics (2014, 2015a, 2015b).

Notes
Total new vehicle sales includes all four-wheeled vehicles.
*   Missing numbers for BMW, Mercedes, Audi and JLR.
** OICA estimate.

Table 1.2 The leading Asian motor vehicle manufacturers and their global ranking in 2014

Global rank	Group	Country	Total production*
1	Toyota	Japan	10,475,338
4	Hyundai	South Korea	8,008,987
6	Nissan	Japan	5,097,772
8	Honda	Japan	4,512,769
9	Suzuki	Japan	3,016,710
13	SAIC	China	2,087,949
15	Changan	China	1,447,017
16	Mazda	Japan	1,328,426
17	Dongfeng	China	1,301,695
18	Mitsubishi	Japan	1,262,342
19	BAIC	China	1,115,847
20	Tata	India	945,113
21	Geely	China	890,652
22	Fuji	Japan	888,812
23	Great Wall	China	730,570
24	FAW	China	623,708

Source: compiled by authors based on OICA statistics.

Note
* The number includes LCV, HCV and heavy buses.

urban planning and middle-class aspirational consumption. As several chapters in this book show, cars greatly impact on how people move around and where and how far they go, and they create new avenues for the expression of social identity and difference. Thus, while some scholars have started discussing the emerging 'post-car system' in the mature capitalist countries (Dennis and Urry 2009), most consumers in Asia have in fact only just entered the age of the automobile.

Automobility

As we indicated above, while the car is certainly a technical-mechanical construct, it is also a social and cultural phenomenon. The modern petrol-powered car took the world by storm, and in Europe and the US became a central symbol in popular culture, tapping into powerful cultural dreams of adventure and freedom (Featherstone 2004) to emerge as key 'toys' (Hagman 2010) through which these dreams are realised. Both film and literature have reflected and generated a passion for cars that extends well beyond their functional use value as means of transportation. Some cars, like some motorcycles, in many cases have their own 'cultures' (see Miller 2001), and some become – at least for a while – national icons, such as Ford's Model T, the German Beetle, the Mini in the UK, and the Ambassador in India (Sardar 2002). Yet as popular symbols, cars may also be highly polysemic and ambiguous. In the erstwhile Soviet Union, for example, the powerful message that a privately owned and privately used car conveyed about individualism and consumption gave it a more conflictual position, even though the Soviet Union developed a large automobile industry of its own (see Siegelbaum 2008). In this book, Notar describes a comparable scenario in China under Mao. This polysemic quality is today perhaps most evident in how the car is upheld as one of the most important threats to global environmental sustainability among environmentalists, even as it remains a central organising principle for consumer aspirations worldwide, as a vehicle that promises a more comfortable life and symbolises upward social mobility.

The car also has profound impacts on how societies are organised, and on the geography and sociality of everyday life. Like all objects, cars too demand context (Appadurai 1986), but the context requirements of motorised transportation in the material form of infrastructure are remarkable and perhaps unprecedented in terms of scope and scale. Cars, most obviously, require roads, but also bridges, car-carrying ferries, mechanics, roadside hotels and restaurants, petrol stations, parking space, traffic police, insurance companies, engineering colleges, and a large oil and iron industry, to name but a few. This context is realised to different degrees in different settings. Cars, in turn, are agentive in shaping spaces and places in novel ways; suburbanisation, drive-ins, and large shopping malls designed for bulk shopping are just some examples of the spatial impacts of cars. Although these phenomena will vary in form and extent, they as a rule emerge wherever cars are a dominant means of transportation. These, and related, impacts of car use and car production simultaneously construe 'the car' as an inherently political site of contestation, informed by often pro-car policy-making and a naturalisation of private automobility in planning processes (see Paterson 2007), while also being subject to sometimes intense popular protests demanding restrictions on car use. Even the earliest of automobiles had led to the imposition of political restrictions because of the perceived danger they represented to public safety – a man waving a red flag was, for instance, required to walk in front of the early British steam cars (Parissien 2013) – but today, popular demands tend to coalesce around environmental concerns, or to find expression in pro-cycling or anti-car movements around the world. The fact that some of the largest Asian cities are also among the most heavily air-polluted in the world, and that the private car to a significant extent contributes to increasing levels of air pollution, has led to the introduction of a few new policy measures intended to restrict car use in, for example, New Delhi, Singapore, Tokyo and Beijing. But, as Notar's chapter shows with particular reference to Beijing, in many Asian cities the transition to a pattern of urbanisation where the private car is the dominant mode of transportation is well and truly over.

For a decade and a half, 'automobility' has been gaining popularity in the social sciences as a concept that captures this wider social and material position of the car. With the 'mobilities turn', or the consolidation of the 'new mobilities paradigm' (Sheller and Urry 2006), this field has produced an impressive array of research, often transdisciplinary in orientation and applying innovative, often mobile methods (Sheller 2011; Sheller and Urry 2006). Several important studies of cars and automobility have critically interrogated the almost taken-for-granted status of 'the car' as the quintessential embodiment of automobility. Scholars have successfully worked to show how cars are, as we alluded to above, embedded in larger 'systems' (Urry 2004) or 'regimes' (Böhm *et al.* 2006) in which factors such as infrastructure, industries, socialities, policies and power work together to project and sustain the car as the ideal, modern and liberating artefact that fulfils core human desires for autonomy, freedom and mobility. According to Urry's well-known definition (2004, 27), 'automobility can be conceptualized as a self-organizing autopoietic, non-linear system that spreads world-wide, and includes cars, car-drivers, roads, petroleum supplies and many novel objects, technologies and signs'. In this system of automobility, the car-driver no longer figures as an autonomous individual in search of freedom, but rather emerges as a 'hybrid assemblage of specific human activities, machines, roads, buildings, signs and cultures of mobility' (Urry 2004, 26).

Much of the existing research on automobility and the social and political dimensions of car ownership and driving has been predominantly focused on European and North American contexts, and in spite of an emerging literature (see for example Edensor 2004; Giucci 2012; Butler and Hannam 2014; Fischer 2014; Monroe 2014; Broz and Habeck 2015), the rise of 'Asian automobilities' beyond automobile industrial development has attracted limited scholarly attention. It is part of the ambition of this book to fill this research gap through empirically rich and grounded analyses of the nexus between cars, automobility and development across a variety of Asian settings. Several chapters find inspiration in debates about automobility, and show the utility of thinking along these lines in the context of emerging Asia. But while they thus reinforce the idea that the 'system of automobility' may be universalising in nature insofar as it appears to spread across the globe in tandem with tectonic economic shifts, the Asian experience that is captured in the chapters that follow illustrates that it does not lead to any immediate uniformity across contexts and domains. If anything, the chapters bring out an extraordinary diversity and variation in terms of, for instance, industrial policy making (Thoburn and Natsuda, Tetzlaff, Hansen), labour organising (Wad), forms of mobility and ways of driving (Roth, Hansen, Talampas, Notar), and aspirational car consumption (Nielsen and Wilhite, Hansen, Fleming and Søborg).

When seeking to bring out this diversity, it has been important to us to suspend for a while the overt expression of anti-car sentiments that have otherwise been common in many previous accounts of cars, written particularly from an environmental or ecological perspective. We adopt this approach not to belittle crucial scholarly efforts to politicise automobility. Indeed, a key contribution of the wave of recent critical scholarship on automobility has been to unmask the nexus of power relations – at both economic, political and symbolic levels – that operates to sustain the 'hegemonic project' (Böhm *et al.* 2006, 6) of automobility that privileges the car over other, alternative means of moving the self in both social and geographical space (see also Paterson 2007). This is no mere exercise in academic deconstruction, but rather a crucial step towards denaturalising the car's privileged position; and it expresses an emancipatory desire to politicise automobility (Böhm *et al.* 2006, 4) in order to better identify and promote viable mobility alternatives that are currently located at the margins of power, but which may eventually unsettle the current ecologically unsustainable and coercive automobility regime, which subordinates other mobilities (Urry 2004, 26–28). This search for a post-car mobility system (Urry 2004; Dennis and Urry 2009) – in academia as well as outside of it – is clearly crucial, and cars obviously do represent a fundamental environmental problem. But, as we seek to untangle and understand the nexus between cars, development and automobility in emerging Asia, it is necessary to take the composite phenomenology of the car – its manufacture, uses, connotations, and implications – seriously, even if it leads us to grapple with experiences and insights that may sit uncomfortably with our own views on global sustainability and social justice. Thus, while the explosion in global car ownership propelled by Asian consumers is justifiably at the core of environmental concerns surrounding the 'rise of the South', the chapters in this book rather seek to bring out how, for the majority of the Asian population, the car remains a symbol for and embodiment of a desired future (Hansen and Nielsen 2014).

Outline of the book

All chapters in this book locate themselves at the interstices of supply and demand, i.e. production and consumption, even as they take one or the other as their empirical starting point. In section two, the chapters start from an exploration of the industrial side of the Asian car boom, a phenomenon that has for long interested scholars working on the car in Asia. They survey the macrodynamics of car production and state policies in select Asian countries, and examine, in a longitudinal perspective, the role of the car industry as a driver of economic development and industrial aspirations in an increasingly globalised Asia. The contributions focus both on the history of policy and planning, but also on the nexus between the car industry and labour organising, and the role of new, globalised accumulation strategies. The chapters in the third section, in contrast, start from an exploration of car consumption and driving practices to show how the rise of the car in Asia has transformed consumer desires and habits, and restructured social practices and urban spaces across a range of scales.

The first chapter in the second section titled 'Driving development: car industries and national development' is by John Thoburn and Kaoru Natsuda. Thoburn and Natsuda analyse automobile industrial development in Southeast Asia and compare and contrast the ways in which especially Thailand, Malaysia and Indonesia, but also the Philippines and Vietnam, have tried to promote the development of their automotive industries. Examining the policies behind the Association of Southeast Asian Nations (ASEAN's) rapid automotive development, they focus on industrial policies and the changing policy space under World Trade Organization (WTO) rules, which different countries have navigated more or less successfully. Japan has played a crucial role in the development of the Asian automobile industry, and Thoburn and Natsuda consider the role played by Japanese auto manufacturers, and the attitudes of Japanese actors towards ASEAN policy making.

Producing cars demands labour, and historically the auto industry has represented an important sector for labour organising. In his chapter, Peter Wad examines the extent to which the Asian automotive industry has provided a platform for independent and powerful trade unionism in a region otherwise known for supressed and relatively weak unions. Through a comparison of Korea, Malaysia, Thailand and the Philippines, Wad carefully documents the significant variations between the different countries, even if the growing consolidation of Japanese-led production networks that dominate domestic production may eventually alter the terrain on which labour struggles are carried out.

Stefan Tetzlaff seeks to fill a significant gap in our understanding of the emergence of the perhaps lesser known Indian automobile industry, debunking the popular myth that India's automobile industry was stagnant during the early post-independence decades. While the yoke of British colonialism certainly stifled the emergence of a domestic Indian car industry, the early five-year plans adopted after independence aimed to strategically develop auto manufacturing and its associated industries through protective measures, an invitation to which key domestic players responded positively. Although the industry lagged behind that of more mature capitalist countries, Tetzlaff shows that some regions of India saw substantial new developments in auto manufacturing at an early stage.

While India now has one of the largest automobile industries in the world, including a number of key domestic players, the growth of the auto industry in Southeast Asia has mainly been driven by foreign investments and the production of foreign brands. Malaysia, however, is an exception as it is the only country in the region boasting a truly national car project. Daniel Fleming and Henrik Søborg take a closer look at the Proton, Malaysia's national car project, and trace its many ups and downs over the past several decades. Examining the many challenges the project has faced, they consider particularly the attempts to develop a new skill formation culture, as well as the future prospects of Proton in a market increasingly defined by global and regional competition and trade liberalisation. Fleming and Søborg also analyse car consumption among the domestic middle class – with very high car ownership ratios compared to overall income levels, Malaysia provides an interesting case study of the role of cars in middle-class lifestyles and consumer aspirations.

Fleming and Søborg's concluding reflections thus gradually move us from the domain of industrial production and into the domain of consumption and everyday life, which are the analytical focal points for the chapters in the third section, titled 'Contested car cultures: consuming automobility'. The chapters in this section approach the car from the point of view of consumption and consumer preferences. They analyse the car as a driver of new social imaginaries and desires among sections of Asia's expanding upwardly mobile middle classes, and unpack the link between historically produced infrastructure; car marketing strategies and symbolism; and consumer aspirations for 'the good life'. Although these 'new middle classes' in many Asian countries still constitute only a fragment of the total population, they are a numerically significant population group nonetheless – were, for example, 'middle class China' and 'middle class India' to secede from the rest of their respective countries, both would in all likelihood make it into the top ten of the world's most populous nations.

This section starts in Vietnam, famous not so much for its cars but for the very high levels of motorbike ownership. Arve Hansen argues that the rapid motorisation of Vietnam's streets can be understood as part of the larger socioeconomic transformation the country has undergone since the market reforms, known as *doi moi*. Examining both Vietnam's industrial aspirations – from the successful motorbike industry to the struggling 'spearhead' automobile industry – and everyday mobility practices in Hanoi, the chapter takes a closer look at both the 'motorbike revolution' and the rapidly emerging automobility. Hansen finds motorbikes and cars, as well as their associated industries, to be symptomatic of both Vietnam's economic development trajectories and the ideological shifts following reforms. Although the motorbike remains the king of the road in Vietnamese cities, the rapidly increasing levels of car ownership may, Hansen argues, signal the start of a new mobility era in 'the land of the motorbike'.

While Hanoi is famous for its rather unruly traffic, overall mobility remains relatively good. Manila is a different story. Here, Rolando Talampas analyses the city's contemporary mobility challenges as a metaphorical Filipino *via crucis*.

By analysing the historical trajectories of the famous jeepney and the tricycle, as well as how cars are now taking over as the preferred means of increasingly private and privatised mobility, he provides unique insights into the history of mobility in the capital city of the Philippines.

Japan is a leading car producing and car consuming country. Toyota is now one of the leading automobile manufacturers in the world and has played a central role in the development of automobile industries in most of the other countries covered in this book. Against this backdrop, Joshua Hotaka Roth proceeds to ask new questions about the relationship between infrastructure, the built environment and driving practices in the Japanese context. Based on observations and interviews he analyses the paradox of a decline in both accidents and fatalities precisely where the infrastructure has been *least* modified, that is, where cars must share the road with bicycles, pedestrians and other modes of transportation. Based on this analysis he explores the question of whether the shared street, often viewed as inherently dangerous and an underdeveloped form of infrastructure, may actually have had a positive impact on Japanese driving behaviour. Roth's findings could be an important inspiration for urban planners and policy makers in other Asian contexts.

China's rapid development since Deng Xiaoping's economic reforms is having profound impacts in the rest of the world as China is now the world's largest producer of cars. Beth E. Notar discusses how the meanings of the car have shifted over time in China, as well as how the car has now completely outcompeted the bicycle, for which Beijing was once so famous. She analyses the political and economic factors that have shaped this transition to automobility, as well as the profound changes in urban space, place and public health this transition has contributed to. Through interviews with Chinese car owners she highlights the particular temporal transformations involved in Chinese automobility, from traffic jams to drag racing.

Kenneth Bo Nielsen and Harold Wilhite bring us back to India, where the development of the ultra-cheap Tata Nano attracted global attention. This 'Indian people's car' was widely predicted to revolutionise the Indian car market, but now, eight years after it was launched, the Tata Nano has barely made an impact and is now widely regarded as a failure. Nielsen and Wilhite offer a detailed case study of the rise and fall of the Tata Nano, mapping out the changing popular expectations and symbolic imaginaries that in India attach to the car as a means to mobility and as an object of identity and social status. They argue that the Nano failed neither because it was a mediocre car, nor because it remained economically out of reach for most Indians. Rather, Nielsen and Wilhite show that its insertion into the lower ranks of a powerful status hierarchy of identity-defining objects precluded it from adequately tapping into new and hegemonic forms of consumer aspiration in middle class India.

In combination, the ten chapters in *Cars, Automobility and Development in Asia* offer rich and stimulating accounts that seek to engage with a large set of issues pertaining to policy, production, planning and consumption in the context of the rapid rise of cars in emerging Asia.

While we have deliberately aimed for a broad thematic coverage, we do not pretend to have offered an exhaustive account of any of these matters. Indeed, no single edited volume will be capable of capturing the diversity of the Asian experience with cars across all domains and national contexts. And, during the years ahead, an entirely new set of pertinent research questions are likely to emerge as new focal points for empirical research. For example, while the majority of Asian car owners still reside in the larger cities, the car may take on new meanings and roles once it starts to properly make its way into rural settings. And, as Asia increasingly plays a leading role in the global economy – and as the Asian middle classes continue to grow – new countries in the region are likely to emerge as global leaders in innovative automobile development. We therefore hope the reader will see this book not as offering the final word on the implications of the rise of the car in Asia, but as an invitation to further comparative research on the many different and shifting implications of the Asian car boom, including the economic, social and cultural 'lives' of cars in different Asian settings.

References

Amsden, Alice. 2001. *The Rise of 'the Rest': Challenges to the West from Late-industrializing Economies*. Oxford: Oxford University Press.

Appadurai, Arjun. 1986. Introduction: Commodities and the politics of value. In *The Social Life of Things: Commodities in Cultural Perspective*, edited by Arjun Appadurai, 3–63. Cambridge: Cambridge University Press.

Auty, Richard M. 1994. Sectoral targeting: Auto manufacture in Korea and Taiwan. *Journal of International Development* 6 (5): 609–625.

Böhm, Steffen, Campbell Jones, Chris Land and Mat Paterson. 2006. Conceptualizing automobility: Introduction: Impossibilities of automobility. *The Sociological Review* 54: 1–16.

Broz, Ludek and Joachim Otto Habeck. 2015. Siberian automobility boom: From the joy of destination to the joy of driving there. *Mobilities* 10 (4): 552–570.

Butler, Gareth and Kevin Hannam. 2014. Performing Expatriate Mobilities in Kuala Lumpur. *Mobilities* 9 (1): 1–20.

Chang, Ha-Joon. 2008. *Bad Samaritans: The Guilty Secrets of Rich Nations and the Threat to Global Prosperity*. London: Random House Business Books.

Dennis, Kingsley and John Urry. 2009. *After the Car*. Cambridge: Polity.

Dicken, Peter. 2011. *Global Shift: Mapping the Changing Contours of the World Economy*. Los Angeles: Sage.

Doner, Richard F. 1991. *Driving a Bargain: Automobile Industrialization and Japanese Firms in Southeast Asia*. Berkeley: University of California Press.

Drucker, Peter F. 1946. *Concept of the Corporation*. New York: John Day.

Edensor, Tim. 2004. Automobility and national identity: Representation, geography and driving practice. *Theory, Culture & Society* 21 (4/5): 101–120.

Featherstone, Mike. 2004. Automobilities: An introduction. *Theory, Culture & Society* 21 (4/5): 1–24.

Fischer, Johan. 2014. Islamic mobility: Car culture in modern Malaysia. *Journal of Consumer Culture*. Doi: 10.1177/1469540514531683.

Flink, James J. 1988. *The Automobile Age*. Cambridge, MA: MIT Press.

Gallagher, Kelly S. 2006. *China Shifts Gears: Automakers, Oil, Pollution, and Development*. Cambridge, MA: MIT Press.

Giucci, Guillermo. 2012. *The Cultural Life of the Automobile: Roads to Modernity*. Austin: University of Texas Press.

Hagman, Olle. 2010. Driving pleasure: A key concept in Swedish car culture. *Mobilities* 5 (1): 25–39.

Hansen, Arve and Kenneth Bo Nielsen. 2014. Cars of future past in Vietnam and India. *Tvergastein* 4: 72–79.

Medlock, Kenneth B. and Ronald Soligo. 2002. Car ownership and economic development with forecasts to the year 2015. *Journal of Transport Economics and Policy* 36 (2): 163–188.

Miller, Daniel. 2001. Driven societies. In *Car Cultures*, edited by Daniel Miller, 1–33. Oxford: Berg.

Monroe, Kristin V. 2014. Automobility and citizenship in interwar Lebanon. *Comparative Studies of South Asia, Africa and the Middle East* 34 (3): 518–531.

Natsuda, Kaoru, Kozo Otsuka and John Thoburn. 2015. Dawn of industrialisation? The Indonesian automotive industry. *Bulletin of Indonesian Economic Studies* 51 (1): 47–68.

OICA. 2014. World Vehicles in Use. www.oica.net/wp-content/uploads//total-inuse-2013.pdf (accessed 11 February 2016).

OICA. 2015a. Registrations or sales of new vehicles – all types (2005–2014). www.oica.net/wp-content/uploads//total-sales-2014-21.pdf (accessed 11 February 2016).

OICA. 2015b. World motor vehicle production by country and type. www.oica.net/wp-content/uploads//Total-2015-Q2.pdf (accessed 11 February 2016).

Parissien, Steven. 2013. *The Life of the Automobile*. New York: St. Martin's Press.

Paterson, Matthew. 2007. *Automobile Politics: Ecology and Cultural Political Economy*. Cambridge: Cambridge University Press.

Sardar, Ziauddin. 2002. The Ambassador from India. In *Autopia: Cars and Culture*, edited by Joe Kerr and Peter Wollen, 209–218. London: Reaktion Books.

Sheller, Mimi. 2011. Mobility. *Sociopedia.isa*. Doi: 10.1177/205684601163.

Sheller, Mimi and John Urry. 2006. The new mobilities paradigm. *Environment and Planning A* 38 (2): 207–226.

Shimokawa, Koichi. 2013. *Japan and the Global Automotive Industry*. Cambridge: Cambridge University Press.

Siegelbaum, Lewis H. 2008. *Cars for Comrades: The Life of the Soviet Automobile*. Ithaca: Cornell University Press.

Urry, John. 2004. The 'system' of automobility. *Theory, Culture & Society* 21 (4/5): 25–39.

Wad, Peter. 2009. The automobile industry of Southeast Asia: Malaysia and Thailand. *Journal of the Asia Pacific Economy* 14 (2): 172–193.

Part II

Driving development

Car industries and national development

2 Comparative policies for automotive development in Southeast Asia

John Thoburn and Kaoru Natsuda

The five automotive producers of ASEAN – the Association of Southeast Asian Nations – have seen their vehicle output grow rapidly in recent years. As Table 2.1 shows, over the period 2000–2014, the output of the Philippines and Malaysia grew less rapidly than that of the other producers in relation to world production, though in Vietnam the rapid growth was from a lower base.

Despite their slightly similar output levels in 2014, however, the Philippines and Vietnam are very different cases. The Vietnamese started their industry in the 1990s, whereas the Philippines' industry dates back as far as that of Malaysia and Thailand. The growth of Thailand, ASEAN's best automotive performer, is understated in Table 2.1 in the sense that if we took the period from 2000 to 2013, before the country's political turmoil and subsequent military coup in 2014, its output rose almost six-fold. In this chapter we shall ask what policies lay

Table 2.1 Total vehicle production, 2000 and 2014

	Numbers of vehicles			Growth (%) 2013–2014
	2000	2014	2014/2000	
Thailand	411,721	1,880,007	4.57	−23.5
Indonesia	292,710	1,298,523	4.44	7.6
Malaysia	282,830	596,000	2.11	−0.8
Philippines	41,840	77,628	1.86	16.5
Vietnam	6,862	41,500	6.05	1.4
Japan	10,140,796	9,774,558	0.96	1.5
South Korea	3,114,998	4,524,932	1.45	0.1
Taiwan	372,613	379,223	1.02	12.0
India	801,360	3,840,160	4.79	−1.5
China	2,069,069	23,722,890	11.47	7.3
World	58,374,162	89,747,430	1.54	2.6

Source: OICA (2015), Production Statistics 1998–2015, www.oica.net/2015-production-statistics/.

Notes

2014 production figures for the Philippines for all vehicles are contentious: they are shown variously for 2014 on the OICA website as 77,628 units and 106,938 units. We also obtained a figure of 86,218 units from the Chamber of Automotive Manufacturers of the Philippines for total 2014 vehicle production (interview 6 February 2015).

behind ASEAN's rapid automotive development.[1] We consider first the rationale for industrial policy, and then look at the region's initial attempts to develop automotive production through import substitution and the various countries' policies towards, and success at, attracting foreign investment. We ask how the countries have been able to carve out 'policy space' under the World Trade Organization's rules from 2000 that try to outlaw previously popular policies such as local content (LC) requirements. As Table 2.1 indicates, Japan's domestic automotive production declined over the 2000–2014 period, but its production overseas, particularly in Asia, increased. We look at the attitudes of the Japanese foreign investors who are so important in shaping the development of the industry in the region, whom we have interviewed extensively, and we draw where appropriate on literature both in English and in Japanese. We focus principally on the three main automotive producers – Thailand, Indonesia and Malaysia – with some additional discussion of the Philippines and the newest producer, Vietnam. We do not cover the motorcycle industry.

Industrial policies

Industrial policy involves governments attempting to shift the economy towards activities they regard as more dynamic at a faster rate than market forces alone will bring about (Rodrik 2004; UNIDO 2013, ch.7). The automotive industry is often seen as a vital stage in industrialisation, when the economy can move beyond labour-intensive activities like textiles towards products requiring more complex technology and engineering skills. Such more advanced industrialisation requires firms and other economic actors to accumulate new industrial capabilities, and governments can aid this process (Cimoli *et al.* 2009, ch.1). Since the Second World War there have been many changing fashions in industrial policy. Interventionist industrial policies – and particularly trade policies related to industrialisation, principally import-substituting industrialisation (ISI) – were strongly favoured in the early period after the war when many Southeast Asian countries were gaining political independence; they fell out of favour under the influence of neoliberal 'Washington Consensus' (WC) views of the 1980s and early 1990s, and have now made a substantial comeback in recent years as the 'market fundamentalist' views of the WC have disappointed (Stiglitz 1998; Thoburn 2016). Active industrial policy has characterised, to varying degrees, the development of the automotive industry in all our five countries. All have a history of ISI, developing the industry behind high tariff walls; even the late starter Vietnam has chosen this way of beginning. All have been influenced to some extent by the trade liberalisation policies advocated by international agencies in the 1990s, though the ASEAN Free Trade Area, AFTA, under which tariffs on vehicles for the original ASEAN four producers were reduced to zero in 2010 (Fourin 2015, 120–121), has probably been a greater force for trade liberalisation (Rasiah 2005). These producers have also been affected by the stricter controls on foreign investment policy and trade-related industrial policy instituted by the WTO in the 2000s.

Early history: import substitution based on foreign investment

The three largest ASEAN producers – Thailand, Indonesia and Malaysia – all started their automotive industries by using import substitution policies to attract foreign investment to serve the domestic market. Thailand started in 1960–1962 under a general investment promotion programme with policies not specific to the motor industry. It set tariffs on completely built up (CBU) imports of passenger vehicles (PVs) at 60 per cent, while kits of components from which cars could be assembled (CKDs, completely knocked down kits) attracted import duty of only 30 per cent. These differential rates raised the effective rate of protection (ERP) – that is, protection on value-added – on the local assembly of motor vehicles substantially beyond the 60 per cent indicated by the nominal tariff (Greenaway and Milner 1993, 79–80). The figures for commercial vehicles (CVs) were 40 per cent for CBUs and 20 per cent for CKDs. Thailand actually banned imports of CBU passenger cars from 1978 to 1991. Even in the late 1980s, when exports had started, according to Kaosa-ard (1993), CBUs remained banned for PVs under 2300 cc, while the tariff on larger capacity PVs was 300 per cent, with CKD kits at 112 per cent, generating extremely high ERPs.

Similarly to Thailand, Malaysia started its automotive industry in the 1960s, with even heavier initial tariff protection, and by the mid-1970s had seven foreign assembly plants, and a further five soon after. Since Malaysian production had only reached 100,000 vehicles by 1980, the industry suffered from its multiplicity of plants, which could not achieve economies of scale.[2]

Indonesia started its automotive industrialisation much earlier, with its first foreign plant built by General Motors of the US in 1928, but this was assembly of a rather notional kind, merely assembling 'kits' of two pieces, with an annual output of only 6,000 vehicles (Sato 1992). Assembly of CKD kits did not start until after the Second World War (Witoelar 1983, 18). GM was nationalised by the regime of President Sukarno, and in the 1960s annual vehicle output was only around 2,000 per year (Hansen 1971, 38). Following the change of government bringing President Soeharto to power in 1967, foreign investors were invited back into Indonesia. Astra, an Indonesian ethnic Chinese-owned company, formed partnerships for vehicle assembly with Japanese companies including Toyota. Like Thailand, Indonesia protected its automotive industry with a ban on finished vehicle imports from 1974 until 1993. Even in the 2000s, tariffs on passenger vehicle imports into Indonesia were at least 45 per cent,[3] and not much reduced thereafter (Natsuda et al. 2015, 58).

The Philippines motor industry, like Malaysia and Thailand, has a long history of import substituting policies. Under the country's first Progressive Car Manufacturing Program in the early 1970s, a ban was imposed on the import of vehicles. Tariffs of 100 per cent were levied on CBUs up to 1980, then cut to 70 per cent in 1981 and 50 per cent in 1982 (Aldaba 2008, 5). One interesting aspect of the Philippines is that its motor components industry dates back to the 1970s, but this industry is mainly oriented towards exports, nowadays mainly of wiring-harnesses (one of the most labour-intensive of automotive components) and manual transmissions, particularly within the ASEAN region and to Japan; local vehicle producers could absorb only a very small percentage of the output.[4]

Vietnam's (commercial) automotive industry dates back to the early 1990s, though there was earlier state production of military vehicles (Hansen 2016). Four-wheeled vehicles are much less in evidence compared to motorcycles in Vietnam than in other countries in ASEAN (Truong and Nguyen 2011), and the road network, especially in major cities, is still hardly conducive to car use at present. There has been heavy tariff protection. Even when Vietnam was preparing to join the WTO – which it did in 2007 – its tariff commitment on CBU imports was 83 per cent, the highest among its commitments (Truong and Nguyen 2011, 276).

Moves towards liberalisation

Moves towards liberalisation in Thailand were associated with a new government that came to power in 1991 after a military coup. The ban on vehicle imports was lifted and tariffs were cut to well under 100 per cent on both vehicles and CKD kits, though CKDs had lower duties still (thus raising effective protection). Restrictions on foreign ownership were lifted (from 49 per cent to 100 per cent) if foreign firms would export 60 per cent of their production, together with some tax exemption measures for exporting. Following these new policies, several American automotive manufacturers and their suppliers decided to set up in Thailand.

Liberalisation was pushed in part because the dominant Japanese auto companies in Thailand appeared to be gaining large economic rents with government collusion, at the expense of Thai consumers (Ikemoto 1994, 173). At the time these criticisms particularly focused on the impacts of LC requirements, which we deal with later. However, LC requirements were, in the event, not reduced under the liberalisation measures, and indeed reached a peak of 72 per cent for diesel pick-up trucks (about which more later) in 1994 (Natsuda and Thoburn 2013, 14–15).

Thailand's attempts to promote exports had started in the 1980s, with domestic production exceeding domestic sales for the first time in 1988, but it was the 1997 Asian financial crisis that proved the main driver of Thailand's later export success by forcing automotive firms to look for sales beyond the depressed domestic market. While the post-crisis exports in a sense continued along a path already set out by policy since the late 1980s (Doner and Wad 2014), the post-crisis export expansion was a step-change. Immediately prior to the crisis exports were well under 100,000 units, but ten years later, in 2008, they had reached 800,000.

Moves towards trade liberalisation in Malaysia came later, and were principally associated with the country's obligations under AFTA. While Thailand, Indonesia and the Philippines had moved automobiles out of AFTA's temporary exclusion list with a view to cutting tariffs to within the range 0–5 per cent by 2003, Malaysia postponed until 2005, though it did finally reduce automotive tariffs to zero by the final 2010 deadline along with the other original ASEAN members of AFTA. Malaysia's hesitation about trade liberalisation sprung from problems with protecting its national car, Proton (see also Fleming and Søborg, this volume), discussed later, and with its export performance.

Indonesia, like Thailand, had had an import ban on CBUs, imposed gradually to cover the whole country over the period 1969–1974 (Sato 1992, 340–341); this ban was removed in 1993. In Indonesia's case, strong liberalisation pressure came following the 1997 Asian financial crisis. The crisis affected Indonesia more severely than other ASEAN members; trade and other liberalisation were required as conditions for loan assistance from the International Monetary Fund and the World Bank.

In the Philippines there was a feeling among our interviewees that the country had liberalised its automotive trade regime more than its ASEAN competitors: during the 1990s tariffs on passenger cars (CBUs) were reduced from 50 per cent to 30 per cent by 2000. In contrast, in Indonesia passenger vehicle tariffs were as high as 40–60 per cent in the mid-2000s (Natsuda *et al.* 2015, 58), at least 50 per cent in Thailand for much of the 2000s (Natsuda and Thoburn 2013, 421), and in 2004 Malaysian CBU tariffs ranged from 80 to 200 per cent, then mostly 50 per cent in 2005 and not reduced to 30 per cent until 2006 (Natsuda *et al.* 2013, 133).[5] These quoted tariffs are MFN tariffs; under AFTA the Philippines cut tariffs from 5 per cent in 2004 to zero in 2010 (Aldaba 2008, 6).

As noted earlier, Vietnam retained high tariffs on CBU imports up to and following its WTO accession in 2007. With regard to AFTA, there is a breathing space before it encounters full competition from other ASEAN countries, as its tariffs fall from 50 per cent in 2015 gradually to zero in 2018.[6] Industry interviews and officials in Hanoi in 2015 were of the opinion that imported models of cars typically were 20 per cent cheaper than locally produced equivalents, so the reduction in tariff protection is a serious threat. Threats from imports from China are limited at the moment by a 50 per cent tariff imposed as an exception under the ASEAN-China FTA.

Foreign investment, national cars and local participation

In the global automotive industry industrial concentration has been increasing, both among assemblers and among their large first tier suppliers of components (Humphrey and Memedovic, 2003). This reflects the need to engage in massive research and development expenditure to develop new models and stay competitive. Nolan (2012, 25–26) estimates that for producing a mass market car, an annual output of five million vehicles is required, and even the luxury car makers BMW and Mercedes each produce over a million cars a year. These figures are significantly greater than the minimum efficient size of plants (see note 2), and they help explain why even developed countries like the UK, previously with a diverse locally owned motor industry, have ones now in the hands of a small number of foreign automotive multinationals.

While Thailand has accepted what seems to be the inevitable, and has an automotive industry dominated by foreign assemblers – Japanese assemblers alone accounted for between 80 and 90 per cent of domestic production, domestic sales and exports in the early 2010s – Malaysia has tried hard since the mid-1980s to develop a national car, the Proton. In the early 2010s Proton and the semi-national (Japanese majority-owned) Perodua – set up later, in 1993, as a joint venture between Daihatsu and various local companies and state agencies – accounted for about 60 per cent of domestic sales. Originally developed in partnership with Mitsubishi from Japan, Proton broke from Mitsubishi in the mid-1990s. Proton started exporting in the late 1980s, with the UK becoming its biggest market; yet from an export of 21,000 units in 1994 its UK sales had fallen to under 1,000 units by 2010 (Fourin 2011, 74). Subsequently, even with its trade preferences in the AFTA market, Malaysia's total world exports were tiny: US$306 million compared to US$6.6 *billion* for Thailand and US$2.1 *billion* for Indonesia. Malaysia's exports of CVs were a negligible US$14 million[7] compared to US$10.6 billion for Thailand.

The protection on the automotive sector under Malaysia's ISI programme was high – an ERP of over 250 per cent in 1989 according to Alavi (1996, 174) – and Proton enjoyed additional protection over and above this. Such protection included lower rates of import duty on CKD kits than for other automotive assemblers, and various other non-tariff measures and tax preferences (Natsuda *et al.* 2013, 122).

Indonesia also tried experimenting with a national car in the late 1990s, in cooperation with a Korean assembler, but the methods used were so blatantly anti-competitive that the countries of its competitors were able successfully to protest to the WTO, and the venture went bankrupt. However, Malaysian press reports in early 2015 record that Indonesia's new president, Joko Widodo, has been to Malaysia to discuss exploratory measures to set up cooperation with Proton to start another Indonesian national car,[8] following which an agreement has been signed with an Indonesian company run by a political figure to study how to set up the operation.[9] At present, Japanese manufacturers account for over 90 per cent of Indonesian automotive production.

In the Philippines, too, there has been a long history of foreign investment, though US producers are much less important now than in the past, Ford – the last one – having left in 2012. Now it is Japanese assemblers who predominate, with Toyota as the largest (Rosellon and Medalla 2011, 280). Japanese cars make up approximately three quarters of domestic sales (including imports), and Korean cars another 13 per cent.[10]

Among Vietnam's 20 vehicles assemblers, Japanese firms predominate, but Ford and Hyundai are present too, though foreign assemblers are often in joint ventures with Vietnamese partners. Denso, the mega-supplier components firm from Japan, also is there.[11] However, the largest assembler, Toyota, in 2006 was reported as having a capacity of only 20,000 units, too small to achieve economies of scale (see note 2). Vietnam, echoing the Philippines in earlier years, has attracted Japanese foreign investment – Sumitomo and Yazaki – in wiring-harnesses for export, using its cheap but high quality labour. In 2013, Vietnam was exporting US$888 million of 'parts and accessories for motor vehicles' (HS 8708), of which 44 per cent was to Japan.[12]

Deepening the industrial structure: local content requirements and mandatory deletion policies in the pre-WTO era

Although in principle a developing country could start an automotive industry by developing the production of labour-intensive components, such as wiring-harnesses, and progress later to assembly, in practice virtually all developing countries have started with assembly (Auty 1994). Assembly can be done on the basis of imported CKD kits. Then, in principle, as local capabilities develop, more and more of the thousands of components that make up a vehicle can be produced locally. Typically components have been importable into ASEAN producers at lower rates of import duty than finished vehicles. As a result, prospective local component suppliers have faced more import competition than assemblers, while – as mentioned earlier – the assemblers enjoyed a higher ERP than the nominal tariff on imported vehicles indicates. However, some countries (in ASEAN, particularly the Philippines and Vietnam) have developed labour-intensive automotive component exports, based on foreign investment, somewhat independently of domestic motor vehicle assembly.

An important aim of all of our producers has been to raise the LC of production by producing more components domestically. This has been done typically by stipulating LC requirements and/or by having mandatory deletion policies (that is, specifying that certain items must be deleted from imported CKD kits and therefore be produced locally). For example, Malaysia introduced a Mandatory Deletion Programme in 1980, under which 30 specified automotive parts had to be deleted from imported CKD kits. Later, in 1992, a Local Material Content Program required the achievement of LC targets of between 45 and 60 per cent by 1996, with penalties in the form of import restrictions for non-compliance (Tham 2004, 55).[13] Thailand introduced an LC requirement of 25 per cent in 1975. This followed its first automotive specific industrial policy in 1971, which placed limits on the number of vehicle models and minimum new capital investment requirements (Adachi 1987; Kaosa-ard 1993). Indonesia, having banned CBU imports nationwide in 1974, introduced a mandatory deletion programme (for commercial vehicles) in 1976. In 1993 a new policy-deregulation package, while ending the ban on importing CBU vehicles, encouraged localisation by cutting tariffs and luxury tax on imported components depending on the level of LC and the type of vehicle. This new system was more flexible than the mandatory deletion policy because it gave assemblers the choice of which components to delete from imported CKD kits (Aswicahyono *et al.* 2000).

Opinions about LC requirements differ sharply among commentators on the automotive industry. Writing with regard to Thailand, the ASEAN country

with the deepest automotive industrial structure, Wad (2009, 190) and Athukorala and Kohpaiboon (2010, 13) appear to regard the end of LC requirements
simply as a desirable move towards economic liberalisation, while Hassler (2009,
2236–2237), for example, thinks they played a key role in the 1990s in
increasing the territorial embeddedness of the automotive industry in Thailand.
LC requirements offer an apparently easy opportunity for 'backward linkage'
investment for import substitution to increase the net revenue from exports (or
reduce the foreign exchange expenditure on imports). However, it has long
been known that such backward linkages sometimes can be 'bad' ones, in
the sense of not generating new activities that would become eventually
internationally competitive without protection or subsidy (Thoburn 1973). We
have argued that the LC requirements, at least in Thailand, have had quite
positive effects in stimulating deepening of the automotive industrial structure
though not necessarily in promoting the growth of locally owned firms (Natsuda
and Thoburn 2013, 2014), an issue to which we now turn.

Complicating the issue of how to raise LC is the fact that for many decades
past the production of vehicles in virtually all major producing countries has
been organised into a series of tiers, following practices developed originally in
Japan at a time when US and European automotive production was more
vertically integrated (Thoburn and Takashima 1992, ch.5). Nowadays the first
tier suppliers are themselves large multinational companies, like Denso from
Japan or Bosch from Germany. Such 'mega-suppliers', especially where Japanese
auto assemblers are involved, organise the lower tiers of generally smaller firms,
thus relieving the assemblers of part of the responsibility of 'governance' in the
automotive global value chain (Humphrey and Memedovic 2003). When policy
is directed towards developing more LC, it is often such suppliers that set up in
the producing country, sometimes pushing existing local firms into lower tiers,
and conditioning the development of lower tier suppliers. While lower tier
suppliers may well have new technology transferred to them by the higher tier
suppliers, we have found the lower tier suppliers may also be restricted in what
new activities they are allowed to develop.

As Table 2.2 indicates, the Thai network of supporting firms is more
extensive than in Indonesia and Malaysia. Only 23 per cent of the first tier firms
are purely Thai, but over half are *either* purely Thai or Thai-majority owned.

Well-known researchers on the Thai automotive industry have suggested
that indigenous Thai suppliers of components have experienced little upgrading,
and that the Thai government has been happy to leave the development of the
automotive industry generally to foreign investors (Doner 2009, ch.7; Lauridsen
2009). Nevertheless, there are certainly instances of Thai firms developing well
as suppliers (Ueda 2007, 2009). Indeed, some indigenous Thai suppliers have
expanded on a regional basis: probably the most famous, Thai Summit, has
made foreign investments in Malaysia, Vietnam, Indonesia and China with a
view to supplying components to Japanese and other assemblers (Fourin 2012,
220–221). In Indonesia typically 20–40 per cent of suppliers for the major
Japanese vehicle assemblers will be purely local firms, though the local share is

Table 2.2 Assemblers, parts suppliers and employment in ASEAN automotive producers

Country	Number of assembly plants	Number of parts suppliers	Employment in assembly and parts
Thailand	16*	2390	400,000
Indonesia	20	850	115,000
Malaysia	15	690	47,947
Philippines	16	265	60,000**
Vietnam	20	300+	n/a

Sources: Natsuda *et al.* (2015, 54), and interviews in the Philippines and Vietnam.

Notes
* The number of assemblers in Thailand in 2010, Malaysia 2011, Indonesia 2012, Philippines and Vietnam 2015.
** Parts only.

understated since other local firms are in joint ventures with Japanese component makers, on which we do not have a more detailed breakdown. Domestic investment in the automotive and parts sector, however, is very low: in 2012 it was equivalent to only 3.2 per cent of the investment being made by foreigners (Natsuda *et al.* 2015, 62).

In Malaysia's case the issue of LC has been closely related to the promotion of its affirmative action programme to help ethnic Malays and other indigenous people (collectively known as *Bumiputera*) improve their economic position in relation to Malaysian ethnic Chinese and Indians, and in relation to foreigners (Segawa *et al.* 2014). Not only has the production of the Proton car itself been used to assist *Bumiputera* into industrial employment, but the Malaysian government has also promoted a network of local parts suppliers ('vendors') who are *Bumiputera*. Of Malaysia's 690 vendors (see Table 2.2), probably only about 30 per cent were foreign or foreign-majority owned, and the rest are either wholly local or majority-local. However, as an empirical study by Rasiah (2009) has suggested, Malaysia's industrial policy to promote local auto parts suppliers (see also Fleming and Søborg, this volume) did not succeed in upgrading their technological capabilities, partly due to the lack of external competition. Similarly, Otsuka and Natsuda (2015) in their analysis of total factor productivity in the Malaysian automotive industry argue that 'the policies to protect the domestic producers from international competition and to favour *Bumiputera* firms seem to have adverse impacts on productivity'.

In the Philippines too, LC requirements were used extensively. They were introduced first in the early 1950s and finally abandoned in 2003 (Aldaba 2008, 1). The producers of the major components that are now important exports are Japanese rather than local companies, though there are also large numbers of small local firms. However, it is claimed that the import content of the production of these export components is very high and that they generate few backward linkages to local firms (Aldaba 2008, 16–17). Compared even to Malaysia's 600 suppliers, the Philippines has some 265 suppliers, of which 90 are in the top tier – of which 60 per cent are joint ventures, 30 per cent foreign and 10 per cent purely local.[14]

In Vietnam, there are probably only about 300 second and third tier suppliers, mostly local but including some foreign from Taiwan. One major motor manufacturer had 18 firms as its first tier suppliers.[15] Given the small size of the market at present, with per capita incomes still very low (see Table 2.3) and with high taxes and fees on cars, not only can assemblers not reap economies of scale themselves but the size of their demand for components would make it hard to attract their component suppliers to establish themselves.

However, as noted earlier, some labour-intensive component production has started for export, not only wiring-harnesses but also batteries and some other items. The Vietnamese government announced LC targets, but without effective policies to enforce them (Hansen 2016).

Responses to new WTO rules and trade liberalisation under AFTA

WTO rules and local content policies

LC policies have become illegal in the 2000s under the WTO's TRIMS (trade-related investment measures) agreement, as have several other trade-related industrial policies.[16] As we have argued elsewhere (Natsuda and Thoburn 2014), there were fears that these new WTO rules would seriously restrict the 'policy space' of developing country governments to intervene in their economies to accelerate industrial development. In the event, the ASEAN automotive industry shows that skilful construction of policies can circumvent these difficulties to a considerable extent while staying – at least broadly! – within WTO rules.

Thailand complied with TRIMs in 2000, as had Indonesia in 1999, while Malaysia complied in stages up to 2004. Note, however, that as free trade under AFTA had been established, LC becomes more important than in the past in the sense that exports from one ASEAN country to another are subject to rules-of-origin as to the ASEAN content of production. While the use of the free

Table 2.3 GDP per head, and population, in ASEAN automotive producers, 2013

Country	US$	US$ (PPP)	Population (million)
Malaysia	10,430	22,530	29.7
Thailand	5,340	13,430	67
Indonesia	3,580	9,270	249.9
Philippines	3,270	7,840	98.4
Vietnam	1,740	5,070	89.9

Source: World Bank, wdi.worldbank.org/table/1.1.

Note
PPP is purchasing power parity.

trade possibilities of AFTA has not been fully taken up by many exporting firms within ASEAN, the motor industry's take-up of market access under AFTA has been relatively high.[17]

Thai automotive policy under the WTO has been strongly connected to its policy of picking product champion vehicles – types of vehicle whose domestic production would be encouraged by policy irrespective of ownership. Under the Thai Board of Investment's 'New Automotive Investment Policy' in early 2002, one-ton pick-up trucks – a vehicle already very popular in the Thai domestic market – together with their supporting components industries became the first product champion.

The development of the first product champion is often associated with the government of Thaksin Shinawatra's (2001–2006) plan to make Thailand into a regional automotive hub (initially to be called the 'Detroit of Asia'); but even after Thaksin was overthrown by a military coup in 2006, the new government selected a second product champion in 2007, the Eco-car. The government has given consumers an incentive to buy these champions by charging lower rates of excise tax on them than on other vehicles, and has given firms (including foreign firms) the incentive of corporate tax exemption. Interestingly, and apparently WTO-compliant (both in terms of TRIMS and 'national treatment'), a car has to meet various LC stipulations before it can qualify as an Eco-car (Natsuda and Thoburn 2014, 14).

While Thailand has been able to give selective help to its automotive industry without openly flouting WTO rules, Malaysia's position is more ambiguous. Selective help to the country's national car, Proton and its vendors, is likely to go against the WTO's 'national treatment' provision, and so Malaysia has relied on policies which implicitly take into account that the LC for Proton is higher than that of its competitors in Malaysia.

Indonesia had been forced to liberalise its automotive policies prior to 2000 as a result of International Monetary Fund (IMF) conditionality and the World Bank structural adjustment programme following the country's difficulties after the 1997 Asian financial crisis. The changes included the abolition of the incentive system for LC, referred to above, and a reduction of import tariffs (Hale 2001, Nomura 2003). In 2006 an interesting new scheme was introduced to encourage LC, the incompletely knocked down (IKD) scheme. Lower tariffs were set for imported parts than for CKD parts, with a particular aim of encouraging the importation of subcomponents for local assembly, rather than importing the complete final component. This addresses the issue of the high indirect import content of cited LC ratios on a CKD basis, which conceal the import content resulting from imported subcomponents of components assembled locally. GAIKINDO (2010) estimates the LC of various models, presumably calculated on a CKD basis, ranging from 21 per cent for a 3-series BMW (which is simply assembled locally from a full CKD kit), to over 70 per cent for several Toyota and over 80 per cent for some Daihatsu models. Import duties for most kinds of passenger vehicles, and all sedans, were 40 per cent on complete vehicles, 10 per cent on CKD kits and 7.5 per cent on IKDs.[18]

Similarly to Thailand's second product champion, the Eco-car, the Indonesian government in 2009 decided to encourage the development of a small, environmentally friendly vehicle, the Low Cost Green Car (LCGC).[19] Demand for the LCGC is stimulated by the government's exempting it from luxury tax, although, unlike Thailand, Indonesia did not offer special incentives to firms in the automotive sector. Also, the Thais tried to target the local production of higher value components such as engines in exchange for tax incentives. The IKD system is to be used to calculate the local content of the LCGC. Incentives for higher local content will be offered in the form of reductions in the luxury tax according to the LC ratio.[20] Interestingly, while Indonesian economic growth has slackened since 2012, LCGC sales have expanded and exports of the LCGC have started, beginning with the Philippines.

The Philippines, as noted earlier, abandoned LC requirements in 2003, but without the subsequent attempts of the larger vehicle producing countries in ASEAN to increase LC by indirect means. Vietnam has not attempted to use excise taxes, or any other effective policy measure, to increase LC.

Trade liberalisation

As we have noted, trade liberalisation in the Southeast Asian automotive producing countries has been strongly driven by AFTA, although domestic considerations (as in Thailand) or pressure from the multilateral agencies (as in Indonesia) have been drivers too. ASEAN trade liberalisation also facilitates regional sourcing. For example, Toyota Indonesia is said to buy its steering systems from Malaysia, its transmissions from the Philippines and its engines in Indonesia.[21]

In the Philippines, the tariff cutting under AFTA has been accompanied by a sharp increase in import competition, with the share of imports in total domestic sales rising from an average of 11 per cent during 1999–2003, to 44 per cent in 2006 and 48 per cent in 2007 (Aldaba 2008, 24). In 2012, it was estimated that of total domestic sales, 60 per cent were of imports. It was estimated that a locally assembled vehicle would cost 14 per cent more than its equivalent imported from Thailand, due primarily to production volumes too small to reap economies of scale, and the inadequacy of the local supplier base.[22]

The Philippines domestic production has also been adversely affected by competition from second hand car imports. Though notionally banned, they can be imported indirectly via the country's free port zones (Aldaba 2008, 4–5). Indeed, the Philippines is the country most affected more generally by import competition in the automotive sector. Vietnam is also seriously threatened by import competition under AFTA, but its tariff reductions will be progressive, falling from 50 per cent in 2015 to 40 per cent (2016) and 30 per cent (2017) before going to zero in 2018.

An additional factor has been the role of Economic Partnership Agreements (EPAs) with Japan, to which all five producers belong.[23] These EPAs include moves towards freer trade, with automotive tariffs between, for example, Indonesia and Japan due to fall to 5 per cent by 2016.[24] These moves have been partly designed to facilitate the relocation of production from Japan to individual Southeast Asian countries with the idea of exporting back to the Japanese domestic market as well as acting as an export platform to other countries both within and outside ASEAN. Yet even for Thailand, the country with the largest automotive exports, exports of passenger vehicles (HS 8703) to Japan in 2013 only accounted for 7 per cent of exports under that HS heading,[25] compared to 23 per cent to Australia,[26] 16 per cent to Indonesia and 10 per cent to the Philippines (and 4 per cent to Malaysia). Similarly, of Indonesia's US$2.1 billion dollars of passenger vehicle exports, only a little under 7 per cent went to Japan, with both Thailand and the Philippines being more important export destinations. The similarity in importance of the Japanese market between Thailand and Indonesia may change somewhat in future, however – with the relative importance of Japan for Thailand increasing – as production of LCGCs in Indonesia and Eco-cars in Thailand expands, unless affected in Thailand by political turmoil.

Another aspect of the EPAs with Japan is that in addition to their provisions for freer trade, they also contain important technical assistance, such as the Malaysia-Japan Automotive Industries Cooperation scheme (MAJAICO) under the Malaysia-Japan EPA (under which automotive tariffs were reduced to zero in 2015). MAJAICO is a scheme to transfer technology and skills to Malaysian component suppliers (and, implicitly, often to *Bumiputera* suppliers). Our interviewees suggest MAJAICO is likely to be more successful than a somewhat similar programme in Indonesia because of the greater commitment of the Malaysian government to it and the lack of a policy in Indonesia to enhance the capabilities of local suppliers.

Conclusions and prospects

This overview of the automotive industry in five ASEAN countries has identified a number of key policy themes. We now conclude by discussing these in turn.

Policies vs market size and market growth

One issue that emerges, particularly based on recent Indonesian experience, is that although policies can influence the plans of automotive producers – whether favourably as in Thailand or negatively as in Malaysia – the prospects of rapid growth of the domestic market can be a more significant influence. As one assembler in Jakarta commented, the opportunity to achieve economies of scale in production is much more important to profits than are tax incentives from government. Domestic incomes – at US$3,580 per head in 2013 (in current US$, see Table 2.3), and perhaps US$10,000 in the capital Jakarta – had reached a level when motorisation becomes feasible and people switch from riding motorbikes to cars. On the basis of the domestic market expansion, expected production will grow rapidly. Although some exports are planned, it would be domestic market growth that would be central.

Another factor is the maturity of the domestic market. Of the three main ASEAN automotive producers, Malaysia has grown much more slowly since 2000 than either Thailand or Indonesia, and the contrast between Malaysia and Indonesia is the more striking because they produced similar numbers of vehicles in 2000 (see Table 2.1). This is, in part, a reflection of the greater maturity of the Malaysian domestic automotive market: in 2014 there were 405 motor vehicles per 1,000 people, which was like the figure for Korea (406), rather than those of Thailand (232), Indonesia (83), Philippines (35) and Vietnam (22), and closer to that of developed market economies, where the ratio is often over 500.[27] Malaysia's failure to export, of course, has been an additional issue, which we return to below.

The foreign investment context of policy

Foreign investors, overwhelmingly Japanese, dominate the automotive industries of all the ASEAN countries except – to some extent – Malaysia. These investors are not only influenced by policy towards foreign investment but by all policies relating to the industry. Here the contrast between such investors' views of Malaysia and of (at least pre-coup) Thailand is striking. The Japanese automotive assemblers we have interviewed tend to have a rather negative view of Malaysian policy, and decline to do more than service the domestic market, strongly preferring the policies of Thailand. Malaysia's attempts to go it alone with Proton have not only produced a relatively inefficient operation, but have failed after some initial successes (when the company was still linked to Mitsubishi) to develop exports of its main national car. Recently there has been talk of Proton linking again to a multinational Japanese assembler, Honda,[28] but we await events.

Import substitution, trade liberalisation and exports

All the ASEAN automotive producers started their production in domestic markets heavily protected from import competition. Some degree of import liberalisation was driven by the sense that it was generating excessive profits for assemblers (Thailand), or by international agencies (Indonesia in the late 1990s), but the main driving force has been the AFTA, the ASEAN Free Trade Area. Only Vietnam does not yet face zero tariffs on vehicle imports from its ASEAN neighbours. Exports have been driven less by explicit policy and more by the decisions of foreign investors; even in Thailand, with pro-export policies in place, the collapse of the domestic market after the 1997 Asian financial crisis was the most important force pushing firms to seek export markets.

Local content policies and 'policy space'

An automotive industry starting with assembly can be an important generator of backward linkages into local component manufacture, and all the ASEAN producers – except, so far in practice, Vietnam – have used LC requirements and mandatory deletion policies actively to promote local suppliers. Although explicit LC policies have become illegal under WTO rules after 2000, some countries, notably Thailand and Malaysia, have used tax and excise duty policy to favour increased LC, creating more freedom of action ('policy space') than might have been expected.

A related issue is that the deepening of the automotive economic structure often is the result of inward foreign investment by large makers of components. It is clear in Indonesia that Japanese automotive assemblers have been persuading their Japanese suppliers to come too, hence the high level of foreign investment in the sector, a process that has already occurred in Thailand, making the automotive industry more embedded in those countries. Some sourcing, though, is regional, and facilitated by AFTA, both in terms of assembled vehicles and in terms of components. Regional automotive trade may be facilitated by the reduction of various remaining non-tariff barriers and restrictions on labour mobility as the ASEAN Economic Community took effect from the end of 2015 (EIU 2014).

Policy conflicts

Policy conflicts can arise among stakeholders. For example, a popular model in the Philippines, far from being encouraged by Thai-style favourable tax treatment, was seen as a promising source of revenue, with adverse effects on the industry. Similarly in Vietnam, our interviews suggest that government proponents of automotive growth are frustrated by the wish of other arms of governments to discourage it by high taxes. However, as Hansen (2016) notes, these conflicts can reflect genuine development dilemmas between promoting industrialisation via the automotive industry and the danger of doing so in a context where urban infrastructure is inadequate and environment impacts are a problem.

National cars and product champions

Unlike Malaysia's experiment with Proton, Thailand's use of its product champions – the one-ton pick-up truck and later the Eco-car – has been an important element in its export success, with skilful tax policies designed to encourage increased LC too. At the time of writing, it is unclear what the longer-term effects will be of Thailand's political turmoil in 2013–2014, but the short run effects on output are already clear from its output fall over those two years of nearly a quarter. Indonesia's low cost green car has been expanding its exports, despite recent slowdowns in Indonesian economic growth.

Prospects for the smaller producers

The Philippines is a much less successful automotive producer even than Malaysia. In part this is due to small market size, despite a population larger than Thailand's (see Table 2.3), but its current output is not much more than half of its 1996 peak, following a fall that occurred after the 1997 Asian financial crisis from which automotive output has not recovered very much.[29] People in the automotive industry felt that the Philippines, like Indonesia, was at a level of income per head which was the threshold of motorisation[30] – where the market for vehicles quickly begins to expand – but this demand might be met by imports. The smallness of the market in the past has made it difficult to achieve the economies of scale necessary for efficient production, and now that imported models are quite well established as a result of the trade liberalisation under AFTA, there are disagreements about policy between the vehicle assemblers and the importers of vehicles. One hopeful sign for the industry is an increased interest in electric vehicles, and the electrification of one of Manila's traditional forms of transport – the famous jeepney – was being discussed seriously in 2014, together with the electrification of Manila's trishaw fleet,[31] and further progress is underway.[32]

Vietnam faces similar problems of small market size, which prevent economies of scale and generate too small a market for components to develop an efficient supplier base though, like the Philippines, it has received some foreign investment for the export of labour-intensive automotive components, whose production is far more than the local market could absorb. Neither the Philippines nor Vietnam has successfully developed 'product champion' models, in Vietnam's case because of lack of agreement between different stakeholders about what sort of vehicle to develop. Neither country has used excise taxes to help the industry develop champions, and has seen such taxation only from the viewpoint of revenue. In Vietnam, domestically produced vehicles are widely thought to be 20 per cent more expensive than imported models, but the industry has some breathing space to reduce costs before AFTA tariffs fall to zero for the country in 2018.

Acknowledgements

We are grateful to the editors for their comments. We also thank Ritsumeikan Asia Pacific University and the Japan Society for the Promotion of Science (KAKENHI Grant No. 15K03496) for research finance. Of course, the usual disclaimers apply.

Notes

1 We shall draw heavily on the following papers: Natsuda and Thoburn (2013; 2014) on Thailand and Malaysia; Natsuda et al. (2013) and Segawa et al. (2014) on Malaysia; and Natsuda et al. (2015) on Indonesia. We also use material from Otsuka and Natsuda (2015). To save space, we shall not give the detailed referencing from these

papers. The papers are based on extensive in-country interviewing. Although we have tried to update wherever possible, the basic data on which this chapter is founded come from field trips in 2010 and 2011 to Thailand, 2012 to Malaysia, 2013 to Indonesia, 2014 and 2015 to the Philippines, and 2015 to Vietnam.

2 Typically a minimum efficient scale for a car plant is cited as 150–200,000 units per year (Natsuda and Thoburn 2013, 417; Natsuda *et al.* 2015, 61). However, for simpler assembly operations, industry interviewees in the Philippines in 2014 suggested that while the current largest annual assembly outputs of particular models of 15,000 units were not enough to achieve economies of scale, an output of 40,000 would be.

3 These are MFN (most-favoured-nation) tariffs – the tariffs imposed on imports from countries with which there are no regional or other trade agreements or preferences. Those on imports from AFTA members would have been lower.

4 In 2014, the Philippines exported US$1.47 billion of parts and accessories for motor vehicles under HS 8708. Of this total, almost a third was exported within ASEAN, particularly to Thailand, and almost another quarter of exports were to Japan. See http://comtrade.un.org/db (accessed 29 April 2015).

5 More work would be needed to estimate the ERPs associated with these nominal MFN tariffs. Probably in the early 2010s for Malaysia for the least protected vehicles it was around 140 per cent (Natsuda *et al.* 2013, 121, 130, note 26).

6 Interview, Ministry of Industry and Trade, Institute for Industrial Policy and Strategy, Hanoi, 5 March 2015.

7 Indonesia was not a significant exporter of CVs either, with exports in 2013 of US$284 million. For this, and other trade data used here, see http://comtrade.un.org/db (accessed 29 April 2015). PVs in the trade statistics are HS 8703 and CVs are HS 8704.

8 See www.thestar.com.my/News/Nation/2015/02/07/Dr-M-takes-Jokowi-for-a-fast-spin-and-president-cool-about-it/ (accessed 15 April 2015).

9 See *Asia Sentinel*, 9 February 2015, www.asiasentinel.com/econ-business/indonesia-ties-up-with-malaysias-proton-car/ (accessed 11 May 2015).

10 Interview, Japan External Trade Organization (JETRO), Manila, 17 February 2014.

11 Interview, Ministry of Industry and Trade, Supporting Industry Enterprise Development Sector, Hanoi, 4 March 2015.

12 See www.comtrade.un.org/db.

13 A further stimulus for such policies, beyond the policy objective of increasing LC for its own sake, was to meet the rules of origin requirements of the Generalised System of Preferences for preferential access to the UK market, which specified 60 per cent LC (Anazawa 1998).

14 Interview, Motor Vehicle Parts Manufacturers Association of the Philippines, Manila, 10 February 2015.

15 Interview, Hanoi, 6 March 2015.

16 TRIMS was the measure most affecting the ASEAN automotive industry, and to a much lesser extent SCM (Subsidies and Countervailing Measures). Although Trade Related Intellectual Property-rights (TRIPS) and the General Agreement on Trade in Services (GATS) in principle could have applied to the motor industry, in practice in ASEAN there appeared to be no prior policies in existence before 2000 that contravened them. The WTO's provision that members should treat foreign and domestic firms equally ('national treatment'), however, is relevant too (Natsuda and Thoburn 2014).

17 See Widnaraja (2015, 190–191), who argues that take up in some other sectors has been low because of ignorance of AFTA and the opaqueness of the rules drafted by ASEAN for the use of AFTA's provisions.

18 2011 tariff figures supplied by GAIKINDO, the Association of Indonesia Automotive Industries (interview, Jakarta, 27 February 2013). According to GAIKINDO, the IKD system is also employed in South Africa and Canada.

19 A reason for the government's interest in the LCGC was to reduce Indonesian fuel consumption and thereby reduce the size of the large subsidy the government gave on domestic fuel. However, in 2014 the fuel subsidy was reduced substantially. There are also plans discussed for a Low Emission Carbon Project car, of a hybrid or electric variety.

20 Interview, Ministry of Industry, Jakarta, 5 March 2013.

21 Interview, GAIKINDO, 27 February 2013.

22 Interview, Philippine Automotive Competitiveness Council (PACCI), 18 February 2014.

23 See www.mofa.go.jp/policy/economy/fta/index.html (accessed 16 June 2015).

24 However, according to Japanese press reports in mid-2015, the Indonesians were delaying their promised tariffs reduction on auto imports from Japan (*Japan News* 27 May 2015).

25 For vehicles for the transport of goods (HS 8704), only US$7.71 million out of US$10.6 billion were exported from Thailand to Japan, a miniscule 0.07 per cent.

26 In Australia's case, also the result of a free trade agreement.

27 See www.oica.net/category/vehicles-in-use/ (accessed 29 April 2016).

28 And also to Suzuki. See http://paultan.org/2015/06/15/proton-suzuki-mou/ (accessed 16 June 2015).

29 137,000 for all vehicles in 1996, falling to 45,000 in 1998. See www.jama-english.jp/asia/asean/1996–2007_Production.pdf (accessed 18 May 2015).

30 Interview, Chamber of Automotive Manufacturers of the Philippines (CAMPI), 22 February 2014.

31 Philippines Electric Vehicle Summit, Manila, 27–28 February 2014.

32 See http://industry.gov.ph/e-vehicle-sector-eyes-p5-b-investments-in-5-yrs/ (accessed 29 April 2016).

References

Adachi, Fumihiko. 1987. Jidosha Sangyo – Konnan na Kokusannka he no Michi [The Automobile Industry – Obstacles for Localisation Process]. In *Tai no Kogyoka: NAIC he no Cyosen* [Industrialisation in Thailand: Challenge for NAIC], edited by Akira Suehiro and Osamu Yasuda, 256–277. Tokyo: Institute of Developing Economies.

Alavi, Rokiah. 1996. *Industrialisation in Malaysia: Import substitution and Infant Industry Performance*. London. Routledge.

Aldaba, Rafaelita M. 2008. Globalization and the Need for Strategic Government-Industry Cooperation in the Philippine Automotive Industry. Philippine Institute for Development Studies, discussion paper 2008–21. Manila: Philippine Institute for Development Studies.

Anazawa, Makoto. 1998. Mareisia Kukuminsha Purojekuto to Susono Sangyo no Keisei [Malaysian National Car Project and the Formation of Supporting Industry]. *Ajia Keizai* 39 (5): 92–114.

Aswicahyono, Haryo, M. Chatib Basri and Hal Hill. 2000. How Not to Industrialise? Indonesia's Automotive Industry. *Bulletin of Indonesian Economic Studies* 36 (1): 209–241.

Athukorala, Prema-chandra and Archanun Kohpaiboon. 2010. *Thailand in Global Automobile Networks*. Geneva: International Trade Centre.

Auty, Richard. 1994. Sectoral Targeting: Auto Manufacture in Korea and Taiwan. *Journal of International Development* 6 (2): 609–625.

Cimoli, Mario, Giovanni Dosi and Joseph E. Stiglitz, (eds). 2009. *Industrial Policy and Development: The Political Economy of Capabilities Accumulation*. Oxford: Clarendon Press.

Doner, Richard. 2009. *The Politics of Uneven Development: Thailand's Economic Growth in Comparative Perspective*. New York: Cambridge University Press.

Doner, Richard and Peter Wad. 2014. Financial Crises and Automotive Industry Development in Southeast Asia. *Journal of Contemporary Asia* 44 (4): 664–687.

EIU. 2014. The Automotive Sector after the AEC. London: Economist Intelligence Unit.

Fourin. 2011. *ASEAN Jidosha Sangyo* [ASEAN Automobile Industry]. Nagoya: Fourin.

Fourin. 2012. *Ajia Jidosha Buhin Sangyo* [Asian Automotive Parts Industry]. Nagoya: Fourin.

Fourin. 2015. *ASEAN Jidosha Sangyo* [ASEAN Automobile Industry]. Nagoya: Fourin.

GAIKINDO (Association of Indonesian Automotive Industries). 2010. *Enter the World Mobility Through Building Competitive Automotive Industry 2010–2013*. Jakarta: Gaikindo.

Greenaway, David and Chris Milner. 1993. *Trade and Industrial Policy in Developing Countries*. London: Macmillan.

Hale, Christopher D. 2001. Indonesia's National Car Project Revised: History of Kia-Timor Motors and Its Aftermath. *Asian Survey* 41 (4): 629–645.

Hansen, Arve. 2016. Driving Development? The Problems and Promises of the Car in Vietnam. *Journal of Contemporary Asia*. Doi: 10.1080/00472336.2016.1151916.

Hansen, John R. 1971. The Motor Vehicle Industry. *Bulletin of Indonesian Economic Studies* 7 (2): 38–69.

Hassler, Markus. 2009. Variations of Value Creation: Automobile Manufacturing in Thailand. *Environment and Planning* A 41: 2232–2249.

Humphrey, John and Olga Memedovic. 2003. *The Global Automotive Industry Value Chain: What Prospects for Upgrading by Developing Countries*. Vienna: United Nations Industrial Development Organization.

Ikemoto, Yukio. 1994. Tai no Jidosha Kumitate Sangyo to Jiyuka Seisaku [The Automobile Assembly Industry and Liberalisation Policy in Thailand]. In *Sangyo Hatten to Sangyo Soshiki no Henka* [Industrial Development and Transformation of Industrial Organisation], edited by Taniura Taeko, 169–190. Tokyo: Institute of Developing Economies.

Kaosa-ard, Mingsarn Santikarn. 1993. TNC Involvement in the Thai Auto Industry. *TDRI Quarterly Review* 8 (1): 9–16.

Lauridsen, Laurids S. 2009. The Policies and Politics of Industrial Upgrading in Thailand during the Thaksin Era (2001–2006). *Asian Politics and Policy* 1 (3): 409–434.

Natsuda, Kaoru and John Thoburn. 2013. Industrial Policy and the Development of the Automotive Industry in Thailand. *Journal of the Asia Pacific Economy* 18 (3): 413–437.

Natsuda, Kaoru and John Thoburn. 2014. How Much Policy Space Still Exists Under the WTO? A Comparative Study of the Automotive Industry in Thailand and Malaysia. *Review of International Political Economy* 21 (6): 1346–1377.

Natsuda, Kaoru, Kozo Otsuka and John Thoburn. 2015. Dawn of Industrialisation: The Indonesian Automotive Industry. *Bulletin of Indonesian Economic Studies* 51 (1): 47–68.

Natsuda, Kaoru, Noriyuki Segawa and John Thoburn. 2013. Liberalization, Industrial Nationalism, and the Malaysian Automotive Industry. *Global Economic Review* 42 (2): 113–134.

Nolan, Peter. 2012. *Is China Buying the World?* London: Polity Press.

Nomura, Toshiro. 2003. Indonesia Jidosha Sangyo no Kaihokatei [Liberalisation Process of the Indonesian Automotive Industry]. *ShoKei Ronshu* 53: 1–64.

Otsuka, Kozo and Kaoru Natsuda. 2015. The Determinants of Total Factor Productivity in the Malaysian Automotive Industry: Are Government Policies Upgrading Technological Capacity? *The Singapore Economic Review*, online ready, DOI: 10.1142/S0217590815500460.

Rasiah, Rajah. 2005. Trade-related Investment Liberalization under the WTO: The Malaysian Experience. *Global Economic Review* 34 (4): 453–471.

Rasiah, Rajah. 2009. Technological Capabilities of Automotive Firms in Indonesia and Malaysia. *Asian Economic Papers* 8 (1): 151–168.

Rodrik, Dani. 2004. Industrial Policy for the Twenty-First Century. www.sss.ias.edu/files/pdfs/Rodrik/Research/industrial-policy-twenty-first-century.pdf

Rosellon, Maureen Ane D. and Erlinda M. Medalla. 2011. ASEAN+1 FTAs and Global Value Chains in East Asia: The Case of the Philippine Automotive and Electronics. In *ASEAN+1 FTAs and Global Value Chains in East Asia*, edited by Christopher Findlay, 275–320. Jakarta: ERIA.

Sato, Yuri. 1992. The Automotive Industry. In *Indonesia no Kogyoka* [Industrialisation in Indonesia], edited by Norio Mihara and Yuri Sato, 336–361. Tokyo: Institute of Developing Economies.

Segawa, Noriyuki, Kaoru Natsuda and John Thoburn. 2014. Affirmative Action and Economic Liberalisation: The Dilemmas of the Malaysian Automotive Industry. *Asian Studies Review* 38 (3): 422–441.

Stiglitz, Joseph E. 1998. More Instruments and Broader Goals: Moving Towards a Post-Washington Consensus. 1998 WIDER annual lecture, Helsinki. www.wider.unu.edu/publications/...lectures/.../annual-lecture-1998.pdf.

Tham, Siew-Yean. 2004. Malaysian Policies for the Automobile Sector. In *Production Networks in Asia and Europe*, edited by Rogier Busser and Yuri Sadoi, 51–70. London: RoutledgeCurzon.

Thoburn, John T. 1973. Exports and the Malaysian Engineering Industry: A Case Study of Backward Linkage. *Oxford Bulletin of Economics and Statistics* 35 (2): 91–117.

Thoburn, John. 2016. Trade and Industrial Policy for Development. In *Comparative Economic Perspectives on Europe and the MENA Region*, edited by Mustafa Erdoğdu and Bryan Christiansen, 25–35. Hershey, PA: IGI Global.

Thoburn, John T. and Makoto Takashima. 1992. *Industrial Subcontracting in the United Kingdom and Japan*. Aldershot: Avebury.

Truong, Thi Chi Binh and Nguyen Manh Linh. 2011. Development of Automotive Industries in Vietnam with Improving the Network Capability. In *How to Enhance Innovation Capability with Internal and External Sources*, edited by Patarapong Intarakumnerd, 273–307. Jakarta: ERIA.

Ueda, Yoko. 2007. Nihon no Cyokusetsu Toshi to Tai no Jidosha Me-ka-no Keisei [Japanese Foreign Direct Investment and the Development of Auto Parts Industry in Thailand]. *Doshisha University Economic Review* 58 (4): 87–117.

Ueda, Yoko. 2009. The Origin and Growth of Local Entrepreneurs in Auto Parts Industry in Thailand. Center for Contemporary Asia Working Paper no. 25. Kyoto: Doshisha University.

UNIDO. 2013. Industrial Development Report 2013: Sustaining Employment Growth: the Role of Manufacturing and Structural Change. Vienna: United Nations Industrial Development Organization.

Wad, Peter. 2009. The Automobile Industry of Southeast Asia: Malaysia and Thailand. *Journal of the Asia Pacific Economy* 14 (2): 172–193.

Widnaraja, Ganeshan. 2015. Regional Trade Agreements and Enterprises in Southeast Asia. In *Routledge Handbook of Southeast Asian Economics*, edited by Ian Coxhead, 181–197. London: Routledge.

Witoelar, Wirmar. 1983. Ancillary Firm Development in the Motor Vehicle Industry in Indonesia. In *The Motor Vehicle Industry in Asia: A Study of Ancillary Firm Development*, edited by Konosuke Odaka, 17–84. Singapore: Singapore University Press.

3 The Asian automotive industry and labour organising

Peter Wad

The automotive industry including the automobile firms, motorcycle firms and their component and parts suppliers has traditionally been considered the 'industry of industries', that is, the key industry of industrial power and technological development that held extensive linkages to other manufacturing industries and had a wide impact on economy and society. The question is if the automotive industry can also be considered the 'industry of labour organising'.

The chapter will examine this question in relation to automotive industries in Asian market economies. More specifically, the question is if the automotive industry provided a sector-based platform for independent and powerful trade unionism in a region where labour and trade unions have otherwise been suppressed and remained relatively weak during the post-World War II Asian economic transformation (Deyo 1989, 2012; Kuruvilla *et al.* 2002).

The proposed structural relationship between the evolution of an automotive industry and labour empowerment is not a new idea. Frederic Deyo suggested that the industrial revolution in East Asia did only breed a weak labour movement because the new working class in light export industries was demobilised structurally due to the use of temporary employment of young unskilled women. Although they did carry out industrial protest, this labour unrest was not offensive or well organised. Strikes and other outbursts were rapidly suppressed by employers and state authorities united by an anti-union policy in line with the industrial policy based on low labour cost and export competitiveness. Yet, with domestic-market oriented heavy industrialisation the East Asian workforces changed toward male employees in more regular jobs in capital intensive industries like automobile manufacturing. Thus, workers became less demobilised by structural transformation, but they still faced a labour repressive political regime that excluded, suppressed, controlled or co-opted worker organising in trade unions, political parties and social networks.

However, the pessimistic view of e.g. Deyo has been criticised by Beverly Silver (2003), contending that the globalisation of capitalism unfolds in a long-term cyclical way with ups and downs for both capital and labour in the market economy at large and within specific sectors and industries. The dynamic of this cycle of industrial evolution was grounded in the power relation between capital and labour where capital tried to control and exploit labour through spatial fixes (geographical location and relocation of production and jobs) and technical-organisational fixes (craft-based production, 'Fordist' mass-assembling or 'post-Fordist' flexible, customised 'lean' manufacturing). Against these capital-driven accumulation strategies for increased expansion, investment and profitability in the auto industry, workers responded individually and collectively to the perceived injustices by employers. Sooner or later they formed organised, strong and militant labour movements which culminated in widespread labour unrest and rising labour wage and working conditions. With worker empowerment and resistance to exploitation, profitability would be squeezed and capital would encourage managers and employers to rationalise, automatise, outsource or off-shore production, components, modules or final products and thus downsize the workforce in 'hot and hard' spots and expand into 'calm and soft' spots.

Beverly Silver describes the transformation of the global automotive industry from the US-dominated Fordist system to the Japanese-lead post-Fordist, 'lean' production system. She notices and explains the exception of the Japanese automotive industry and its industrial relations by way of the Japanese techno-organisational fix to govern the workforce. Basically, the two manufacturing systems raise production vulnerability to selective labour actions and interruption of the flow processes in the factory. The lean manufacturing system is even more vulnerable to stoppages due to its geographical and organisational dispersal of production activities. But the legitimacy of the two systems is perceived differently by their workforces due to the divergence of employment and industrial relations, thus conditioning widespread dissatisfaction in North American 'lean-and-mean' factories and collaboration and work motivation in the core workforce of the Japanese 'lean-and-dual' factories.

The *claim* of the chapter is that, contingent on the structural significance of the industry and the institutional space of collective labour action, the automotive workers in East Asian market economies have formed relatively strong labour organisations domestically in a sea of weak and/or declining union movements, but with large differences in auto workers' power position across countries depending on the structural and political demobilisation of auto workers. Moreover, we contend that the auto industrial relations between labour and management have changed toward 'responsible' enterprise unionism Japanese style due to Japanese industrial dominance in the region, except in 'economic nationalist' countries where local corporations have led the industry and market.

The chapter is structured in the following way: The next section presents and discusses the methodology applied selecting the automotive industries and workforces in South Korea, Thailand, Malaysia and the Philippines as the field of analysis. The third section analyses the organisational power of auto workers in these four countries. In the fourth and fifth sections we take on the similarities and divergences of auto workers' structural and institutional powers. In the sixth section, we try to explain the patterns and changes of auto worker organising at first in a static, comparative perspective and then we enlarge the analysis to the dynamic-relational perspective of the regional and global auto industry to see if international production chains and global labour networking improve our understanding and explanation of the momentum of auto workers' organisational power before and after 2005. The seventh section concludes the chapter.

Methodological approach

In broad terms we are arguing with Arrighi and Silver (1984), Silver (2003), Deyo (2012), Wright (2000) and others that *workers' power* is constituted by their organisational, structural, institutional and social powers, and that workers' organisational power that forms the potential for workers' coordinated collective action (agency) is conditioned by their structural, institutional and social power.

Workers' organisational power is formed by its capacity for collective decision-making, bargaining and action, which will be operationalised into trade union intensity and trade union centralisation and rank-and-file participation. *Workers' structural power* is considered a composite of their *industrial-strategic* power infused by the sector's political-strategic importance for the government's economic development strategy, their *industrial-productive power* formed by its economic-technological capacity and linkages to other industries and sectors within and across the national boundary from the industrial cluster down to the workplace, and their *marketplace power* due to the skill level, employment conditions and unemployment situation of the employable industrial workforce. Workers' *institutional power* is framed by the country's adoption of international labour rights, their implementation and enforcement in labour and industrial relations legislation and administration and the freedom to form and participate in political parties and civil society associations to the point of taking state power. Finally, workers' *social power* is determined by workers' networks, alliances and coalitions with other civil society groups and social movements within and across borders. In our analysis, we delimit our scope of analysis from including auto workers' social power in a systematic way and will include it if necessary under the analysis of auto workers' organisational power.

The chapter aims to analyse the formation and power of auto workers' organisations, first through a rather *static-comparative analysis* of the correlation between their structural, institutional and organisational powers in the EA-four group of countries, and then through a *dynamic-relational* analysis of regional impact of Japanese automakers' advancement in these countries and auto workers' international organising and networking with other national, regional and global trade unions and labour networks.

Taking workers' structural power to be the key factor explaining workers' organisational power, we *select and compare* four market economies in East Asia based on their industries' varying political-economic significance around our baseline, 2005, that is, between the East Asian and the global financial crises. These four countries are South Korea (henceforth Korea), Malaysia, Thailand, and the Philippines (henceforth the 'EA-4' countries). Korea has a significant and strategic-important auto industry; Thailand has an important economic but politically insignificant auto industry; Malaysia has a politically important, but economically less important auto sector; and the Philippines has a rather weak automobile industry in both economic and political terms. This selection is based on two core components of the crucial independent factor, structural power, for explaining variance in organisational power of auto workers across the four countries, allowing for testing our claims of conditional causation.

Then we broaden our analysis in time and space looking at the historical and international processes influencing the formation of auto workers' unions with particular reference to Japan with its regionally-dominant automotive industry and to cross-border labour networking within and beyond the region. Thus, we take organisational power as the dependent factor in the static-comparative analysis and as an interdependent factor in the dynamic-relational analysis, delimiting ourselves from investigating workers' influence on the structure and dynamic of the automotive industry in East Asia.

Comparative data on employment and industrial relations in the automotive industry are fragile and dated by a decade which makes the year 2005 the most appropriate comparative baseline for the cross-country analysis. The study delimits itself from making a straight qualitative comparison between Asian developing countries with and without automobile manufacturing or assembling (e.g. Singapore), or countries where local auto components and parts production have been the key segment of the auto industry (e.g. Taiwan). The horizon of comparison is East Asia, not East Asia to North America or Europe. Thus, in East Asia Korean auto workers possess 'high' organisational power relative to auto workers in other EA-4 countries, but if compared to German auto workers, the level may be 'medium'.

Organisational power of auto workers in EA-4 around 2005

Based on International Labour Organization (ILO) statistics and other country specific sources (with Thailand displaying relatively weak employment and industrial relations statistics) a comparative snapshot of auto workers' organisational power can be established for the years around 2005 indicating relative strengths of Korean and Malaysian auto workers and the relative weakness of Thai and Philippine auto workers and their unions across the countries.

Union intensity among auto workers

The relative status of Korea and Malaysia recurs in the general organisational level with around 1.5 million union members in Korea and half the number in Malaysia, but this translates into a general union density of around 10 per cent in both countries. When it comes to the unionisation of the auto industry workers the two countries converge again and at a relatively high level among the EA-4 countries. In the Korean automobile industry 120,000 workers were unionised out of 266,500 employed, equal to a union density of 45 per cent in 2005, while in Malaysia 21,000 employees were organised out of 53,700 employed, equal to 37 per cent in union density calculated with a base in employed and not in employees which lowers the intensity level a bit (ILO 2010).

In both countries union density was much higher in the auto industry than in the overall economy, and this is a general trend in the global automobile industry. Within the auto industry, union density was much higher among the automakers than among auto supplier firms. In 2001 union densities in the Korean auto industry were estimated at 74 per cent and 19 per cent in the auto-maker and the component and parts segments respectively (Jeong 2007).

Considering the general level of unionisation, the Philippines does much better than Thailand, anyway, with the Philippines numbering nearly two million union members compared to Thailand's half a million, translating into a nearly four times higher total union density in the Philippines (11.7 per cent) relative to Thailand (3.3 per cent)! However, the Philippine numbers may be inflated by the reporting trade unions, considering that only around 250,000 employees were covered by collective agreements making up for 1.5 per cent union density nationwide. Around 2010 Thai private sector union density was below 4 per cent with more than 350,000 unionists relative to a workforce of 9 million, while state enterprise unions claimed 180,000 members, equivalent to 64 per cent union density (Brown and Sakdina 2013).

Thai auto unions mustered around 40,000 members in 2005 compared to Philippines auto unions that numbered below 3,000, whereby the auto union densities are estimated at 20 per cent in Thailand and 10 per cent in the Philippines at that time. These levels of organising indicate that although the Philippines auto workers were relatively weakly unionised they were anyway on a par with the relatively high level of national union density. Thai auto unions were able to organise well above the relatively low density at the national level and the private sector, but well below the state-enterprise unions.

Organisation of auto workers' unions

The majority of automotive workers in all EA-4 countries were organised in enterprise unions around 2005, yet with a large minority united in industrial unions in Malaysia and Korea. In fact, the Korean Metal Workers' Union, KMWU, united the majority of auto workers in 2006 after the large carmakers' enterprise unions merged into the KMWU. In Japan enterprise unionism has been one of the pillars of the Japanese model of industrial relations, and Japanese enterprise unions are often accused by Western unions of being weak, docile or 'yellow' 'company unions', that is, dependent on employers' will and support. Yet sometimes workplace-based unions as enterprise unions have also displayed high independence, collective militancy and resilience in industrial disputes, e.g. in Korean workers' Great Worker Struggle 1987–1989 (Koo 2001).

Although the workers of the Philippine auto companies seemed to fragment into many enterprise unions they were mainly affiliated into two union federations, the independent Auto Industry Workers' Alliance (AIWA) and the

KAR-AID federation affiliated to KMU (the radical First May Movement). AIWA was a rather loosely organised federation and the KAR-AID was dwindling. Contrary to Korea and Thailand the Philippine union federations did not coordinate workers' unions in a vibrant industry with large workplaces, and they were competing with other union federations and alliances in the metal industries and embedded in a politicised climate within a landscape of pluralistic social movements with conflicting ideologies and practices.

When Thailand switched to a more liberal and open auto industrial policy in the early 1990s, four autoworkers' unions from Toyota, Hino, Denso and NHK formed a loose union association. Just before the combined democratic breakthrough and financial crisis in Thailand in 1997, auto worker enterprise unions established the Federation of Thailand Automobile Workers' Union (TAW) in 1996. The Toyota Thailand Workers' Union (TTWU), that registered in 1982, joined the union federation but it did also build a TTWU-centred union network, or what could be called a 'supply chain union' network. In 2003–2004 the Federation of All Toyota Thailand Workers' Union was constituted by TTWU and around 80–90 trade unions in more than 50 per cent of the component and parts companies affiliated or linked to the Toyota Motor Thailand (TMT) and reflecting the Toyota *keiretsu* production cluster in Thailand (Arnold 2006). While the Nissan worker unions later stopped collaborating with the TAW unions prioritising the activities of their own federation of Nissan-related unions, the Toyota union chose to stay within the TAW federation.

In 2002, the TAW-membership numbered 15,672 members in 24 enterprise unions including Toyota, Mitsubishi Motor, Isuzu, Hino, Kawasaki and Honda (Ofreneo and Wad 2010). In 2004–2005 TAW had increased its member base to 30 unions and 22,448 members (Arnold 2006). The Toyota union also engaged in broader union networks as well, e.g. the Confederation of Thai Electrical Appliances, Electronic, Automobile and Metalworkers (TEAM). TEAM was affiliated with the International Metalworkers' Federation (IMFmetal) where the Japanese Autoworkers' Union (JAW) was an important member (Arnold 2006). All in all, the TTWU took a leading role in the developing of labour-management relations in the Thai-based and Japanese dominated auto industry, but at the same time the TTWU aimed to sustain the competitiveness of Toyota in Thailand and to promote mutually trusting and beneficial relations between employers, employees and unions. In fact, employers of auto companies in Thailand are reported to support enterprise unionism in the mid-2000s (Brown and Sakdina 2013).

In post-colonial Malaysia, industrial unions have dominated from the outset of Independence. The situation changed towards a more decentralised union structure in Malaysia due to the state support for enterprise unions in general and the specific state-driven establishment of a national automobile programme in the early 1980s. The government and managements supported the formation of enterprise unions in the new national automaking firms. Facing setbacks among the new national automakers, the industrial union increased its organising efforts in the auto component and parts subsector (Wad 2004).

Concomitantly, the industry-wide collective bargaining and agreement (CBA) system withered and gave birth to two CBA models: industrial union-company CBA and enterprise union-company CBA. In the early 2000s consultations to form an auto workers' federation for the enterprise and industrial unions did not mature. However, the industrial union's CBAs in the non-national auto subsector seemed to set the standard for negotiations within the national auto sector.

In Korea the opposite trend of union centralisation has been pursued deliberately by one of the core national labour centres. Militant enterprise unions have merged into militant industrial unions in, for example, the metal industry including automobile industry workers (Wad 2007). In the metal industries the Korean Confederation of Metal Unions (KCMU) had been formed in 1997 (Jeong 2007) but it was soon followed by the Korean Metalworkers' Federation (KMWF), also known as the Korean Metal Labour Union Federation, KMLUF (Lee and Yi 2012), in 1998, only to be surpassed by the Korean Metalworkers' Union (KMWU) in 2001. The KMWF's mission was to form an industrial union for the metal industry and establish industry-level collective bargaining.

This agenda was especially important in the automobile industry that was dominated by five automakers: Hyundai, Kia, GM Daewoo, Ssangyong and Renault Samsung. Only Renault Samsung stayed unorganised in 2005 even after it was acquired by French Renault, thus following the anti-union policy of the Samsung business group (*chaebol*). Kia was unionised way back in 1960, Daewoo in 1963, while Hyundai and Ssangyong were organised during the political upheavals in 1987. These automakers' workplaces were much better unionised than auto component and parts suppliers, but in the industrial federation it was the smaller unions in workplaces of supplier firms that pushed for more centralisation of union structure and collective bargaining. When KMWF's leadership decided to form the KMWU in 2001 only around 20 per cent of KMWF's membership joined the new industrial union, equal to a bit more than 30,000 members in 108 smaller unions, mostly in the auto components segment (Lee and Yi 2012). The big automakers' unions would not give up their independence and authority to negotiate collective agreements with their individual employers, and they continued as members of the umbrella union of KMWF until they finally joined KMWU in 2006, yet kept their workplace organisation.

Although KMWU did not control the larger auto unions it pushed for industry-wide bargaining, facing a counterpart of employers in the metal industries, the Korean Metal Industrial Employers' Association (KMEA) based on members from small and medium sized companies and only including 14 per cent of KMWU's membership (Lee 2011). KMWU at first pursued regional-level negotiations from 2001 to 2002 and then moved to national industry bargaining in 2003, pursuing a three-tier structure of collective bargaining (national, regional, enterprise). The bargaining processes were combined with threats or launches of industrial strikes every year from 2003 to 2006, thus following the same pattern of industrial action as the Japanese enterprise unions with their 'Spring' offensive (*Shunto*) but conducted in a much more militant way than the Japanese did in the 2000s.

By the mid-2000s, then, collective bargaining in the Korean auto industry took place at the enterprise level between management and enterprise unions in the automakers segment, and at a more centralised regional and industry level among auto suppliers between KMWU and the KMEA representing smaller metal firms.

Auto workers and the labour movement

The trade union movements of EA-4 have maintained peak union unity only in Malaysia (the Malaysian Trades Union Congress, or MTUC), while it is divided into two peak centres according to union ideology in Korea (moderate FKTU and radical KCTU) and several national centres in Thailand and the Philippines where Christian-oriented unions played a larger role around 2005. The employers of the automakers and component suppliers had only organised an employers' association in Korea and only among the small and medium sized suppliers. The auto firms primarily organised in business associations, and most often their associations took place within the automakers segment of private (and non-national) firms on the one hand and among the auto component and parts suppliers on the other hand. In Malaysia, the non-national automakers and auto traders' associations merged in 2000 in order to improve lobbying of the government on the brink of the ASEAN Free Trade Area (AFTA), but this did not spur the auto workers' unions enough to form a federation of enterprise and industrial unions by 2005, although they did try.

Metal workers' federations or industrial unions played a key role in the Korean labour movement while the enterprise unions and federations of metal workers and auto workers did not take a leading role in Thailand or the Philippines, where labour organising and mobilisation was linked to the larger political and social movements, e.g. the Thai Labour Solidarity Committee and the Philippine Alliance of Progressive Labour (Deyo 2012). In Malaysia, the industrial union of autoworkers (NUTEAIW) had left the MTUC during the 1980s aiming to build a more grass-root oriented union movement (Dass 1991), but NUTEAIW returned in the 1990s. With its union allies it achieved a significant victory in the election of top leadership to the MTUC in 2004 when the executive secretary of NUTEAIW was elected president of the MTUC. However, the Metal Industry Employees' Union kept the more powerful position of general secretary leading an alternative union alliance.

In general, the emerging layer of non-regular contract workers did not join trade unions of regular workers and regular employees, as temporary jobs did not encourage union membership and also unions were often hesitant if not outright negative about allowing non-regular workers union membership. In the Korean auto industry unions responded to the new non-regular workers in a multitude of ways: 'exclusion' where the existing union did not organise, nor represent contract workers; 'proxy' in the sense of representing the non-regular without allowing for union membership; 'inclusion' whereby the contract workers were unionised but not represented in union leadership and negotiations; and finally 'integration' whereby unions both organised and empowered the new workers in leadership and practices (Yun 2011). From the early to mid-2000s contract workers started their own unions at the automakers (Lee 2014). The same happened in Thailand.

Summing up, the organisational power of auto workers was highest in Korea and Malaysia due to the high level of union density on the one hand and the co-existence of industrial unions and large auto workers' enterprise unions in key automaking workplaces. Auto workers in Thailand and the Philippines were qualitatively on par at a lower level of associational power due to low union density, fragmented enterprise unions and firm level collective bargaining, yet with some kind of industry-level union networking.

The momentum for organisational centralisation lay anyway in the Korean auto industry. Korean enterprise unions joined the industrial union in 2006, while informal consultations to form a federation of enterprise unions and the industrial union failed in Malaysia. However, in Thailand some kind of 'supply chain unionism' evolved by 2005 linking enterprise unions in the lead assembling firm with unions in the firm's supply chain. Supply chain unionism contrasts with industrial unionism where unions align or merge across competing lead firms and their auto component suppliers, as well as enterprise unionism where workers stand together within the boundaries of the firm, be it at the workplace, company or corporate levels of the firm.

In the following section we will outline the structural and institutional powers of auto workers, aiming for a static-comparative analysis of the varying organisational power of auto workers in the EA-4 countries.

Structural power of auto workers in EA-4 around 2005

Industrial-strategic significance of the auto industry

The EA-4 automobile industries evolved for long behind protectionist walls of quota and tariff regulations, depending on sales in their domestic markets, and aiming for a gradual industrial upgrading from assembling to local component production and further on to export motor vehicles and parts (Doner 1991). Building a national automotive industry was part of the heavy industrialisation policy pursued by the Korean state from the 1970s (Wad 2002). Imitating both Korea and Japan that demonstrated huge automotive competitiveness in the late 1970s and the early 1980s, Malaysia embarked on heavy industrialisation in the 1980s that included the establishment of a national automotive industry with automakers Proton, Perodua and MTB, and motorcycle making Modenas plus hundreds of indigenous auto suppliers mostly of ethnic Malay origin (Wad and Govindaraju 2011). By 2005, Proton had become a wholly Malaysian owned company after Japanese partners had left while other national carmakers had been acquired by Japanese auto transnational corporations (TNCs). Proton was controlled by Malaysian state capital after it was privatised in the mid-1990s, renationalised during the East Asian financial crisis, and it was privatised for a second time in 2010 (Doner and Wad 2014), an outcome very contrary to Korea where no Japanese transplants had ever established a production platform.

In Thailand and the Philippines policies to develop national auto firms and industries were abandoned in the 1980s and early 1990s and these countries turned to foreign direct investments in building a domestic auto industry (Doner 2009; Ofreneo 2016). Thailand made it in alliance with especially Japanese automakers and their demand management policy promoting a 'product champion' (one tonne pick-up truck) (Natsuda and Thoburn 2013). The Philippines stumbled in both national and foreign auto assembling, partly due to import of second hand vehicles, but the country did succeed in building a specialised auto component industry and export during the 2000s (Ofreneo 2016).

Industrial-productive capacity of the auto industries

In the middle of the 2000s between the East Asian crisis of 1997–1998 and the global financial crisis of 2008–2009, the political-economic significance of the automobile industries in South Korea, Thailand, Malaysia and the Philippines varied considerably and so did the structural power of the auto workers. The Korean auto industry was relatively advanced compared to the Southeast Asian auto industries and it performed much better in terms of production, export and domestic market share than its nearest EA-4 competitor, the Japanese-controlled Thai auto industry.

In comparison, the Korean auto industry is on par with the Thai auto industry in its relative weight in the manufacturing sector (11–12 per cent of manufacturing GDP and a total workforce of around 200,000) while a bit ahead in terms of share of manufacturing export (15 compared to 10 per cent). Yet the Korean auto workers count much more relatively in manufacturing sector employment than the Thai workforce (6 compared to 4 per cent) reflecting the larger (triple) output and export in Korea relative to Thailand and the lower labour productivity of the Thai automotive industry.

Korean auto firms have embarked on a strategy of lean production and modularisation at home and the skill levels of auto workers may diverge quite a bit (Lee and Jo 2007). Korean firms conduct R&D at home and worldwide, where Japanese subsidiaries in Southeast Asia are confined to product adjustment and technical services. Anyway, the technological level of automotive manufacturing may not be that different between the Korean and Thai auto industries due to the impact of Japanese transfer of technology, management and production systems to Thai transplants (Doner 2009; Sadoi 2015). Thailand has also achieved a global mandate for manufacturing and development of pick-up trucks by Japanese automakers (Natsuda and Thoburn 2013). For Malaysia data available indicate that the Malaysian auto industry is still a 'screw driver' industry with low skill requirements and only 7 per cent of the workforce being skilled workers (Wad and Govindaraju 2011). The same overall low level of skills in the workforce is assumed to prevail in the Thai and the Philippine auto industries, too, yet with some upskilling taking place in Japanese transplants in Thailand (Sadoi 2015).

Marketplace power of auto workers

Korea and Malaysia are the two countries with the most capitalist relations of production indicated by a labour market where wage employment counted for 75 per cent of the Malaysian workforce and 66 per cent for the Korean workforce in 2005. The Korean labour force is double the size of the Malaysian labour force with Korean auto industry employment to manufacturing employment (6.4 per cent) again double sized relative to Malaysian employment (2.9 per cent) but with nearly the same share (<20 per cent) of the workforce in manufacturing employment to total employment. Korea is in a phase of 'positive' de-industrialising where a transition to a high-productive service and knowledge economy is accompanied by a smaller but highly productive manufacturing sector, while Malaysia is facing 'negative' de-industrialising in the 2000s with a declining share of manufacturing in overall GDP combined with stagnant or falling labour productivity in manufacturing in general and in transport equipment in particular (Rasiah 2011).

In the foreign-dominated auto industries of Thailand and the Philippines the situation was different from the national-dominated auto industries of Korea and Malaysia. Auto manufacturing took place in societies that were less capitalist in terms of capital-labour relations as wage earners only represented half or less of the workforce in both countries. Both the labour force and the wage workers counted around the same numbers, above 30 million employed and above 15 million wage earners, but the share of manufacturing employment was 50 per cent higher in Thailand (15 per cent) than in the Philippines (10 per cent). Moreover, the Thai auto industry employment to manufacturing employment was much higher (3.7 per cent) than the Philippine share (0.1 per cent), higher than in Malaysia but much lower than in Korea.

The use of temporary workers or contract labour increased dramatically after the East Asian financial crisis as firms aimed for cost reduction, especially in South Korea. The recruitment of contract workers – including immigrant workers – for manufacturing jobs was already emerging in the 1990s in Southeast Asia due to labour shortages and immigrant labour recruitment policies in Thailand and Malaysia. In contrast, the Philippines has been a net-labour exporting country. In 2005 unemployment had again fallen in the EA-4 countries and shortages of skilled workers were widespread as reflected in numerous training programmes and human resource development funded by the authorities and employers.

'Flexibilisation' of employment conditions and increasing shares of non-regular employees became a global and regional trend in the 2000s, and it was also manifest in the EA-4 countries. The worst case of non-regulated employment in the EA-4 countries is found in the Philippines where one estimate says that 50 per cent of total employment was in the informal sector in 2005, and another estimate came up with 77 per cent of all employed being part of the informal sector in 2006 (Ofreneo 2015, Table 6–7). However, no data are available for the Philippine automotive industry. The share of non-regular employment in Korean auto industry went beyond 30 per cent by 2005 and probably reached around 50 per cent at the time of the global financial crisis. In 2008 the Thai auto industry employed 350,000 employees of which 50,000 (or 14 per cent) were subcontract workers (Serrano 2014, 133). In Malaysia manufacturing contract workers to total production workers amounted to 12 per cent in 2005 up from 7 per cent in 2000 (Rasiah et al. 2015, Figure 1), and the number of foreign contract workers rose to 30–40 per cent in the larger automakers like Proton, Perodua, Toyota and Honda over the 2000s (Kishnam 2009). This use of contract workers opened up the way for downward pressure on regular employment, on wage levels and social benefits, and it created new obstacles for unionisation because the immigrants were often told not to become members of any association, contrary to their legal right to join trade unions according to Malaysian trade union legislation.

In sum, the structural power of auto workers in the AE-4 countries varies from the relatively high level in Korea where auto workers are part of an industry that musters both economic and political significance, to a medium level in Malaysia and Thailand where the auto industries are significant in one way only, Malaysia's being political important and Thailand's being economically important, down to the Philippines where the auto industry and its workers are insignificant both economically and politically. In all countries, marketplace power is medium due to relatively low unemployment for industrial workers combined with low (Thailand, Malaysia, Philippines) to medium (Korea) skill levels and reverse levels of contract and temporary employed labour. But the general labour marketplace witnesses rising use of irregular employment, challenging the dominance of regular employment and thus the core basis of trade union membership and empowerment.

Institutional power of auto workers in EA-4 around 2005

The institutional context of labour organising in general and specifically in the focal industry of automobile manufacturing around 2005 demonstrates similarities and differences across the EA-4. The most manifest difference seems to be regarding the recognition of international labour rights and especially the so-called enabling rights about union organising and collective bargaining (covenant 87 and 98) and the practices and situation on the ground. Paradoxically, all four core ILO labour rights were adopted only by the Philippines, where the suppression of organised labour was also the most extreme, including killings of unionists.

Korea had not ratified either of the two enabling covenants but the Korean government claimed that the Korean legislation provided for free unionising and bargaining (like the situation in the USA). With Korea's membership of the OECD in 1996 Korea had to comply with the ILO conventions within a decade, but the government dragged its feet in this 'catching-up' process. Union pluralism at the enterprise level was only allowed in 2011, and several normal union practices are criminalised and brutally suppressed by police intervention and punished by courts with heavy sanctions (fines, imprisonment). However, Korean (auto) workers did gain much more institutional space with the demo-cratisation process that formally began in 1987 and finally consolidated with the election of the oppositional candidate for president and the peaceful transfer of power around 1997/1998. A popular backlash against labour militancy followed during the 1990s in the wake of economic globalisation and industrial restruc-turing. Trade union density declined, and the unions' counter strategy to cen-tralise organisationally turned out to be a difficult process even in the auto industry that faced social inertia or path dependence of enterprise-based col-lective organising and bargaining since the early 1980s (Jeong 2007).

The Thai labour laws reflected the historical legacy of shifting short demo-cratic regimes and longer repressive military regimes, allowing private sector employees to organise unions and bargain for collective agreements with cir-cumscribed space for collective actions. With the democratisation process during the 1990s and the new constitution of 1997 labour rights were on the political agenda. The populist-oriented Thaksin-government (2001–2006) com-mitted itself to ratifying the core ILO enabling labour rights, and state-enterprise employees obtained permission to form unions, yet without gaining the right to strike. Yet by 2005 the Thaksin government had switched to a neoliberal policy which promoted privatisation of state enterprises and liberalisation of the labour market and discouraged labour organising and mobilisation (Brown and Hewison 2005). In 2006 the Thaksin government was expelled by a military coup instigated by massive opposition among urban royal, state and business elites, middle-class people and selected trade unions and labour networks (Brown and Ayudhya 2013; Deyo 2012).

Contrary to the other EA-4 countries, the Malaysian labour legislation and industrial relation system is path dependent on British colonial policy that aimed at suppressing the rebellion of the Communist labour movement in the late 1940s and early 1950s. Malaysian governments rejected the ILO core labour right to freely form trade unions (Covenant 87), and they tightened step by step labour laws to stifle the development of strong trade unions in new manufac-turing industries, to impede collective actions and to sever the integration of trade unionism and labour politics. Industrial unions were prohibited in export industries like garments and component electronics, and enterprise unions were promoted by government and employers if unions knocked on the factory gate of e.g. government-linked companies like automaker Proton. In this way, Malay-sian employment and industrial relations law and practice converged toward a legalistic labour regime à la USA and Philippines. The outcome was a labour regime of control and not the labour regime of commitment for workers and their organisations that seemed to be needed for the Malaysian transition into a developed society by 2020 (Todd and Peetz 2001; Todd *et al.* 2006). Excluding trade unions as partners for societal tripartism except in times of economic emergency (1998), Malaysia displayed political stability as an 'ethnocracy' (authoritarian consociationalism) in the middle of the 2000s. Claims for justice and reform (*reformasi*) were articulated by an increasingly stronger partisan opposition and civil society, and the dissatisfaction was reflected in parliamentary elections over the 2000s.

With a legacy of Spanish and American post-colonialism, the Philippines labour legislation and administration was modelled after the US legalistic labour regime. The Philippine political system went through two political revolutions from the mid-1980s to the early 2000s. The First People Power movement toppled the autocratic Marcos regime in 1986 and the Second People Power movement forced President Estrada out of office in 2001 after serving only three years (Deyo 2012). The first revolt was a democratic revolution while the second revolt against a populist government was rather a palace coup by factions of the political elite with support from mass demonstrations including the radical labour movement, KMU. The rather liberal but legalistic industrial relations framework contrasted with the militant and violent clashes of interests between labour and capital in the Philippines that testify to the supremacy of power constellations relative to regulative institutions in a highly unequal society. Huge income and asset inequalities are rooted primarily in high land concentration, and confrontational industrial relations dominate, especially in rural areas between commercial landowners and poor landless labourers.

In sum, the institutional power of workers in general and auto workers in particular was relatively high in Korea around 2005 while it was medium in Thailand and low in Malaysia and the Philippines. The legalisation or expansion of contract work and labour agencies employing and supplying contract workers for in-factory jobs posed a threat to regular auto workers and their unions in all EA-4 countries in the mid-2000s.

Explaining the organisational power of auto workers in East Asian EA-4 around 2005

As argued theoretically, the organisational power of auto workers is conditioned by the combination of their structural power and institutional power while the labour movement forms an institutional-organisational context of workers' organisational power at the sector level. The question is if the empirical evidence corroborates or falsifies our claim about auto workers' organisational power in the EA-4 countries interpreted in a static-comparative perspective of the mid-2000s and in a dynamic-relational perspective across time and space in East Asia and beyond.

The static-comparative explanation

Overall, both Korean and Malaysian auto workers ranked high in terms of organisational power; Thai auto workers had a medium level of organisational power while the Philippine auto workers were low on organisational strength.

This variety in organisational power of the Korean, Thai and Philippine auto workers correlates by and large with their variation in structural and institutional power:

- Korea ranked high on all factors because Korean auto workers worked in a structurally important industry, they had achieved relatively large institutional space for collective organising and action, and they had achieved a high organisational level.
- The Thai auto workers were deemed medium in all respects with medium structural power due to the little political-strategic but high economic significance of the auto industry with large production, export and employment, and with medium institutional space in the private sector due to liberal union legislation combined with an anti-union environment of operation due to formal and informal institutions, translating into a low level of enterprise-based unionisation and fragmented union federations and confederations. However, some inter-union coordination is emerging in the Japanese transplant subsector in the form of 'supply chain' union networks and union federations among enterprise unions in Japanese transplants and affiliated Thai auto suppliers.
- The Philippines ranked low on all measures because Philippines auto workers were positioned in a domestically insignificant industry, they had not much space for collective action in practice although the Philippine state had recognised all core ILO covenants, and they were weakly unionised and highly fragmented.

Malaysian autoworkers deviate significantly from our theory-based expectations with a position of high organisational power contrary to their structural position as medium due to the industry's economic insignificance, but political-strategic salience as a core part of the development of a *Bumiputera* (Malay) commercial and industrial community economically on a par with the Chinese-Malaysian business community. The institutional space for worker organising and collective actions is narrow non-partisan in purpose, form and action and thus low, being strictly controlled politically, legally and administratively including being marginalised in tripartite processes. Explaining the Malaysian exception, recently corroborated by the election of the general secretary of the Malaysian auto workers' industrial union, NUTEAIW, to general secretary of the Malaysian peak union organisation, MTUC, will require a broader historical-dynamic and international perspective, as will a deeper understanding of the expected pattern, too.

The dynamic-relational explanation: global auto capital and labour

Since the 1980s the global automotive industry has reorganised towards the Japanese lean and just-in-time production system allowing for above average wage and work conditions for the core, regular workforce in unionised workplaces and 'mean', more precarious employment conditions for an increasingly larger non-core, non-regular and non-unionised workforce. No wonder that the auto industry's employment and industrial relations in East Asia have been impacted by the lean and mean systems of advanced auto production due to the regional dominance of Japanese auto transnationals and the hegemony of the Japanese development model into the 1990s. This Japanese development model was constituted by a strong developmental state, internal and external production networking, productivity-related wages and micro-corporatism if necessary.

In Malaysia we have seen a deliberate political attempt to adopt selected parts of this model from the 1980s, including the development of a national auto industry substituting the foreign assembly transplants and restructuring the Western inspired industrial relations regime through a double decentralising manoeuvre of union devolution to 'in-house' unions and to 'in-house' collective bargaining (Wad 1988). In line with the principles of the New Economic Policy the 'national' auto industry was 'denationalised' and Proton was privatised to a Malay industrialist in the mid-1990s, renationalised after his death during the East Asian financial crisis and then again aims to be privatised to local interests in the 2000s. Contrary to the vision of the original privatisation policy, Japanese transplants also became the beneficiaries of the privatisation of auto joint ventures in the inter-crisis period 1999–2007, acquiring majority equity control of manufacturing facilities while sustaining supplier networks of foreign and local vendors (Perodua, MTB) (Wad and Govindaraju 2011). The adjustment to the competitive conditions of the evolving AFTA automobile market was also set to continue (Natsuda et al. 2013).

Thus, the problems facing the Malaysian auto workers' industrial union are not only rooted in the state-Japanese business collaboration but also in the industry's constrained production for the domestic market and its low productivity and export competitiveness even in the regional market of Southeast Asia (Wad 2009). This situation is again conditioned by the government's 'ethno-industrial nationalism' and the reactions by Western and Japanese automakers, abandoning Malaysia as a production base in favour of the Thai auto industrial cluster for domestic and export manufacturing. The success of the Malaysian auto ethno-industrial nationalism in the 1980s–1990s affected the auto industrial union negatively while allowing for expansion of enterprise-based unions, but the failure of Malaysian auto policy from the late 1990s impacted all auto workers and all their unions negatively from 1997.

The leverage of the Korean auto workers was rooted in the most successful national auto industrial developments in East Asia since the Japanese automakers changed the international way of manufacturing motor vehicles. With an active pro-national auto industrial policy from the 1970s the Korean government deliberately linked up with Japanese and American auto TNCs until the Korean joint ventures could do it alone, overtaking the domestic market and then moving into export production in the 1980s, and finally internationalising effectively through foreign direct investments in the 1990s. The upgrading of the Korean auto industry went hand in hand with labour militancy, union organising and improved employment conditions, but labour empowerment was counter-acted by corporate restructuring and labour flexibilisation.

The militant trade unions of the KCTU tried to drive the Korean industrial relation system toward centralisation against the global trend of organisational centralisation and decentralisation of collective bargaining. Aiming for a centralised industrial union (KMWU) and industry-wide collective bargaining at national or regional levels, substituting enterprise based negotiations, the radical faction of KMWU unionists were resisted by an unholy and implicit alliance between employers of the automakers and local enterprise-based workers unwilling to give up their vested interests and local identities for a larger cause of industrial unionism. In this impasse contract worker unions turned more militant than the regular worker unions (ILO 2010). The contract labour issue became a public issue in the middle of the 2010s but the level of unionisation among non-regular workers was still only around 3 per cent in 2013. Regular workers accounted for a union density of around 17 per cent while the whole workforce lay at around 10 per cent in 2012 (Lee 2014).

In the Japanese-dominated auto industries of Thailand and the Philippines all unions were enterprise-based unions and collective bargaining, if any, took place at the company level (Arnold 2006; Haruhi 2006). No industrial union of auto workers existed in these countries although the Philippine AIWA federation claimed to aim for industrial unionism. Thai auto workers' unions appeared to be linked via auto production networks and supply chains. Japanese automaker enterprise unions seemed to follow their own policy in favour of their own corporate viability, as auto production networks formed by Japanese transplants at the core and local Thai suppliers in the periphery of the domestic production network. In this way, auto workers' unionism in Thailand took a relatively new route of domestic 'supply chain' unionism.

At the federal level two organisations existed in 2005: TAW, the Federation of Thai Auto Workers, where the Toyota union (TTWU) was the lead union until mid-2000s, and the Federation of Thailand Siam Motors Automobile Industry Workers' Union. In the late 2000s Japanese and non-Japanese unions seemed to be split into the TAW unionising auto workers' unions at GM Thailand, Ford and Mazda Thailand among others, and the Automobile Labour Congress of Thailand (ALCT) that counted many more unions including the Toyota Thailand Workers' Union, the Denso Thailand Workers' Union and the Honda Labour Union of Thailand (Thai Labour Database 2015). The Japanese auto workers' unions seemed to have shifted sides toward the more royalist-oriented unions including ALCT following the accelerating political conflict between Thaksin and anti-Thaksin supporters in the second part of the 2000s into the first military coup in 2006–2008 and again in 2014. Finally, enterprise unions in Japanese transplants and affiliated firms seemed from the mid-1990s to engage in more cordial relationships with the management in favour of the competitiveness of the company and the employment conditions of the workers.

This evolution toward 'responsible' unionism was paralleled by increased flexibilisation of auto industry employment relations. While the Thai based

Japanese auto transplants reoriented from domestic to export markets, especially after the 1997 financial crisis, the labour force was gradually changed from regular employment to a mix of regular and temporary employment. The rising share of contract workers in the Thai auto industry aimed probably to drive down the average wage level. In Toyota's affiliate TMT the mix of employees was around 50–50 in the middle of the 2000s although the company had a policy to transfer contract employees to regular employment after two years.

Thus, in all select EA-4 countries the Western automakers and their auto workers played second hand after having had some leverage in the 1970s. Taking control of Daewoo Motors in the end of the 1990s, the American auto TNC General Motors (GM) restructured and downsized its Korean activities during the Global Financial Crisis 2008–2009, and it abandoned domestic assembling in the Philippines as well as Indonesia. While both GM and Ford stayed in Thailand, Ford severed its ties with Mazda in their joint venture, and Ford gave up its assembling activity in Malaysia, thus closing down the auto assembling factory that had been the abode of the industrial union in Malaysia and workplace for its two long serving general secretaries.

Japanese TNCs tried to enter the Korean market but failed. A joint venture between Samsung and Nissan in the 1990s failed and French Renault took charge of the transplant (Renault-Nissan) substituting Nissan, and this automaker was the last one in Korea to become unionised (in 2011). In Southeast Asia Japanese auto TNCs prioritised Thailand even when facing a natural disaster in 2012. With enduring political turbulence Japanese and other foreign automakers may increasingly have second thoughts about the viability of Thailand as the 'Southeast Asian Detroit' (Busser 2008) and look around for alternative locations. With decreasing auto industrial nationalism in Malaysia, a regional auto market is emerging within the ASEAN region where Indonesia's large and rapidly growing automobile market presents a new opportunity for foreign automakers.

In sum, the regionalisation of Japanese production networks into a dominant position in Southeast Asia has been accompanied by a trend toward enterprise, 'responsible' and even 'supply chain' unionism which fits post-Fordist auto manufacturing with its more disintegrated production chains and creation of global production networks where automakers' value added share of total vehicle value has declined from 75 per cent in 1955 to 25 per cent in 1995 (Wad 2008). In Korea, the exception to Japanese auto hegemony among our EA-4 countries in 2005, industrial and militant unionism affects labour-management relations in the auto industry where employers also pursue anti-union policies, generating an environment of adversarial industrial relations. In Malaysia, with creeping Japanisation of the auto industry, the auto industrial union is pressured by foreign and local firms' restructuring and support for enterprise unions to prevent or get rid of industrial unionisation (NUTEAIW 2009).

In general transplant managements seem to prefer non-union workplaces, but if this cannot be accomplished they accept enterprise unions when the alternative is industrial union. Japanese auto TNCs like Toyota accepted 'responsible' enterprise unions if necessary for implementing their Toyota Production System, but avoided, resisted and eliminated militant enterprise unions, industrial unions and centralised negotiations (Fumio 2006). Contrary to US electronics TNCs that are known for their anti-union policy, Western auto TNCs accepted enterprise or industrial unions especially if they could establish working labour-management relations, e.g. the Ford affiliated joint venture in Malaysia. However, this was not always the case. At the Ford-Mazda joint venture in Thailand, AutoAlliance, auto workers had to call on assistance from the American auto workers' industrial union, UAW, in order to become recognised and enter collective bargaining agreement.

Thus, Beverly Silver's thesis of the Japanese exceptionalism is corroborated for the EA-4 countries. But the question remains if this outcome is due to dynamic industrial internationalisation and restructuring and domestic worker mobilisation alone, or whether cross-border labour networks also matter.

The dynamic-relational explanation: global union networks and auto workers

Until 2012 the International Metal Workers' Federation (henceforth IMF-metal) has been the global union federation that affiliated auto workers' unions across the world, including the unions in EA-4. IMFmetal is headquartered in Europe and traditionally dominated by European and American metal workers' unions with a strong automotive group.

The IMFmetal intervened at a late moment in the Philippine dispute on union recognition between Toyota's (TMC) joint venture (TMPC) and the enterprise union (TMPCWA) trying to mediate between the Philippine union and the Japanese TNC, and the Japanese enterprise unions of the Toyota production network and the Confederation of Japanese Automobile Workers' Unions (JAW) (Wad 2014). With the Japanese unions leaving the 'transplant' issue to the TMC, and thereby the Philippine transplant TMPC, the IMFmetal could not persuade the TMC HQs to recognise the TMPCWA and reinstate the dismissed workers. The IMFmetal finally decided to launch a worldwide campaign for the reinstatement of the dismissed workers at TMPC, but it failed and withered with the certification of the second union (TMPCLO) and the collective bargaining and agreement in 2006. After the 2006 campaign IMF-metal tried to facilitate union collaboration in the Philippines, in line with the ICFTU-WCL (International Confederation of Free Trade Unions-World Confederation of Labour) collaboration and foundation of the new International Trade Union Confederation (ITUC) in 2006 that also brought several peak labour organisations into the same fold.

A more successful intervention by IMFmetal took place in Malaysia. Unionising of the auto TNC component supplier, German Robert Bosch's subsidiary in Malaysia, lasted several years. At first, the industrial union, NUTEAIW, started building a local union base at the company with support from the American Confederation for International Labor Solidarity that ran a campaign to organise Bosch subsidiaries in the USA and globally (NUTEAIW 2009). Followed by visits of Bosch unions in 2010 and then with decisive assistance by the European Works Council of Bosch, resistance by local and HQs management and the Malaysian authorities was overcome. The certification election held in 2011 showed that around 75 per cent of the nearly 500 employees favoured recognition of NUTEAIW as the legitimate union of the Bosch employees (IndustriALL 2011).

With the merger of IMFmetal and other manufacturing sector unions into IndustriALL in 2012 the new global union federation adopted an action plan to establish company-recognised World Work Councils which include unions of the corporation and representatives of IndustriALL (IndustriALL 2014). The new global union federation formed an automotive working group which takes as its objective to bring together auto TNC HQs unions from e.g. BMW, Daimler, Renault and GM with their transplants' local unions to improve mutual knowledge and understanding and to integrate these unions in the particular global union corporate network. In addition non-unionised plants are spotted and organising efforts of the local unions are supported by the global union federation and the TNC HQs union. Thus, the Automotive Working Group of the IndustriALL is operating as 'a stable international network of all auto unions to support each other in organising campaigns and strengthen unions by including them in the different company networks' (email from IndustriALL officer, 12 March 2015).

The IndustriALL has union networks in most major global auto TNCs. Global union corporate networks have been recognised by Western firms like BMW, Daimler, Ford, GM/Opel, PSA Peugeot Citroën, Renault, Volkswagen (and Volvo AB) plus Bosch as one of the leading first tier auto suppliers and by Japanese corporations like Honda, Nissan and Toyota (IndustriALL 2014). Italian/American Fiat/Chrysler and Korean Hyundai/Kia have not recognised the global union corporate network. Finally, mostly European automakers have entered Global Framework Agreements with the IndustriALL, while neither GM/Opel and Fiat/Chrysler nor the Japanese automakers and Korean Hyundai/Kia had agreed to sign a global framework agreement with IndustriALL by 2014.

The Japanese auto workers' unions, organised in the Japan Autoworkers' Unions (JAW), probably perceived the IMFmetal's automotive group as a group aligned informally with Western auto TNCs. JAW stepped out of the TMPC dispute with TMPCWA and lined up with 'responsible' TMPCLO in the end. Recently, the Japanese auto workers' unions have set up the JAW Asia Auto Network as an automotive working group for Japanese TNCs' unions and counterparts in Asia: 'The JAW Asia Auto network is something similar [to the IndustriALL's automotive group – PW] but only focused on Asia' (email from IndustriALL officer to PW, 12 March 2015).

While Japanese transplants achieved Japanese standards of 'responsible' industrial relations in Thailand from the mid-1990s and in the Philippines from the mid-2000s, the political environment in the two countries turned more turbulent and violent and thus against Japanese production philosophy in particular and global automakers in general.

In all EA-4 countries the consolidation of the two global union confederations of ICFTU and WCL into the ITUC in 2006 and of several global union federations, including IMFmetal, in the manufacturing sectors into IndustriALL in 2012 has opened new space for intra-country and cross-country union collaboration and support. The ITUC consolidation was not complete in the Philippines where the World Federation of Trade Unions (WFTU) is supported by KMU. Most recently four national federations within the Thai manufacturing sector formed the Confederation of Industrial Labour of Thailand, including the TEAM and the ALCT that together bridge auto worker unions based in Western and Japanese transplants.

Yet the merger of global union federations within the global manufacturing industry has not overcome the differences between Western and Japanese trade unions below the global level of regional unionism. The Western and Japanese IndustriALL affiliates engage primarily with auto workers and their unions in East Asia in their own way and within their related corporate automotive production networks.

Conclusion

This chapter aimed at analysing the power of auto workers' organisations in East Asian market economies through static-comparative and dynamic-relational perspectives on the pattern and evolution of the automobile industry and auto workers' power position in the EA-4 countries: Korea, Malaysia, Thailand and the Philippines.

In the mid-2000s the automotive industries boomed in East Asia (except the Philippines auto assembling industry). Their growth started well before and ran high after the East Asian financial crisis in 1997–1998 and their expansion was only briefly suspended by the global financial crisis in 2008–2009 that primarily hit the Global North, as did a second slump in 2011–2012 due to the European debt crisis (Wad 2010). At such fortunate economic junctures, workers and trade unions should be able to advance their cause and strengthen the organisational power of auto workers. A snapshot of auto workers' power around 2005 indicates anyway that auto workers' organisational power was relatively high in Korea and Malaysia, at a medium level in Thailand and at a low level in the Philippines. This variation in organisation power fits the variation in structural and institutional power of auto workers, except in the case of Malaysia, indicating that the structural-productive evolution of auto industries had mostly taken place in Korea and Thailand, modified by the rise of non-regular employment, the dependence of Japanese transplants, and the lack of political-strategic salience of auto industry in Thailand.

Auto workers' unions in the structurally more autonomous and politically-strategic auto industries of Korea and Malaysia have been partly able either to build an industrial union from enterprise unions (Korea) or to sustain industry level unionisation from the past (Malaysia), in both cases obtaining or sustaining relative high union density. The processes of organisational centralisation or decentralisation, manifested in the competition between enterprise unions and industrial unions, may have interfaced in Korea and Malaysia in a way that has generated higher overall union density. No such inter-union competition has taken place in Thailand and the Philippines because there were only enterprise-based unions, and auto workers had no industrial union as an alternative choice.

In the two dependent auto industries of Thailand and the Philippines, worker organising has been lower and enterprise based, and after a period of adversarial labour-management relations more conducive labour-management relations emerged in Thailand's auto industry from the mid-1990s and in the Philippine auto industry from the mid-2000s. In fact, in Thailand micro-corporatism with 'supply chain' unionism (assembly-union lead networking with supplier enterprise unions along the supply chain of the automakers) emerged in the 2000s among Japanese-related firms, partly reflecting the new global competition between specific global auto value chains or networks and the regional dominance of Japanese auto TNCs. However, the evolution of 'auto industrial peace' in the two Japanese dominated domestic auto industries contrasted with and is challenged by the broader social movement unionism prevailing in both these countries, together with tense and turbulent political environments, with military coups in Thailand and People Power movements in the Philippines.

With the creeping 'Japanisation' of the Malaysian auto industry, the last Southeast Asian national auto industry uncaptured by Japanese automakers, the Malaysian industrial union is under siege as the Japanese TNCs and their local suppliers prefer 'responsible' enterprise unionism to militant industrial unionism. The Malaysian exception of high auto worker organisational power is very much conditioned by the institutional-organisational path of Malaysian auto industry unionism. The union history reflects the transformation of the Malaysian auto industry from a Western dominated one in the late 1960s to the mid-1970s, where industrial unionism and centralised collective bargaining was established, into a highly competitive foreign Japanese-Western dominated industry during the next decade, where industry-wide bargaining withered while the industrial union prevailed, further on into a Malaysian state-owned industrial hegemony in the late 1980s to the early 2000s where enterprise unions gained ground among automakers. In the 1990s the industrial union shifted strategy making inroads into the auto component and parts subsector and returning to the Malaysian peak labour centre, the MTUC. With the strengthening of Japanese automakers' structural position in the 2000s the industrial union has been challenged once again by employer-supported or -instigated enterprise union 'coups' in local auto suppliers or Japanese transplants previously organised by the industrial union.

Thus, in the emerging regional automotive industry and market of Southeast Asia, Japanese-led production networks dominate domestic production, and they seem to further Japanese-inspired 'responsible' enterprise unionism to the point where new forms of 'supply chain' unionism evolved in Thailand's large auto industry, although it is unclear if they had been sustained. In the 'uncaptured' Korean auto industry, more militant industrial unionism is progressing, yet with a strong inclination to decentralised, enterprise based collective bargaining at the large carmakers' workplaces with strong union locales.

Acknowledgements

Highly appreciated critical comments on former drafts were received from the editors, Byoung-Hoon Lee, Daniel Fleming, Rene Ofreneo and Rick Doner. The usual disclaimers prevail.

References

Arnold, Dennis. 2006. Toyota in Thailand: Capital and Labour in 'Harmonious' Globalised Production. In *Labour in Globalising Asian Corporations: A Portrait of Struggle*, edited by Dae-oup Chang, 215–246. Hong Kong: Asia Monitor Resource Centre.

Arrighi, Giovanni and Beverly Silver. 1984. Labour Movements and Capital Migration: The US and Western Europe in World-Historical Perspective. In *Labor in the Capitalist World-Economy*, edited by Charles Bergquist, 183–216. Beverly Hills: Sage.

Brown, Andrew and Kevin Hewison. 2005. 'Economics is the Deciding Factor': Labour Politics in Thaksin's Thailand. *Pacific Affairs* 78 (3): 353–375.

Brown, Andrew and Sakdina Chatrakul Na Ayudhya. 2013. Labour Activism in Thailand. In *Social Activism in Southeast Asia*, edited by Michele Ford, 104–118. London: Routledge.

Busser, Rogier. 2008. 'Detroit of the East'? Industrial Upgrading, Japanese Car Producers and the Development of the Automotive Industry in Thailand. *Asia Pacific Business Review* 14 (1): 29–45.

Dass, Arokia. 1991. *Not Beyond Repair: Reflections of a Malaysian Trade Unionist*. Hong Kong: Asia Monitor Resource Centre.

Deyo, Frederic. 1989. *Beneath the Miracle*. Berkeley: University of California Press.

Deyo, Frederic. 2012. *Reforming Asian Labor Systems: Economic Tension and Worker Discontent*. Ithaca: Cornell University Press.

Doner, Richard. 1991. *Driving a Bargain: Automobile Industrialization and Japanese Firms in Southeast Asia*. Berkeley: University of California Press.

Doner, Richard. 2009. *The Politics of Uneven Development: Thailand's Economic Growth in Comparative Perspective*. New York: Cambridge University Press.

Doner, Richard and Peter Wad. 2014. Financial Crises and Automotive Industry Development in Southeast Asia. *Journal of Contemporary Asia* 44 (4): 664–687.

Fumio, Kaneko. 2006. Toyota and Asian Automobile Workers. In *Labour in Globalising Asian Corporations: A Portrait of Struggle*, edited by Dae-oup Chang, 181–214. Hong Kong: Asia Monitor Resource Centre.

Haruhi, Tono. 2006. Toyota in the Philippines: Drive your Dream or Drive to the Bottom. In *Labour in Globalising Asian Corporations: A Portrait of Struggle*, edited by Dae-oup Chang, 247–271. Hong Kong: Asia Monitor Resource Centre.

ILO. 2010. The Global Economic Crisis: Sectoral Coverage. Automotive Industry: Trends and Reflexions. Working Paper No. 278. Geneva: ILO.

IndustriALL. 2011. NUTEAIW Wins Union Vote at Bosch Malaysia. www.industriall-union.org/archive/imf/nuteaiw-wins-union-vote-at-bosch-malaysia.

IndustriALL. 2014. Building Global Union Power in the Auto Industry. *Global Workers* 1.

IndustriALL. 2015. Email from IndustriALL officer to Peter Wad, 12 March 2015.

Jeong, Jooyeon. 2007. *Industrial Relations in Korea: Diversity and Dynamism of Korean Enterprise Unions from a Comparative Perspective*. London: Routledge.

Kishnam, Gopal. 2009. Personal email correspondence, 28 September.

Koo, Hagen. 2001. *Korean Workers: The Culture and Politics of Class Formation*. Ithaca: Cornell University Press.

Kuruvilla, Sarosh, Subesh Das, Hyunji Kwon and Soonwon Kwon. 2002. Trade Union Growth and Decline in Asia. *British Journal of Industrial Relations* 40 (3): 431–461.

Lee, Byoung-hoon. 2014. Militant Activism on the Margins: Struggles of Non-regular Workers in South Korea. Paper presented at the seminar on 'Militant Activism at the Margins: Struggles of Non-regular Workers in South Korea' at the Centre for Business and Development Studies, Copenhagen Business School, Denmark, 13 June.

Lee, Byoung-hoon and Hyung-je Jo. 2007. The Mutation of the Toyota Production System: Adapting the TPS at Hyundai Motor Company. *International Journal of Production Research* 45 (16): 3665–3679.

Lee, Byoung-hoon and Sanghoon Yi. 2012. Organizational Transformation Towards Industry Unionism in South Korea. *Journal of Industrial Relations* 54 (4): 476–493.

Lee, Joohee. 2011. Between Fragmentation and Centralization: South Korean Industrial Relations in Transition. *British Journal of Industrial Relations* 49 (4): 767–791.

Natsuda, Kaoru and John Thoburn. 2013. Industrial Policy and the Development of the Automotive Industry in Thailand. *Journal of the Asia Pacific Economy* 18 (3): 413–437.

Natsuda, Kaoru, Noriyuki Segawa and John Thoburn. 2013. Liberalization, Industrial Nationalism and the Malaysian Automotive Industry. *Global Economic Review* 42 (2): 113–134.

NUTEAIW. 2009. Report of the Executive Council 2006–2009. Shah Alam: NUTEAIW.

Ofreneo, Rene. 2015. Growth and Employment in De-industrializing Philippines. *Journal of Asia Pacific Economy* 20 (1): 111–129.

Ofreneo, Rene. 2016. Auto and Car Parts Production: Can the Philippines Catch up with Asia? *Asia Pacific Business Review* 22 (1): 48–64.

Ofreneo, Rene and Peter Wad. 2010. Industrial Relations and Labour Market Conditions. In *The New Political Economy of Southeast Asia*, edited by Rajah Rasiah and Johannes Dragsbaek Schmidt, 169–197. Cheltenham: Edward Elgar.

Rasiah, Rajah. 2011. Is Malaysia Facing Negative Deindustrialization? *Pacific Affairs* 84 (4): 715–736.

Rasiah, Rajah, Vicki Crinis and Hwok-Aun Lee. 2015. Industrialisation and Labour in Malaysia. *Journal of Asia Pacific Economy* 20 (1): 77–99.

Sadoi, Yuri. 2015. The Strategies of Japanese Automobile Manufacturers in Thailand under the Technology Transfer and the Raising of the Thai Wage System. *Meijo Asian Research Journal* 6 (1): 19–30.

Serrano, Melissa, (ed.). 2014. *Between Flexibility and Security: The Rise of Non-standard Employment in Selected ASEAN countries*. Jakarta: Friedrich Ebert Stiftung and ASETUC.

Silver, Beverly. 2003. *Forces of Labor: Workers' Movements and Globalization since 1870*. New York: Cambridge University Press.

Thai Labor Database. 2015. Thai Labor Database. www.thailabordatabase.org/en/affiliate.php?c=detail&t=congress&id=2.

Todd, Patricia and David Peetz. 2001. Malaysian Industrial Relations at Century's Turn: Vision 2020 or a Spectre of the Past? *International Journal of Human Resource Management* 12 (8): 1365–1382.

Todd, Patricia, Russell Lansbury and Ed Davis. 2006. Industrial Relations in Malaysia: Some Proposals for Reform. *Philippine Journal of Labor and Industrial Relations* 61 (1): 70–84.

Wad, Peter. 1988. The Japanization of the Malaysian Trade Union Movement. In *The Trade Unions and the New Internationalization of the Third World*, edited by Roger Southall, 210–229. London: Zed Books.

Wad, Peter. 2002. The Political Business of Development in South Korea. In *Political Business in East Asia*, edited by Terence Gomez, 182–215. London: Routledge.

Wad, Peter. 2004. Transforming Industrial Relations: The Case of the Malaysian Auto Industry. In *Labour in Southeast Asia: Local Processes in a Globalised World*, edited by Rebecca Elmhirst and Ratna Saptari, 235–264. London: RoutledgeCurzon.

Wad, Peter. 2007. Globalization and Trade Unions: Transformation of Automobile Trade Unions in Korea and Malaysia. In *Global Challenges and Local Responses: The East Asian Experience*, edited by Jang-Sup Shin, 163–183. London: Routledge.

Wad, Peter. 2008. The Development of Automotive Parts Suppliers in Korea and Malaysia: A Global Value Chain Perspective. *Asia Pacific Business Review* 14 (1): 47–64.

Wad, Peter. 2009. The Automobile Industry in Southeast Asia: Malaysia and Thailand. *Journal of the Asia Pacific Economy* 14 (2): 172–193.

Wad, Peter. 2010. Impact of the Global Economic and Financial Crisis over the Automotive Industry in Developing Countries. UNIDO Working Paper no. 16. Vienna: UNIDO.

Wad, Peter. 2014. Solidarity Action in Global Labor Networks: Four Cases of Workplace Organizing at Foreign Affiliates in the Global South. *Nordic Journal of Working Life Studies* 4 (1): 11–33.

Wad, Peter and V. G. R. Chandran Govindaraju. 2011. Automotive Industry in Malaysia: Evolution and Impact of Global Crisis. *International Journal of Automotive Technology and Management* 11 (2): 152–171.

Wright, Erik Olin. 2000. Working-Class Power, Capitalist-Class Interests, and Class Compromise. *American Journal of Sociology* 105 (4): 957–1002.

Yun, Aelim. 2011. Building Collective Identity: Trade Union Representation of Precarious Workers in the South Korean Auto Companies. *Labour, Capital and Society* 44 (1): 155–178.

4 Revolution or evolution?

The making of the automobile sector as a key industry in mid-twentieth century India

Stefan Tetzlaff

India's automotive industry witnessed considerable growth after the implementation of economic reforms in the 1990s. Almost all global manufacturers have started vehicle assembly or production in the country since 1991 and production figures have more than doubled since 2006 to almost four million passenger and commercial vehicle units in 2015 (Government of India 2006, 18; Government of India 2015). India's passenger car and commercial vehicle industry became the sixth largest in the world in 2010, partly fuelled by the fact that its automobile market was the second fastest growing in the world after China (OICA 2015; *The Hindu BusinessLine* 2010). These figures establish India as an important global automobile production and market place and reflect several important and new trends since the 1990s. Overseas companies drove the growth of the industry to some extent, but several partly (Maruti Suzuki) or fully Indian-owned (Tata Motors, Mahindra & Mahindra) manufacturers are now among the world's 30 largest producers of vehicles (OICA 2014). The growth of industry and private enterprise also had immense repercussions on the global importance of the country's automobile industry. India became Asia's fourth largest exporter of passenger cars after Japan, South Korea and Thailand (Nair 2009), and an important part in the global automotive supply chain with a strong position in ancillary production (ACMA 2015). Global financial capital and consultancy firms as well as foreign governments interested in export promotion increasingly regard India as an important automobile production and market place (KPMG 2010; Schade *et al.* 2012). In 2014, the industry was responsible for 7.1 per cent of India's GDP, for 4.3 per cent of overall exports and for creating an additional 19 million jobs since 2006 (Government of India 2015, 1). The production of the cheap Tata Nano car from 2008 together with the promise of 'universal car ownership' for a growing consumer group including Indian lower middle class households showed how the automobile influenced both industrialisation and consumption (Chakraverti 2008), even if the Nano project turned out to be largely unsuccessful (Nielsen and Wilhite, this volume).

Overall, these reports and figures reflect not only substantial industrial change, but also a new attitude of the government in pushing the industry and substantially increasing demand for automobiles from old and new consumer classes. Being of comparatively recent nature, however, this trajectory of India's automotive industry more or less suggests a sudden revolution with regard to automobiles in the realm of industrial manufacture, capital formation and consumer behaviour over the past two and a half decades. This view has also been the mainstay of the most recent research literature on the subject. It follows the assumption that the coming of international capital in the form of Japanese investments in vehicle manufacture in the 1980s was the decisive shift for the automotive industry and that the industry became substantial only after the 1990s economic reforms (D'Costa 2005). One reason for privileging these decades over earlier decades might be that the role and extent of industrialisation as well as its interplay with the private business sector in India after independence has not been thoroughly addressed and understood so far. Instead, the research literature on this period differentiates between industrial policies for large and small industries and their effect on large-scale and small-scale industrialisation (Tyabji 1980, 2015). However, this literature has not inquired if and where these industries came together, and only a few studies have looked at the automobile industry as a subject. Two studies that did so either explained the comparative lack of an indigenous automotive industry in India as a result of the unwillingness of Indian industrialists to come forth for automotive manufacture (Chibber 2003), or neglected political ideas around automobile manufacture and repercussions of the new industry on ancillary industrial development (Kathuria 1987).

The previous discussion shows that the research literature has largely neglected the evolution of the automobile industry in the intervening period between independence and 1980. The research literature sees this earlier industrial legacy by and large as one of false planning objectives, dis-allocations of state and private investments and of stagnation in automotive manufacture. However, the early making of this industry cannot be studied without referring to the emergence of national plans and of several Indian companies for automobile manufacture. The literature has not only overlooked the specific environment in which this took place, but also whether and how this impacted ancillary industrial development and the economy more generally. However, these transformations were the product of a longer legacy of the automotive manufacturing sector roughly from the period after the Second World War, and were important in the making of an industry that saw yet another transformation in the 1980s and 1990s.

Assumptions about the revolutionary impact of the 1990s economic reforms will therefore need to be revisited by looking at advances in automobile manufacture in the early planning period and how important the economic effects of the automobile industry on the Indian economy were in general at the time. This chapter analyses the emergence of the automotive sector as a key industry in mid-twentieth century India. Its main purpose is to highlight several specific contexts in this recent historical period in which automotive manufacture emerged and developed, and to bring to the general attention the fact that the larger history of automobile manufacture in India is under-researched. In doing so, the chapter commences with a comparative approach to the automobile industry, which looks at the emergence of this industry and the idea of a key sector in industrialised countries, and why it emerged comparatively late and then did not take off to a larger extent in India. The second part of the chapter looks at how the Indian government and its planning apparatus addressed the automobile industry in the early post-independence period. National plans for automotive manufacture recurred on earlier plans that did not mature during the colonial period, and these plans tried to shut down foreign competition and increase in-house manufacture to boost the indigenous industry.

This chapter is therefore not only concerned with why India's automobile industry emerged comparatively late as a key sector. It also looks at the contexts in which it became a key sector in India and what its specific characteristics have been. The third part of the chapter shows how the industry developed in India in the short and medium run and how it affected several other sectors of the economy such as ancillary industrial units. The current literature particularly regards the initial plans for a small car project under Indira Gandhi and eventually the collaboration between Maruti-Suzuki in the production of the Maruti car as a turning point in the trajectory of automotive manufacture in India. This new collaboration did indeed start an entirely new phase in terms of capital investment and output capacity, but the automobile industry had a much longer historical trajectory with relevant repercussions that have been neglected so far. In particular the political contours and repercussions of industrial development at the local and regional level have been neglected so far. This part shows that despite a much smaller automobile industry compared with the US and Europe, specific localities and regions in India saw substantial new developments in automobile manufacture and with more wide-ranging repercussions on other sectors of the economy.

Vagaries in the making of a key industry

The history of industrialisation and capitalist production in the US and Europe over the past century is inextricably connected with automobile manufacture. The making of Henry Ford's Model T in Detroit from the early 1900s established not only new forms of mass production, but also provided the basis for increasing automobile consumption in the US. Europe had a number of automobile manufacturers before the Second World War, but several countries increasingly promoted automobile manufacture in the war environment. Strategic interests made the Nazi regime in Germany invest heavily into the Volkswagen factory, and this provided the grounds for making the Beetle car after the war. Several industrialised countries saw a major boom in automotive industry and markets over a 50 year period after the Second World War in particular, and the automotive industry remains important in these countries. While the industry as such is important, even more important from the viewpoint of economic growth are the multiplier effects of the automobile industry on specific industrial sectors and the economy at large. Among these count the large number of ancillary production units emerging alongside the automotive industry, the role of the industry in creating employment and the promotion of technology research and development. In the post-war period, state institutions and economists became increasingly aware of the industry's potential to instil economic growth in other sectors and the economy at large, and geared political and economic activities towards this industry. Thus, there was an interdependent process in many industrialised countries in designating automobile production as a key industry.

Ideas for establishing an automobile industry in India existed from as early as the 1920s. The engineer-politician Mokshagundam Visvesvaraya explained early on that 'a great motor-car industry could be established in India within a year ... [and] ... firms [are] ready to start if only they could be assured of Government co-operation and support' (Visvesvaraya 1920, 210). The considerable growth of motorised road transport in the following two decades then instilled a growing demand for vehicles, which was primarily satisfied by US and UK imports. American companies like General Motors and Ford had established several plants for assembling imported vehicle parts and thus clearly led the market ahead of smaller UK manufacturers (Tetzlaff 2015). Visvesvaraya continued to advertise plans for automobile manufacture more vigorously in the 1930s and early 1940s based on this growing demand (Visvesvaraya 1934, 1937), also because of a conviction that the industry could influence other economic sectors and thus act as a motor for industrial progress in India more generally (Krishnamurti 1941, 69; M. V. 1960, 148–149). Several industrialists, including the western India-based Walchand Hirachand and the eastern India-based G. D. Birla, joined Visvesvaraya in his demand for an Indian automobile industry in the late 1930s (Sardesai 1942; Khanolkar 1969; Ray 1979, 176–183; Piramal 1998).

However, plans for an indigenous automotive industry did not materialise in the late colonial period due to several implicit or explicit reasons. More implicitly, arrested development in colonial India led to not only lower industrialisation levels, but also lower levels of consumer expenditure and to a much smaller middle class segment capable of affording vehicles (Dewey 1988). Moreover, the government did not sufficiently promote, and even neglected, forward thinking policies of industrial and technological development, something that contributed to the lack of industrialisation more generally (Lamb 1955; Dewey 1979; Headrick 1981; Macleod and Kumar 1995; Arnold 2000). Most importantly, however, the Government of India did not encourage indigenous automobile manufacture in the 1920s and 1930s, also due to interests of the British government and vehicle manufacturers in expanding their market shares in India (Chatterji 1992; Tetzlaff 2015). During the Second World War, the Government of India then did not want to help Indian politicians and industrialists in establishing the industry as an important war industry and even repeatedly thwarted their plans in this period (Ghosh 1941; Visvesvaraya 1951, 97; Zachariah 2001; Nair 2011, 2013, 12–13). Nationalist politicians such as Jawaharlal Nehru and industrialists such as G. D. Birla argued that an Indian automobile industry did not develop because the Government of India rather followed strategic wartime interests and vested interests of the American and British motorcar industry in keeping the status quo. International manufacturing concerns could make higher profits by selling cars from imported and assembled vehicle parts than by producing them in the country, which is why they had no interest in establishing full-phased manufacture (Birla 1944, 123–124; Gopal 1979, 548–558). This combined action of the colonial state and the interests of global manufacturers in the Indian market further retarded the industry and made it imperative, according to Visvesvaraya, for post-war reconstruction to focus on establishing an automobile industry (Visvesvaraya 1943, 1944).

Two of the most important industrialists in India, Walchand Hirachand and G. D. Birla, had floated enterprises for automobile manufacture – Premier Automobiles Ltd (PAL) and Hindustan Motors Ltd (HML) – in the early 1940s as automobile production seemed to provide a lucrative ground for the diversification of earlier business interests during the war. It was only after the Second World War, however, that both companies established factory sites in Kurla (Mumbai) and Uttarpara (West Bengal) and commenced to assemble shipped vehicles of their respective cooperation partners Chrysler and later Fiat (PAL) as well as Morris Motors (HML) from around 1948–1949 (Kidron 1960; Piramal 1998). These two companies were the two most important manufacturers in the passenger car market until the 1980s, when the collaboration between Maruti and Suzuki set new standards in car production and sales. Another important manufacturer emerging in this period was the Tata Engineering and Locomotive Company (TELCO), which began cooperating with Mercedes-Benz in truck manufacture and established a factory site in Jamshedpur in 1954. The company entered the market roughly ten years after PAL and HML and in an entirely different environment. TELCO emerged in 1945 out of a large industrial conglomerate with interests, among others, in iron and steel production since the nineteenth century, primarily to manufacture locomotives in India (Fraser 1919; Keenan 1943; Menon 1948; Verma 1988). However, the company soon realised not only the heavily fluctuating railway demand for rolling stock and equipment, but also that the demand for commercial vehicles and trucks grew exponentially due to commercialisation in agriculture and upscaling inland trade and transport. At the same time, the Government of India declared the indigenous production of trucks to be of special importance and urgency. Nothing short of an invitation under the given circumstances, TELCO seized the promising opportunity of adding trucks to its manufacturing portfolio in the early 1950s and began a process at the end of which saw it leaving locomotives behind and switching to automobiles entirely (Lala 1993; Nath et al. 2004). Despite advanced knowledge in heavy and machine engineering, TELCO needed external technical cooperation to start the new manufacturing line. At the same time, Daimler-Benz was in search of a production partner in Asia to develop the regional market. Both companies eventually established a joint venture with a majority stake of 85 per cent for Tata in March 1954, to which Daimler agreed to give full technical assistance for 15 years.

National plans and the emergence of automobile manufacture, 1947–1953

The last section pointed out why the Indian automobile industry did not take off before and during the Second World War. The introduction to this chapter, on the other hand, discussed arguments in the more recent literature concerning the absence of a substantial automobile sector after the industry finally came into existence from the late 1940s. This literature mainly tried to explain why the development of the industry in India deviated from that in the US and Europe. The main reasons given were political and business aspects of the industry. Unlike in many other socialist countries, the Indian state never owned the automobile industry or undertakings in it so that the industry remained entirely in the private sector. Nonetheless, the state controlled capitalist enterprise through several important policies such as import substitution and price control since the 1950s.

Plans for the automobile industry itself received a major push in the period after war and independence when politicians and industrialists promoted plans for post-war reconstruction and Indian economic development (Thakurdas *et al.* 1944; Sanyal 2010; Kudaisya 2014). Up to this period, all companies – including smaller Indian companies and bigger foreign manufacturers such as General Motors and Ford – were importing vehicle parts in completely-knocked-down condition for assembly in plants in India. These assembly plants employed a large number of skilled workers and to some extent instilled ancillary industrial development, such as the tyre industry. However, the full potential of the automobile industry was not exhausted in this period, because of the limited production range inside the country. There was little or no on-site manufacturing involved as such, apart from building and fitting of bodies suited to local conditions. Indian companies, thus, continued to depend on the engineering and manufacturing expertise of foreign firms.

In this context of increasing attention to economic reconstruction, the Indian government also to a great extent focused on the automobile industry. The National Planning Committee reports of 1947 were the main policy documents, as they discussed the unfulfilled plans for indigenous automobile manufacture of the late 1930s and of the Second World War. The plan for manufacturing industries designated heavy engineering industries for making automobiles one of the 'vital' key industries (Shah 1947a, 54). The subcommittee on engineering industries recommended a state-sponsored automobile factory in Bombay, as the place served this intermediate industry in terms of material supply and sales market (Shah 1947b, 37–39). The committee estimated that this automobile factory could provide new employment to nearly 33,000 skilled and unskilled workers, supervising staff as well as specialists (ibid., 34). The high demand for steel and other ancillary products to make automobiles was to create additional growth, and the growth of the industry more generally would provide for increasing employment. There was to be a time, therefore, 'when having gained sufficient experience, Indian labour will be able to pilot this industry to success through independent endeavour' (ibid., 40–47).

This greater political recognition of automobile manufacture in comparison with earlier periods had several immediate and long-lasting repercussions also in other areas. Central and state governments not only actively promoted the engineering and automotive sector and tried to attract factories. They also tried to steer education and manpower planning for engineering industries such as automobile manufacture, as is shown by the fact that the National Planning Committee put relevant technical education and the engineering profession on top of the planning agenda (Shah 1948; Ramnath 2007). This was based on the recognition that establishing industries would not work without increasing technical education. Surveying India's basic industries, the economist P. J. Thomas argued: 'India's progress [in the making and repairing of machines and other mechanical appliances] has been greatly delayed by inadequate equipment and lack of proper technical knowledge' (Thomas 1948, 168). These plans were the basis for the first set of five-year plans coming out in 1952 and for the further policy of the Indian government in dealing with the automobile industry.

In the 1950s, planning initiatives at the central and state levels began to forefront the necessary connection between industrialisation and education, and increasingly addressed issues of higher education and technical manpower training for the mechanical and heavy engineering sector. In 1955, the Engineering Personnel Committee estimated that India was short in supply of such personnel to the extent of several thousand graduates and diploma holders, and suggested an increase in the capacity of existing training institutions and the addition of completely new institutions. The Second Plan picked up and implemented many of these recommendations. While the first Indian Institute of Technology had opened at Kharagpur in 1951, many more institutes were established across India in quick succession in the late 1950s and early 1960s, which added substantially to the number of engineering graduates for the mechanical and heavy engineering sector (Sebaly 1972; Joshi 1977).

Thus, there was an immediate connection in the post-independence period between state policies addressing industrial development and engineering, and those addressing education and training of engineering personnel. They coalesced and influenced the development of specific sectors of the economy in differential ways, of which automobile manufacture was one and possibly one of the more important. This sector not only had the potential to instil the growth of ancillary industries and engineering more generally. As a forward-looking industry, it also necessitated an advanced standard of technology and expertise. Once these standards were achieved, they could be transplanted to other industrial sectors and would thus have an even greater impact on industrialisation and education. However, much of this technology and expertise did not yet exist in automobile manufacture.

The main aim of the post-independent Indian state was, thus, to industrialise the country and to reach the necessary technology and expertise in automotive manufacture. The primary means to achieve this was in the way of import substitution of foreign made goods by homemade goods. India's national plans and relevant policy making in the early planning period were therefore immediately informed by the experience of the Second World War of a denial of an indigenous automotive industry. As far as the automobile industry was concerned, politicians still primarily perceived of foreign capital as dominating the industry in the early 1950s. The communist politician, B. T. Ranadive, expressed this concern in a review of the first five-year plan. According to him:

> The purpose of British investment in manufacture of textile machinery, automobiles, etc. is only to keep its control and hold over these lines so that they are confined within the limits set by the interests of the metropolitan industry. Automobile manufacture is mainly assemblage of cars and nothing more.
>
> (1953, 103)

According to Ranadive and the contemporary political sentiment more generally, American companies such as General Motors and Ford in particular did not want to go beyond simple vehicle assembly in India. However, only the manufacture of components in India would have based the industry on firmer ground, and would have resulted in linkage effects with the economy in general (ibid., 131).

The scenario gradually changed in the early 1950s when Indian politicians had formulated the first five-year plan and started developing industries and heavy engineering as well as related fields such as the improvement of technical education. With regard to developing the automobile industry, the post-independent Indian state had a two-pronged strategy in particular. One was a move towards complete market protection not only for automobiles, but also for relevant products of ancillary industries. In 1953, the Government of India decided to allow only full-phased automobile manufacturing in India, a move that was primarily meant to instil the emergence of an indigenous automobile and ancillary industry. This basically put a halt to the assembly of vehicles that the big American producers of General Motors and Ford had been doing since the 1920s. These companies eventually shut down their operations and retreated entirely from the Indian market. Another move was the permission to some of the designated Indian companies to continue cooperating with foreign companies in technology and expertise for some time under specific conditions. In 1953, the Indian government neglected the advice of a German automobile engineer for only a partial protection of the indigenous automobile industry. Instead, in an attempt to gain greater economic benefits from and to instil indigenous expertise in automobile production, the state abolished all foreign manufacturing companies that neglected to comply with a gradual shift to full-phased production cycles in India by 1956 (Government of India 1953a, 1953b). As a result, major companies like General Motors and Ford stopped their production entirely and left the country, while the state issued new licences for the production of passenger cars and commercial vehicles to five designated companies in different localities across India. Among these, HML and PAL received one for the production of passenger cars, and TELCO one for the manufacture of trucks. This changed only slightly in later years. However, none of the prospected companies had yet reached a sufficient level of experience and expertise in automobile manufacture. Indian companies could, therefore, not dispense with contributions from foreign companies and thus necessitated a further technical import of foreign technology and expertise through cooperation to make the leap forward. This was tied to the specific demand by the Indian state that all manufacturers were to introduce complete phased-manufacturing within a certain period and to gradually increase the share of India-made vehicle components (Government of India 1953a, 1953b).

The government decision to promote automobile manufacture in post-independent India was not without contemporary criticism. Several politicians and economists found the state approach a rather haphazard attempt and questioned the economic and technical wisdom in hurriedly setting up this industry without developing necessary basic industries first. One of the main points of criticism was that seven units in the automobile industry in 1952 represented an investment of some INR 880 million, while ancillary industries for components and accessories were absent and the volume of demand on the domestic market small. It was nearly impossible for companies to reach break-even point under these circumstances (Rangnekar 1959, 111). Another criticism was that the main factors behind establishing the industry were the urge to develop an engineering industry of some sort and the strategic importance of the industry. However, this demand for the industry was not borne out by the demand for vehicles for transport purposes.

According to Rangnekar 'the conclusion seems inescapably to be that the stimulation of domestic demand for motor vehicles has been viewed largely, if not solely, from the point of view of the manufacturing programme of the installed plants. The potential transport requirements have scarcely any mention' (ibid., 179).

Effects of the new policy on automobile production and industrialisation, 1953–1969

The current state of government and company records make it a challenging task to detail the actual effects of the new government policies on the automobile industry and on other sectors of the economy. Moreover, there is no way to calculate the variances in production in case given policies had not been implemented. It remains a fact that the number of total units produced in India in the mid-twentieth century and even later remained comparatively low despite the new policy for automotive manufacture of 1953. However, this policy had the overall effect of substantially increasing the number of vehicles and components that were actually produced in India. These ambitious plans and their enactment became visible in state planning documents of the period and the actual trajectory of the automobile industry. Vehicle production figures tripled within ten years from 16,000 in 1950 to 55,000 units in 1960; and they were projected to double again by the end of the third five-year plan in 1966. The third five-year plan targeted the production of 30,000 passenger cars, 60,000 commercial vehicles and 10,000 jeeps and station wagons. Most noteworthy was the primary focus on the commercial vehicles sector rather than the private car sector. While the estimated capacity and production of commercial vehicles increased more than four times between 1950 and 1965–1966, the relevant figures for passenger cars grew only by 50 per cent. Of this overall production up to the late 1960s, HML and TELCO produced the largest number of vehicles in their respective categories (Government of India 1956, 1960b, 1962).

Fuelled by growing production figures and in-house manufacture, the ancillary industry grew substantially in the 1960s and thus increasingly replaced items that were still imported in 1959. While the value of annual ancillary production came to less than INR 50 *lakh* in the early 1950s, it increased to well over INR 10 *crore* by the early 1960s (Planning Commission 1960). The proportion of domestic production in the total supply in the automobile industry increased from 59 per cent to 80 per cent between 1950 and 1966 (Ahmad 1968, 360). The government forecasted ripple effects of an expansion in automobile and ancillary production on other sectors and on industrialisation more generally. For example, the government took a greater interest in expanding small industries as ancillaries to large industries in the 1960s, and one of the main industries for such schemes was the production of automobile and diesel engine parts. Moreover, new capacities in the private sector were to satisfy the demand for steel of this expanding industry (Government of India 1962, 436, 472).

This growing complex of automotive and ancillary industrial production had important repercussions on the number of motor vehicle factories and ancillary units, and by extension also on average daily employment in these units across India. The figures in Table 4.1 provide only a limited insight into the trajectory of automobile and ancillary industrial units and their employment in total and in four important states specifically between 1950 and 1961, as the term motor vehicle factories includes all manufacturing and repairing units. However, a more than ten-fold increase in the number of motor vehicle factories and a

Table 4.1 Distribution of motor vehicle factories in India and average daily employment, 1950–1961*

Year	Total	Madras	Maharashtra	West Bengal	Bihar
1950	133 (13,973)	9 (228)	25 (2,413)	8 (3,468)	–
1953	771 (53,068)	245 (14,024)	151 (15,196)	58 (6,883)	39 (896)
1956	1,022 (69,187)	245 (14,916)	216 (18,374)	67 (8,994)	79 (1,524)
1959	1,419 (82,177)	332 (18,294)	270 (23,106)	93 (9,774)	108 (1,795)
1961	1,564 (100,753)	324 (20,701)	196 (23,865)	100 (12,059)	135 (2,434)

Source: Labour Bureau report (1965, 2–3), Government of India.

Note

* Figures of motor vehicle factories include units manufacturing and repairing motor vehicles; employment figures indicate number of workers employed in them.

nearly ten-fold increase in average daily employment in factories across India indicate a massive growth of the automotive industry in this period.

The regions displayed in the table witnessed the largest growth around automobile manufacture compared with other regions in the 1950s and 1960s. Automobile clusters mainly developed around four cities with one or several main companies in the sector. The large cities of Bombay, Calcutta and Madras had important companies already from the late 1940s. The growth of automotive manufacturing in the 1950s and 1960s had a further substantial impact on these cities, so that they developed into the main automotive manufacturing hubs in India in the period up to 1960. The tariff commission of 1953 basically brought about the concentration of automotive manufacture in these specific cities by giving production licences to companies located in them. The only novelty was that the 1953 commission also gave TELCO a licence for the production of trucks in Jamshedpur so that this city was added to the list of automotive hubs (Government of India 1953b). The following growth of automobile and ancillary industrial production in these localities had a substantial impact on the economic and spatial setup of the larger production regions.

The city and region of Madras (Chennai) recorded the most drastic change in factory and employment numbers in the 1950s and 1960s, as this city became the basis of a large and sophisticated automotive and ancillary industry in this period. Madras had been an important hub of automotive assembly and trade even in the late colonial period. Simpson & Co. was a leading assembler and repairer of vehicles, whereas TVS Sundaram Iyengar specialised in trade. The Indian state nationalised and Indianised Simpson & Co. after independence and continued operations in the public utility company Amalgamations Group from the 1950s. The development of the region as an automotive engineering hub was largely a result of this company and of its manager, the former Simpson employee S. Anantharamakrishnan. Later on, the city was referred to as the 'Detroit of India', and the most important figure in this transformation, Anantharamkrishnan, was in later decades referred to as the 'Henry Ford of India' (Sriram 2011).

Factory and employment figures were largest in Bombay and the larger Maharashtra region. This was rather the continuation of an earlier trend, in which the city became one of India's main hubs of automotive assembly and trade from the late 1920s (Tetzlaff 2015), and then continued to be one of the most important production locations for automobiles in India long after independence. The decision of the 1953 tariff commission to give PAL licences for the production of passenger cars and trucks and Mahindra & Mahindra licences for Jeep manufacture even increased this existing tendency for the location of production sites in this region (Government of India 1953b). Once PAL started producing vehicles more extensively in the Kurla area of Bombay from the late 1940s, the old neighbourhood gradually developed into an automobile and engineering industrial zone. By the 1980s, there were also large engineering plants of Kamani Engineering and Larsen and Toubro Engineering as well as a large number of small and large sized engineering units such as automobile accessories units apart from PAL (Government of Maharashtra 1986). PAL not only expanded its main factory site in the Kurla area of Bombay in the 1950s, but also added ancillary units in Kalyan and Wadala to the larger production complex. From the late 1960s, several new manufacturing areas belonging to PAL and other manufacturers added to Bombay's automotive industry and engineering scene. The most recent area of Mumbai to develop was along the western outer suburbs and along the Western Express Highway, to where several units of older city units such as Mahindra's Jeep unit relocated as the old city became too congested (ibid.).

The state demand for greater in-house manufacture of automobile parts changed not only unit production capacities as well as the spatial location of industries, but also the technical know-how for vehicle manufacture within specific companies. The most important pacemakers in this know-how and the companies with the most recent production locations were HML in Uttarpara and TELCO in Jamshedpur. HML's advance in manufacturing had already been substantial and the most developed of all companies when the tariff commission demanded higher in-house production. HML produced important components (engine, transmission and axle) all by itself already in 1950–1951 and increased the share of in-house to production to 45 per cent in 1953. The company also established a foundry and forging plant around this time, while other accessories (castings for cylinder blocks, cylinder heads) were made in factories in the vicinity (Government of India 1960a). This trajectory became even more pronounced after the tariff commission of 1953. Within six years, the company raised the indigenous content of cars from 56 per cent (1956) to 70 per cent (1962) so much so that they 'have in fact made all the components which an automobile manufacturer normally produces' (Government of India 1962, 178). There is no evidence on whether HML could substantially add to this in-house manufacturing range in later periods. The company continued to use specifications of Morris Motors and did not alter design and functioning of the car, introducing only a few innovations in engines and gearboxes in the decades after starting the production of the Ambassador car in 1956.

Nonetheless, government policies inculcated not only greater in-house production of vehicle manufacturers, but also significantly affected the larger production and industrial environment of Calcutta at the time. The rising demand for indigenous parts instilled the development of other industrial clusters of automobile and ancillary industries. The overall number of West Bengal's motor vehicle and ancillary factories grew immensely from eight units in 1950 to 100 units in 1961 (Government of India 1965). Moreover, the number of workers in the industry increased and the employment situation changed. While average daily employment scaled up from 3,500 to 12,000 workers between 1950 and 1961, the total number of workers even came to 17,000 in 1961. More than 7 per cent of them were professional and technical personnel, while another 7 per cent were clerical workers, more than in any other region in India at the time. The number of production workers came to 82 per cent, which was lower than elsewhere in the country (ibid.). These figures may have differed from other motor vehicle production areas in India for various reasons, but they certainly show that not a small amount of this growth in factories and employment resulted from the company's increasing in-house manufacture and emerging ancillary industries.

TELCO in Jamshedpur saw a similar trajectory in the extent of in-house production. Production of Tata-Mercedes Benz trucks really began from scratch on the Jamshedpur shop floor in October 1954, when the factory site was still being erected. A group of Mercedes engineers and Tata workers engaged from other plants assembled the first vehicle parts shipped from the Mannheim factory in order to deliver finished products to waiting customers without delay. Tata-Mercedes-Benz trucks became so popular within a short period that the company sold 25,000 vehicles up to 1959 and quadrupled its initial annual production capacity of 3,000 units to 12,000 units in 1961 (Wuttke 1961). Over this period, the company gradually increased the share of in-house production according to agreements with the government. The vertical range of manufacture was to reach three-quarters in two phases up to 1959, successively including the local manufacture of frame, sheet-metal components, chassis small parts, cardan shaft, front and rear axle, and the establishment of a cast-iron foundry and forge. By October 1959, all vehicles were effectively fitted with locally made gearboxes and engines (Mondkar 1995). State officials found TELCO to have achieved all required targets by 1960, while managers of Daimler-Benz compared its management and factories favourably with their own sites in Europe. This was primarily a result of the high standards and new factory equipment introduced by Daimler-Benz managers and engineers that made TELCO's manufacture unique in India and Asia (Wuttke 1961; Mondkar 1995).

Moreover, the early development of the company exhibited a much wider connection between the development of production and labour employment/ training in this place than elsewhere. This was on the one hand a direct result of the new government policy, but also part of the cooperation agreement between the two companies. TELCO, thus, commenced a vocational training programme modelled on the German system to increase the number of trained workers and technicians. Five hundred apprentices had passed through the factory's programme by 1960, and 500 more were being trained at the time as fitters, turners, mechanics, and toolmakers. Some of these and another hundred trainees were also sent to factories in Germany for further training and to take over the Jamshedpur plant eventually in its entirety by the end of the cooperation period. By 1961, this pool of locally and foreign-trained employees encompassed 'young engineers, technicians and workers, all of who had shown utmost commitment to make the factory a success' (Wuttke 1961, 100, author's translation). The effect of the government policy to establish indigenous automobile manufacture and stop foreign participation in the Indian market thus became visible in the 1960s. While South German expertise and staff had been crucial for setting up production in the early stages, TELCO's engineering personnel increasingly took over production and engineering tasks in this decade

(Mondkar 1995). Daimler gradually stopped shipping material from Germany and Tata produced virtually complete diesel-engine trucks with local manpower and from materials made in India in the last period of the cooperation before Daimler-Benz retreated from India entirely in 1969 (Grunow-Osswald 2006).

When TELCO was to produce trucks entirely on its own from 1970, it did not need foreign vehicle manufacturing expertise any more. Instead, it independently expanded its manufacturing range to include a light truck suitable for Indian conditions. Presenting plans for an expansion in the manufacturing programme to the Indian government, TELCO's director, Sumant Moolgaokar, gave assurances that the new vehicle 'has been developed entirely with our own know-how and does not involve any collaboration or import of technology'. Tata was to use Indian engineering knowledge to manufacture the truck, which would also 'help to expand the engineering base in India and promote and develop engineering expertise aiming at the highest standards of quality' (Correspondence dated 8 December 1970, Tata Central Archives). TELCO's trajectory in truck manufacturing suggests that the company had inculcated sufficient engineering knowledge and could tap into a larger pool of motor and mechanical engineering personnel in order to expand operations by itself in 1970. This was seemingly not the case upon the start of the joint venture, when TELCO had to rely on outside expertise. Arguably then, it was the interdependency of an adequate industrial policy by the state and technical cooperation with a foreign manufacturer that eventually allowed for the emergence of an indigenous truck and of the company's engineering personnel.

Conclusion

This chapter has analysed the specific circumstances and repercussions of the making of the automobile sector as a key industry in mid-twentieth century India. While the literature has so far tended to ignore this historical phase, I have shown how the late colonial state and vested interests were unwilling to establish in-house production for vehicle manufacture in India. This in itself was reason enough for the government of India after independence to espouse a new policy of establishing the automobile industry.

While this exercise in studying the intervening period has used the historian's method to scrutinise official and unofficial documents, the findings should also interest social scientists and economists working on India and other industrialising countries. The chapter calls, in particular, for a more rigorous use of state planning documents and of business records as an important element in the analysis of Indian economic development since the late colonial period. The findings suggest that the state's new policy helped to make the automobile industry a viable primary industrial sector, and that the industry in return had a substantial influence on the development of ancillary industrial units and educational institutions as well as employment. More implicitly, the chapter also contributes to a new understanding of what economic development might mean in countries that are often discursively cast as either 'industrialised' or 'industrialising'.

Historically, while India's automobile industry was certainly far behind that of the US, Europe and Japan for a long time, the state's recognition of the automobile sector as a key industry, and the repercussions of this industry on other sectors of the economy since the early 1950s, suggests new ways to study economic development in India after independence, and possibly also in other parts of Asia.

References

Ahmad, Jaleel. 1968. Import Substitution and Structural Change in Indian Manufacturing Industry, 1950–1966. *Journal of Development Studies* 4 (3): 355–372.

Arnold, David. 2000. *Science, Technology and Medicine in Colonial India*. Cambridge: Cambridge University Press.

Automotive Component Manufacturers Association of India (ACMA). 2010. Industry Statistics, Turnover and Exports of the Auto Component Industry, 2010–15. http://acma.in/docmgr/ACMA_Industry_Data/Industry-Statistics.pdf (accessed 2 December 2015).

Birla, G. D. 1944. Industrialization in India. *Annals of the American Academy of Political and Social Science* 233 (1): 121–126.

Chakraverti, Sauvik. 2008. Four Wheels for All: The Case for the Rapid Automobilisation of India. Liberty Institute, occasional paper no. 18. New Delhi: Liberty Institute.

Chatterji, Basudev. 1992. *Trade, Tariffs and Empire: Lancashire and British Policy in India, 1919–1939*. Delhi: Oxford University Press.

Chibber, Vivek. 2003. *Locked in Place: State-Building and Late Industrialization in India*. Princeton: Princeton University Press.

D'Costa, Anthony. 2005. *The Long March to Capitalism: Embourgeoisement, Internationalization and Industrial Transformation in India*. Basingstoke: Palgrave Macmillan.

Dewey, Clive. 1979. The Government of India's 'New Industrial Policy', 1900–1925: Formation and Failure. In *Economy and Society: Essays in Indian Economic and Social History*, edited by K. N. Chaudhuri and Clive Dewey, 215–257. Delhi: Oxford University Press.

Dewey, Clive. 1988. *Arrested Development in India: The Historical Dimension*. Delhi: Manohar.

Fraser, Lovat. 1919. *Iron and steel in India: A chapter from the life of Jamshedji N. Tata*. Bombay: The Times Press.

Ghosh, J. C. 1941. War Efforts and the Key Industries of India. *Current Science* 10 (2): 57–63.

Gopal, S. 1979. *Selected Works of Jawaharlal Nehru, Volume Twelve*. New Delhi: Orient Longman.

Government of India (Ministry of Commerce and Industry). 1953a. Automobile Manufacture in India. Delhi: Government of India.

Government of India (Tariff Commission). 1953b. Report on the Automobile Industry. Bombay: Government of India.

Government of India (Tariff Commission). 1956. Report on the Automobile Industry. Delhi: Government of India.

Government of India (Ad-hoc Committee). 1960a. Report on the Automobile Industry. Delhi: Government of India.

Government of India. 1960b. Second Five Year Plan. Progress Report, 1959–60. New Delhi: Government of India.

Government of India (Planning Commission). 1962. Programmes of Industrial Development 1961–66. Delhi: Government of India.

Government of India (Ministry of Labour and Employment, Labour Bureau). 1965. Report on Survey of Labour Conditions in Motor Vehicle Manufacturing and Repairing Factories in India. Simla: Government of India.

Government of India (Ministry of Heavy Industries & Public Enterprises). 2006. Automotive Mission Plan 2006–2016: A Mission for Development of an Indian Automotive Industry. http://india.gov.in/automotive-mission-plan-2006-2016 (accessed 2 December 2015).

Government of India. 2015. Review of Automotive Mission Plan 2006-2016. www.siamindia.com/uploads/filemanager/19ReviewofAutomotiveMissionPlan2006-2016.pdf (accessed 2 December 2015).

Government of Maharashtra. 1986. Maharashtra State Gazetteers, Greater Bombay District, vol. 1. https://cultural.maharashtra.gov.in/english/gazetteer/greater_bombay/volume1.html (accessed 24 February 2016).

Grunow-Osswald, Elfriede. 2006. Die Internationalisierung eines Konzerns: Daimler Benz 1890–1997 [The Internationalisation of a Business Group: Daimler Benz, 1890–1997]. *Wissenschaftliche Schriftenreihe, DaimlerChrysler Konzernarchivs* 10.

Headrick, Daniel R. 1981. *The Tools of Empire: Technology and European Imperialism in the Nineteenth Century*. New York: Oxford University Press.

Joshi, K. L. 1977. *Problems of Higher Education in India: An Approach to Structural Analysis and Reorganization*. Bombay: Popular Prakashan.

Kathuria, Sanjay. 1987. Commercial Vehicles Industry in India: A Case History, 1928–1987. *Economic and Political Weekly* 22 (42/43): 1809–1823.

Keenan, John L. 1943. *A Steel Man in India*. New York: V. Gollancz.

Khanolkar, G. D. 1969. *Walchand Hirachand: Man, His Times and Achievements*. Bombay: Walchand Group.

Kidron, Michael. 1960. *Foreign Investments in India*. Bombay: Oxford University Press.

KPMG. 2010. The Indian Automotive Industry – Evolving Dynamics. KPMG in India, Automotive, 2010.

Krishnamurti, Y. G. 1941. *Sir M. Visvesvaraya: A Study*. Bombay: Popular Book Depot.

Kudaisya, Medha. 2014. 'The Promise of Partnership': Indian Business, the State, and the Bombay Plan of 1944. *Business History Review* 88 (1): 97–131.

Lala, R. M. 1993. *Beyond the Last Blue Mountain: A Life of J.R.D. Tata*. Delhi: Penguin.

Lamb, Helen B. 1955. The 'State' and Economic Development in India. In *Economic Growth: Brazil, India, Japan*, edited by Simon Kuznets, 464–495. Durham: Duke University Press.

M. V. (Dr. M. Visvesvaraya). 1960. *Birth Centenary Commemoration Volume, by his Contemporaries and Admirers*. Bangalore: Visvesvaraya Centenary Celebration Committee.

Macleod, Roy M. and Deepak Kumar, (eds). 1995. *Technology and the Raj: Western Technology and Technical Transfers to India 1700–1947*. Delhi: Sage.

Menon, Aubrey. 1948. *Sixty Years: The story of the Tatas*. Dehra Dun: Tata Industries.

Mondkar, K. R. 1995. *Telco Story*. (Unpublished company history). Pune: Telco.

Nair, Janaki. 2011. *Mysore Modern: Rethinking the Region under Princely Rule*. Minnesota: University of Minnesota Press.

Nair, Janaki. 2013. Mysore's Wembley? The Dasara Exhibition's Imagined Economies. *Modern Asian Studies* 47 (5): 1549–1587.

Nair, Vipin V. 2009. Suzuki, Hyundai's Indian Car Exports Beat China's. Bloomberg.com., 7 September 2009.

Nath, Aman and Jay Vithalani, with Tulsi Vatsal. 2004. *Horizons: The Tata-India century, 1904–2004*. Mumbai: India Book House.

Organisation Internationale des Constructeurs d'Automobiles (OICA). 2014. World Motor Vehicle Production by Country and Type. http://oica.net/wp-content/uploads/all-vehicles-2010-provisional.pdf (accessed 2 December 2015).

Organisation Internationale des Constructeurs d'Automobiles (OICA). 2015. World Motor Vehicle Production: World Ranking of Manufacturers, Year 2014. www.oica.net/wp-content/uploads//Ranking-2014-Q4-Rev.-22-July.pdf (accessed 2 December 2015).

Piramal, Gita. 1998. *Business Legends*. New Delhi: Penguin Books.

Ramnath, Aparajit. 2007. Breaking Free: Technical Education Policy in India Immediately Before and After Independence. Unpublished M.Sc. dissertation, University of Oxford.

Ranadive, B. T. 1953. *India's Five-Year Plan: What It Offers*. Bombay: Current Book House.

Rangnekar, D. K. 1959. *Poverty and Capital Development in India*. London: Oxford University Press.

Ray, Rajat Kanta. 1979. *Industrialization in India*. Delhi: Oxford University Press.

Sanyal, Amal. 2010. The Curious Case of the Bombay Plan. *Contemporary Issues and Ideas in Social Sciences*, June.

Sardesai, B. D. 1942. *Walchand Diamond Jubilee Commemoration* Volume. Bombay: Walchand Group.

Schade, Wolfgang, Christoph Zanker, André Kühn, Steffen Kinkel, Angela Jäger, Tim Hettesheimer and Thomas Schmall. 2012. Future of the Automobile Industry. Working report no. 152. Berlin: Office of Technology Assessment at the German Bundestag.

Sebaly, K. P. 1972. The Assistance of Four Nations in the Establishment of the Indian Institutes of Technology, 1945–1970. PhD Dissertation, University of Michigan.

Shah, K. T. 1947a. National Planning Committee Series (Report of the Sub-Committee on Manufacturing Industries). Bombay: Vora & Co. Publishers.

Shah, K. T. 1947b. National Planning Committee Series (Report of the Sub-Committee on Engineering Industries). Bombay: Vora & Co. Publishers.

Shah, K. T. 1948. National Planning Committee Series. (Reports of the Sub-Committees on 'Labour' and on 'General Education and Technical Education and Development Research'). Bombay: Vora & Co. Publishers.

Sriram, V. 2011. *The Rane Story: A Journey of Excellence*. Madras: Rane Holdings Ltd.

Tata. 1970. Correspondence dated 8 December 1970, Tata Central Archives.

Thakurdas, Sir Purshotamdas, J. R. D. Tata, G. D. Birla, Sir Ardeshir Dalal, Sir Shri Ram, Kasturbhai Lalbhai, A. D. Shroff and John Matthai. 1944–45. *A Memorandum Outlining a Plan of Economic Development for India*. Harmondsworth: Penguin Books.

Tetzlaff, Stefan. 2015. The Motorisation of the Mofussil: Automobile Traffic and Social Change in Rural and Small-Town India, c. 1915–1940. Unpublished PhD Dissertation, University of Göttingen.

The Hindu BusinessLine. 2010. India second fastest growing auto market after China. 9 April, www.thehindubusinessline.com/todays-paper/article988689.ece (accessed 2 December 2015).

Thomas, P. J. 1948. *India's Basic Industries*. Calcutta: Orient Longman.

Tyabji, Nasir. 1980. Capitalism in India and the Small Industries Policy. *Economic and Political Weekly* 15 (41/43): 1721–1732.

Tyabji, Nasir. 2015. *The Politics of Industry in Nehru's India*. New Delhi: Nehru Memorial Museum and Library.

Verma, S. D. 1988. *To serve with honour: My memoirs.* Bombay: S. D. Verma.

Visvesvaraya, Mokshagundam. 1920. *Reconstructing India.* London: P. S. King & Son.

Visvesvaraya, Mokshagundam. 1934. *Planned Economy for India.* Bangalore: Bangalore Press.

Visvesvaraya, Mokshagundam. 1937. *Nation-Building: A Five-Year Plan for the Provinces.* Bangalore: Bangalore Press.

Visvesvaraya, Mokshagundam. 1943. *Prosperity Through Industry: Move Towards Rapid Industrialization.* Bombay: All-India Manufacturers' Organisation.

Visvesvaraya, Mokshagundam. 1944. *Reconstruction in Post-War India: A Plan of Development All Round.* Bombay: All-India Manufacturers' Organisation.

Visvesvaraya, Mokshagundam. 1951. *Memoirs of My Working Life.* Bombay: G. Claridge & Co.

Wuttke, Hans. 1961. Erfahrungen bei der Erstellung und dem Betrieb des Tata-Mercedes-Benz-Werkes in Jamshedpur [Experiences with the Creation and Operation of the Tata Mercedes-Benz Plant in Jamshedpur]. *Intertechnik: Archiv für Entwicklungshilfe/ Mitteilungen des Forschungsinstituts für Internationale Technische Zusammenarbeit,* June: 95–104.

Zachariah, Benjamin. 2001. Uses of Scientific Argument: The Case of 'Development' in India, c. 1930–1950. *Economic and Political Weekly* 36 (39): 3689–3702.

5 Proton – Malaysia's national car project

Between success and failure?

Daniel Fleming and Henrik Søborg

Before the Malaysian national car project Proton Saga was designed in the beginning of 1980s as an integral part of the larger national heavy industry project (HICOM), the government had already in the 1960s encouraged the setting up of automobile assembly plants in Malaysia (Mahidin and Kanageswary 2004) – the first with Swedish Motors (Volvo) in 1967. In 1980 there were 11 assembly plants in Malaysia producing 25 car brands and 122 models (Athukorala 2014, 4). The aim of the national car project was twofold. On the one hand the government sought to stimulate and accelerate the transformation of Malaysia to an industrial developed economy by transfer of knowledge to build automobiles. On the other hand the government would favour a system of automobility. This system comprises of components that in their combination generate and reproduce the 'specific character of domination' that the car exercises. The first and essential components are the use of cars and their production by carmakers. The other components such as infrastructure (roads, bridges, parking places etc.) and institutions supporting family life, housing, city life, commuting, leisure, pleasure of movement etc. adapting to the use of cars, constitute, together with car production, the system of automobility (Urry 2004). In order to favour this system the government has built a dense network of roads, particularly in and outside the greater cities, and has, through its policies of easy car credits and fuel price subsidies, promoted private transportation (Barter 2004) and given special support to the national car project.

Thus, the story of the national car project is a journey back to the government's early attempts to establish Malaysia as an independent industrial nation. Until the 1980s, manufacturing had concentrated on processing imported raw materials, food and chemicals, and assembling imported components, such as electronics and vehicles. In contrast to Singapore, Malaysia's government did not want to rely only on cooperation with multinational companies and export-oriented industrialisation based on foreign investments. It wanted to have its own industries, following an import-substitution industrial (ISI) strategy like many other newly industrialising countries. Early on in the 1970s Japan was viewed as the best model to follow (the 'Look East' policy). At that time, Japan was seen as a world leader in industrial productivity, technical quality, work process organisation and industrial export (Johnson 1982).

HICOM signalled that Malaysia would embark on an industrialisation process, which did not aim to harvest short-term benefits. The former Prime Minister Mahathir, who was the architect and driver of the HICOM project, believed in the value of a long-term effort. For him, the national car project was a testimony of Malaysia's commitment to an independent modernisation process, and at the same time it was an important leverage in building up national confidence and pride, especially among the underprivileged Malay population, *Bumiputera*, ('sons of the soil'; the name given to the indigenous Malays), the majority Muslim population to whom jobs and ownership were to be transferred to balance the strong socio-economic position of the ethnic Chinese Malaysians.

In exploring the history of the national car project our focus is on the above-mentioned twin aim of the project. We examine the challenges and turbulence that the project has faced in searching for collaboration and partnership to get technological and managerial capacity to build a national car, and to create a skill formation culture that enhances Proton's capability.

Another crucial aspect of the national car project is the market and demand side. Our focus is on the prospects of Proton in an automobile market with increased global competition and regional trade cooperation and trade liberalisation in ASEAN. We examine whether this market development is a leverage or barrier for Proton, which has enjoyed the advantage of high duty on completely built-up foreign car units on the domestic market. Can Proton find regional partners to bolster its competitiveness? We look into possibilities and difficulties in developing a partnership with leading car firms, and, as announced in 2015, an ASEAN car project with Indonesia (Associated Press 2015).

We also throw light on internal market demand. The focus here is on the middle class and its demand for cars, and the impact that this demand exercises on the system of automobility. How does this class give priority to purchase cars? Is it willing to use a relatively large part of its income to purchase them? And how does the government underpin the system of automobility and give priority to the national car, for instance through easy access to credits and subsidies?

In the literature on Proton Saga the interest is highly concentrated on the upstart period in order to explore the difficulties that a newcomer meets in an industry dominated by Western and Japanese carmakers (Bartu 1992; Jomo 1994b; Schmitz 2007; Wad and Govindaraju 2011). Much attention is devoted to the control that the large carmakers exercise through global production and value chains. They have made control more centralised, production more large scale, and concentrated on a limited number of brands and production platforms. Their market dominance makes it more difficult to start up and sustain more independent national car industries which do not have a very large domestic market (Gereffi *et al.* 2005).[1] We deal with the difficulties derived from the large carmakers' hierarchical governance of their global production and value chains. We focus on the vulnerable position that Proton Saga occupied, especially in the beginning, because of its lack of technological and managerial capacity and capability. Bartu and Jomo have inspired our discussion on these issues, and our analysis of Proton Saga's partnership with Mitsubishi.

The analysis is structured as follows. First, we give an account of Proton's successes and failures in developing a national car project. We look at the ways in which the government has sought to nourish and support the project by an ISI policy, and at its search for collaboration and partnership to get technological and managerial capacity and know-how to move the project from idea to reality. Second, we explore the Malaysian skill formation culture compared to the one of Mitsubishi, Proton's Japanese partner. The focus is on the short-term training tradition in Malaysia in relation to the continuous learning tradition in Japan. How do these two traditions meet in a partnership? Third, we examine the middle class and its demand for cars, and the impact of the system of automobility on the demand for cars. Fourth, in the conclusion, we reflect on the current status of the national car project and its impact on Malaysia's development.

The national car industry

The first Malaysian national car project began at a 900 hectare HICOM industrial estate in Shah Alam, some 15 km outside Kuala Lumpur; and on 9 July 1985 the first Proton Saga Saloon 1.3 L went out from the assembly belt. It was based on the 1983 Mitsubishi Lancer Fiore sedan platform and was powered by a 1.3 L Mitsubishi Orion 4613 engine (Bartu 1992). This car was aimed at fulfilling a middle class family dream of an affordable family car. It was, because of the ISI policy, 20 to 30 per cent cheaper than similar types of cars manufactured by non-national local assemblers.

Former Prime Minister Mahathir coined the concept of a national car in 1979 and has since been the main driver of the project. He considered a national car as an important step forward in Malaysia's transformation to an industrial developed economy and an upper middle-income consumption society. The main model of inspiration for this transformation was Japan, but also South Korea. In both countries a close cooperation between the public and the private sector was an important driver in their transformation to industrial developed economies. Inspired by these two industrial success stories, the Malaysian government built up the national car project, based precisely on a close cooperation between the public and private sector (Jomo 1994a). This cooperation was also leveraged to increase the Malay population's participation in the industrial transformation process. The aim was to bring up *Bumiputera* entrepreneurs, managers, local suppliers and workers to a competence level comparable to the more advanced industrial nations. This ethnically oriented industrial policy was closely connected to the New Economic Policy, which in the beginning of the 1970s introduced ethnic preference policies to support the rise of the poor Malay population to the level of the more wealthy ethnic Chinese population (Case 2005). Proton and its suppliers were designed to have an important role in this ethnic redistribution of ownership and jobs.

The overall financial foundation for the national car project has been gener-ous government spending. This has been possible, among other things, because of huge revenues from the state-owned oil and gas company, Petronas. In 2008, its payment to the Federal Government represented 44 per cent of total federal revenues (Chin 2008). This revenue is also the foundation of most other government-linked companies shaping the connection between *Bumiputera* businesses, the ruling UMNO party and the government (Chin 2015).

In the following two subsections the focus is on how the Malaysian govern-ment has sought to nourish and support the national car industry, and especially the Proton car project. First, we examine protection measures with an emphasis on the ISI policy which aimed to protect the national car industry from com-petition of foreign carmakers, especially in the upstart period. Second, we go into the government's efforts to establish partnerships and facilitate a transfer of technological capacity and know-how.

Protection measures

The government's ISI policy towards the national car industry has run through two stages. The first stage was in the 1960s and 1970s. It aimed to make foreign carmakers establish local assembly plants by letting local completely knocked down (CKD) car units have a lower import and excise duty than imported com-pletely built-up units (CBU). There was also a deletion programme for parts and components that could not be imported, but had to be produced locally. The protection rate for the whole transport and equipment sector in Malaysia was estimated to be 252 per cent in 1987 (Alavi 1996, 174). The protection policy was especially directed towards import of CBU of the same type and engine capacity as Proton Saga. The import duties on these cars were 140 per cent. This helped make Proton Saga more affordable than imported CBU passenger cars (Mahidin and Kanageswary 2004). Table 5.1 shows the large variation span in import duties on cars according to engine size prior to 1 January 2004.

To protect Proton as an infant industry, the government also used non-tariff barriers such as import quotas for an Approval Permit system (AP) and for manufacturing licences (ML). AP and ML were used to limit imports of CKD

Table 5.1 Import duties on automotive vehicles (CBU)

Type/engine capacity cc	ASEAN and non-ASEAN import duty (%)
Passenger cars	
1,800	140
1,800–2,000	170
2,000–2,500	200
2,500–3,000	250
3,000–	300

Source: The Automotive Industry in Malaysia. MIDA Working Paper 2004. Malaysian Industrial Development Authority (MIDA).

kits and CBU vehicles. Discriminatory incentives were used for national cars, Proton and later Perodua. Until 2003 they enjoyed 50 per cent discount on excise duties. After the AFTA agreement on trade liberalisation was implemented, the government had to limit its use of the ISI policy to protect the national car industry (more on this below).

Instead, other discriminatory measures were used to give Proton advantages compared to other locally assembled CKD cars in terms of imports of engines and other parts and components. As we will elaborate later, the Proton car project was very vulnerable because it lacked the technological capacity and capability to make an engine. It was totally dependent on a partner who could deliver an engine and other more advanced parts. The government protected and promoted the project by giving Mitsubishi exemption from import duties to export its Japanese produced engine and other parts and components, and then sell them to Proton Saga at an overprice (Bartu 1992; Jomo 1994b).

The second ISI stage is connected to ASEAN's free trade agreement with AFTA in 1992. This agreement aimed to abolish all tariffs and non-tariff protectionist measurements in 2008. This deadline was later reset to 2003. To coordinate reductions of tariff and non-tariff protection, a Common Effective Preferential Tariff (CEPT) was established in 1993. The Malaysian government was much in favour of AFTA but was worried about Proton's and the *Bumiputera* vendors' possibility of surviving under the free trade agreement. Thailand, Indonesia and the Philippines complied with the 2003 liberalisation programme, setting 0 to 5 per cent tariff goals by 2003, and 0 per cent by 2010. Only Malaysia decided to continue to protect its national car industry (Natsuda *et al.* 2012, 22), postponing tariff reductions to 2005 and abolishing local contents and deletion programmes by 2004.

In practice, the Malaysian government has not yet stopped protecting the national car project. In line with tariff reductions on CBU vehicles and CKD kits under CEPT, it has imposed excise duties on cars. In 2015, the excise duties on cars were in the range of 75 to 105 per cent (MIDA 2015). Dependent on the degree of local content, national car producers could have excise duties refunded. In addition, other supportive measures were adopted that would not be in direct conflict with WTO rules. The Malaysian government set up an Automotive Development Fund providing low interest loans to vendors in order to help mergers and acquisitions of weak vendors. This helped Proton to reorganise its suppliers. Another fund, the Industrial Adjustment Fund, was set up to give interest free loans and grants linked to local content, production scale, and sustainable *Bumiputera* participation (Natsuda *et al.* 2012).

Another more indirect type of protection was the Vendor Development Programme of 1988, which supports start-up *Bumiputera* firms in establishing industrial linkages. The number of vendors increased rapidly, from 17 firms in 1988 to 186 in 1999. Eighty per cent of vendors were registered with Proton and supplied more than 3,000 locally produced parts and components (Rosli and Kari 2008, 108). Extra support was given by the government to develop high-tech components (Abdulsomad 1999, 292). However, these protective measures did not help Proton and its vendor network much in the long run. Proton's market share of a growing domestic market fell from 53 per cent in 2001 to below 20 per cent in 2014, overtaken by Perodua by a full 10 percentage points. Non-national brands were, in 2014, ahead of these two national brands (Sze 2015).

Partnership and technological capacity

In the beginning of the 1980s a feasibility study made by the Industrial Development Authority showed that the national car project did not on its own have the technological capacity to produce a car (Jomo 1994b). Therefore, it was imperative to search for a partnership with an overseas carmaker. The first proposal went to Daihatsu Motors, which after long negotiations was only willing to put up a body stamping plant, and to offer technical assistance (Jomo 1994b). This proposal did not meet Mahathir's dream of building a national car. Mahathir then turned to the Mitsubishi Corporation's president in Japan, and after a negotiation phase they reached an agreement in 1982 of a joint venture between HICOM and Mitsubishi Motor Corporation (Jomo 1994b). The agreement was that HICOM contributed 70 per cent of the total paid-up capital of RM 150 million, while Mitsubishi and its subsidiaries shared the last 30 per cent (Jomo 1994b). The first Proton Saga Saloon 1.3 L was fully built by Mitsubishi in Japan and delivered to Malaysia by night in secrecy – a mere token of a national car (Bartu 1992, 73).

In the beginning the factory in Shah Alam produced at only 25 per cent of full capacity because of lower sales than an optimistic sales projection had estimated, and because of the difficulty of entering the export market. Bartu, who in *The Ugly Japanese* has made a study of the partnership between Mitsubishi and Proton, is very critical of the partnership agreement, and of Mitsubishi's motives:

> Mitsubishi had installed an obsolete plant in Shah Alam which produced second-class vehicles made of thin and inferior steel, composed of many light plastic parts and equipped with an overall technology that was not sufficient to enable the car to pass the strict regulations prevailing in overseas market, especially in the United States. Even the engine was of inferior quality in terms of noise and pollution emissions.
>
> (Bartu 1992, 76)

There were serious conflicts of interest between Proton-HICOM and Mitsubishi regarding exports, engine and technological upgrading. Mitsubishi did not want to compromise its new upgraded models and its brand reputation on overseas and Asian export markets because of an inferior Proton Saga model and therefore made it difficult for Proton to export its Proton Saga Saloon 1.3 L. But in addition, Proton also faced problems in Malaysia. It was pressured by the economic downturn in 1986; by low capacity utilisation of plants; and by higher import prices due to the appreciation of the Yen in September 1985. However, after a former Mitsubishi Motor executive was appointed managing director, production increased and several new models were launched: The Proton Saga Iswara in 1992 and the Proton Wira in 1993 (a fourth generation Mitsubishi Lancer).

After launching these new models, Proton faced new challenges in the domestic market. In 1994 a second national car, Perodua, was launched. The chief partner was Daihatsu, and soon Perodua was selling more cars than Proton. Proton-HICOM tried to counter the challenge by making an acquisition of a foreign company and bought an 80 per cent stake in the Lotus group in 1996 (100 per cent stake in 2003), assisted by the government. Proton felt it necessary to get hold of technology so as to upgrade its models, and to finally be able to produce its own engine (Proton also had a short joint venture with Citroën-Peugeot to produce a super-mini called Proton Tiara, but that collaboration stopped in 1997).

In 1995, Proton was privatised and sold to Diversified Resources Bhd (DRB) and Mega Consolidated. DRB was owned by Yahaya Amad, a close friend of Prime Minister Mahathir. DRB promised big changes and a new 'Proton City', but did not have the capital for large investments (Tan 2008, 166, 171). According to Tan (2008), the privatisation in 1995 came too soon and did not help Proton tackle its main problems concerning knowledge transfer, discipline, discouraging rent-seeking, and supporting efficiency and technological upgrading among vendors and suppliers. In 2000, the ownership of Proton Saga went back to the government with the government-owned oil and gas company Petronas becoming financially responsible; this ownership was succeeded later by Khazanah Nasional, the holding company of the government, who, however, in 2012 sold Proton Saga for RM 1.2 billion back to DRB-HICOM who, at the same time, acquired all of Petronas' engine technologies and patents for RM 63 million.

Under DRB-HICOM ownership, Proton started serious negotiations on establishing new international partnerships. These partnership negotiations should be seen in the light of Malaysia's attempts to adapt to global market competition, which included a compromise between domestic interests (the ISI strategy) and export market interests. Larger exports were a necessity for large-scale production, which again was necessary to make Proton profitable. In trade agreements with ASEAN, AFTA and WTO, Malaysia had to accept liberalisation rules, lower tariffs and reduced subsidies. As a consequence, the price differences between national cars and foreign cars levelled out and, as mentioned, by 2013–2014 foreign cars had gained a larger market share than national cars (Sze 2015). These market conditions stress how Proton is in desperate need of partnerships and cooperation with global lead firms in the auto industry to overcome its difficulties. But its attempts to find partners have not been an encouraging story.

After Mitsubishi sold off its Proton shares, Proton (and the owner, Khazanah Nasional) negotiated for new agreements with Volkswagen, but this failed in 2006. This was followed by negotiations with Citroën-Peugeot and General Motors, but they also fell through. Proton then reached a technical partnership with Mitsubishi in 2008, and a production sharing agreement with Detroit Electric in 2009 (Athukorala 2014, 15). The main problem was to upgrade suppliers in the production chain. Therefore, the government had accepted, in 2006, a close cooperation with the Japanese Automotive Industry, which set up ten training programmes in lean production and functional improvements (*kaizen*). Later, the programmes came to include all vendors in the industry.

DRB-HICOM, Proton's owner since 2012, plans to restructure Proton over a five year period, with an investment of over US$1 billion. This may be the last chance for Proton to become profitable and more integrated in the global value chains of the auto industry lead firms. DRB-HICOM has a long experience of assembling cars in Malaysia as a partner with several brands like VW, Honda, Suzuki, Isuzu and Mercedes Benz (Athukorala 2014, 16). DRB-HICOM has negotiated with possible new leading car firms for closer collaboration, starting with Volkswagen (an agreement that eventually failed again), and then with Honda Motor which led to a collaboration agreement (Lim 2012). Details of the agreement are secret, but include collaboration on technology enhancement, new product line-up, and platform and facilities sharing. After using Honda's previous Accord model for launching a new Proton Perdana model in 2016 it seems that this collaboration will end. Instead, a new licensing agreement with Suzuki looks more promising. Proton will assemble a Suzuki compact and then later rebrand the model as a Proton compact, sold by Proton's dealer network. The agreement also includes evaluation of potentials in sharing engine and transmission platforms with Proton (Hans 2015). In addition, Proton also wants to develop an electric vehicle – a Proton Iriz EV – still at the prototype stage. This model is developed in partnership with Korean LG Electronics and expected to launch in late 2016 or in 2017 (Tan 2015). Proton – under former Prime Minister Mahathir as re-entering chairman – also intends to enter into a partnership with Indonesia's renewed national car project to establish a stronger market position, not only on the Indonesian market – which is much larger than the Malaysian market – but also in ASEAN and other export markets, mainly Asian (Lee 2015; Associated Press 2015). These partnership negotiations include a plan to sell Proton under a new brand label (FMT Reporters 2015). But in addition, Proton partnerships with Chinese carmakers present a new possibility for building an ASEAN car, and this may be a stronger partnership than the Indonesian one (Lim 2015). A potential barrier in these negotiations, however, is the issue of foreign majority ownership. Until now Proton and the Malaysian government have not accepted foreign majority ownership, in contrast to what has been the case with Perodua (owned by Daihatsu/Toyota).

From the very beginning Proton has thus sought to establish collaboration and partnerships because it has needed the transfer of technological and managerial knowledge. This transfer of knowledge is vital when a newcomer enters a very competitive industry. Protection measures may help for a while, but in the long run, access to advanced technological and managerial knowledge is essential. In this context, a crucial question is whether the skill formation culture in the Malaysian industry underpins or supports this transfer of knowledge. We explore this question in the following section.

The skill formation culture

Like many other industries in Malaysia, the automotive industry has a shortage of educated and advanced skilled workers (Sadoi 1998; Natsuda et al. 2012). This is somewhat of a paradox insofar as the pool of higher educated graduates is in fact very large (Fleming and Søborg 2014). Before we look closer into the skill formation culture in the Malaysian automotive industry, and more generally, we outline the educational baggage of advanced skilled workers in Malaysia, and unpack the paradox outlined above.

The large number of higher educated graduates is a result of the government's huge investments in the educational sector (Malaysia Economic Monitor 2014; Fleming and Søborg 2014). In the last decades, the education budget as a percentage of GNP has been larger than in the neighbouring countries (including Singapore), and even in comparison to developed countries like the US and the UK (Lee and Nagaraj 2012). This is reflected in the number of universities and graduates. Currently, there are 20 public and 26 private universities (Economic Planning Unit 2010). These institutions have produced a great number of graduates with higher education. In 1982, the number was 331,800, or 6 per cent of the total labour force. In 2010 the number had increased to 2.788 million, or 24 per cent of the total labour force. This corresponds to approximately 16 per cent of the population (Department of Statistics, Malaysia 2013b; Gasnier 2013).

The great leap forward in the enrolment of students to higher education has, however, led to an over-production of graduates whose qualifications do not match demand. This is because of students' choice of study field and the quality of education (Economic Planning Unit 2010, 192). It is difficult to recruit students to the natural sciences, and to technical and engineering study fields, in which the demand for graduates is very high. The majority of students choose arts and social science, information technology and communications. This explains the paradox mentioned above. This mismatch between supply and demand is alarming for the Malaysian Federation of Manufacturing. The Federation does not only complain about the mismatch, but also about the quality of the students' qualifications (Fleming and Søborg 2014). Studies of skill formation in the Malaysian automotive industry also emphasise these problems of quality and, in particular, the shortage of advanced skilled workers (Sadoi 1998; Natsuda et al. 2012). This shortage is remarkable insofar as the national car project in fact aimed to *increase* the pool of skilled workers, especially among *Bumiputeras*. Skill formation was an essential part of the agreement between Proton Saga and Mitsubishi Motor Corporation (Jomo 1994b), and many Proton workers have had longer training periods (12 months) at Mitsubishi's factories in Japan. The transfer of knowledge from these workers and staff trained in Japan has been important for gaining knowledge of operations and maintenance. But this skill formation has been limited to specific machines, and the training did not include design, research and the development of skills, which Mitsubishi reserved for its own workforce (Jomo 1994b).

Although the transfer of knowledge from Mitsubishi to Proton – and later from Daihatsu to Perodua – has helped build up an on-the-job-training skill formation culture in the automotive industry, the shortage of advanced skilled workers is still identified as a great problem in the industry. In his study of skill formation in the Malaysian automotive industry, Sadoi found that the lack of advanced skilled workers was closely connected to the way the automotive industry was established, and to the Malaysian skill formation culture. By the time Malaysia started developing its automotive industry, many manual skills had been replaced by numerical control machines, and manual mould-making was replaced by wire-cut and electric cutting machinery (Sadoi 1998). According to Sadoi, this replacement of advanced skills by mechanisation has had a profound influence on the skill formation culture that developed in the automotive industry. In contrast to Japan, where on-the-job-training skill formation is a long, continuous process with an emphasis on industrial master-level skills, the skill formation process in Malaysian companies typically consists of short-term training periods.

The government has, through the National Automotive Policy which was introduced in 2006 and revised in 2009, encouraged and supported the automotive industry to develop a skill formation culture. The Malaysia Automotive Institute has been an important driver in building up this culture. In collaboration with tertiary education institutions such as Universiti Malaysia Pahang and Unversiti Teknologi MARA, the institute established the Automotive Apprenticeship Programme. It aims to build a more advanced level of skills among automotive industry workers, and to support the industry to produce more value-added products.

The Malaysia-Japan Partnership Agreement is another driver in building up a skill formation culture in the automotive industry. This agreement has helped to develop the technical skills of *Bumiputera* vendors, among whom the technical skill level is much lower than in Japanese car supply chains. The agreement consists of an extensive auto cooperation programme, including a technical assistance programme, a mould and die centre, an automobile skill training centre – one in Malaysia and one in Japan – a component and parts testing centre, a business development programme, market information cooperation, automotive expo cooperation and joint venture consultation. The programmes involve Japanese lead firms such as Toyota and Nissan, which set up training in lean production systems and master training programmes in skills centres. After completing a master training programme, a Malaysian skilled master is able to train local trainees in mechanical, electric and manufacturing technologies and quality control (Natsuda *et al.* 2012).

These more extensive, long-term training programmes are up against the above mentioned short-term training culture in the automotive industry, and in vocational training in general. This culture is supported by the Human

Development Fund, which since 1992 has been promoting training in companies with more than 50 employees (Fleming and Søborg 2002). The Fund normally supports short-term, in-house training programmes, but unlike in Japan, these programmes are not anchored in a skill formation culture with continuous follow-up training (Sadoi 1998). Many employers are not interested in investing in more continuous training because of the job-hopping on the Malaysian labour market: If employers cannot make a binding agreement with their employees after the completion of a longer course, they fear losing their training investment to another employer who may entice newly trained employees with a higher salary (Tan 2001). And, while the government has, as mentioned above, sought to counter this short-sighted and negative attitude towards investments in long-term training (Economic Planning Unit 2010), the automotive industry shows that it takes time to change employers' attitudes.

Middle class consumption and the demand for cars

Domestic demand is important for a national car. Here, our focus is on the middle class demand because its huge appetite for consumer goods is a widespread phenomenon in emerging economies (Kharas 2010). The middle class has a preference for consumer durables like cars, not only because of the freedom of transportation that cars provide, but also because of more personal concerns with identity, social status and image (de Mooij and Hofstede 2011; Nielsen and Wilhite this volume). Since the 1980s the Malaysian middle class has grown, and after 2000 the Malaysian middle class income has been in the upper end of the middle-income range in developing countries, in a belt between US$15 to 20 a day per capita (Ravallion 2010; Fleming and Søborg 2014).

The middle class demand for cars has a great impact on the system of automobility, a system that has developed in tandem with the national car project. The first Proton Saga Saloon 1.3 L was in 1985 launched into a society that was moving from a low to a middle-income economy, and from rural to urban ways of life (Fleming and Søborg 2014). There was a car market, and demand was relatively high in light of Malaysia's level of economic development level and population size. In 1984, Malaysia had a person-to-car ratio of 1 to 20.8, second only to Singapore in the ASEAN region and, remarkably, much higher than in South Korea (1 to 146) and Taiwan (1 to 51) (Jomo 1994b). According to Proton Saga's estimates, car sales would increase in the future, and the demand for cars would be large enough for a national car project to be viable (Jomo 1994b). Retrospectively, these estimates did indeed anticipate the remarkable annual increase in car sales over the next decades. In 2010, the total sale of cars was 605,156 units (Malaysian Automotive Association 2010), of which 57 per cent were national brands (Proton and Perodua).

Car sales have been strongly nurtured by the government. The infrastructure planning in bigger cities has the private car as its pivotal point (Barter 2004). Until recently, public or collective transportation has had low priority (Economic Planning Unit 2015). Kuala Lumpur, for instance, reflects the fact that access by private cars has high priority not only in the city centre – which has no restraints on private car traffic – but also in major urban development areas that are located in close proximity to major expressway interchanges or exits. Moreover, the fuel prices are subsidised, something which promotes private vehicle sales and supports the national car and motor cycle industry (Barter 2004).

In Malaysia, the private car has become a dominant part of modern consumption and lifestyle. In general, income levels determine when cars become a dominant part of consumption. Ohmae (1995) has defined income threshold categories in order to identify when specific vehicles become part of household consumption. We have modified his categories to Malaysia, and the following income thresholds may be applied for the purchase of transportation vehicles: People below RM 4,573 a month are more inclined to buy a motorbike, while for incomes below RM 1,847 bicycles are within economic reach. But above RM 4,573, people become focused on car ownership. Many people in Malaysia have now crossed this threshold, as Table 5.2 shows. The table also suggests that Malaysia is moving from being a middle to being an upper middle-income economy.

Consumption patterns in an upper middle-income economy are typically diverting from Fordist mass production of standardised goods to more customisation of products (Streeck 2012). Like other carmakers Proton Saga's production series have been increasingly customised along with re-engineering product ranges and accelerating product design (Mahidin and Kanageswary 2004). In the 2000s in particular, Proton Saga launched several facelift models in order to compete with other carmakers having new facelifts every year. This customisation of products fitted into the growing individualism of the heterogeneous urban middle class in particular.

A recent survey on household income distribution reveals that an increasing number of people in Malaysia are in occupational categories that make them economically fit to take part in modern consumption (Department of Statistics 2013a). Fifty-nine point nine per cent of the workforce is in the reach to buy a car, according to Ohmae's threshold category and 11.9 per cent is at a take off stage to buy a car. In the last decade the occupational groups that are within

Table 5.2 Mean monthly household income of top 20 per cent, middle 40 per cent, and bottom 40 per cent of household by ethnic groups and strata, Malaysia, 2012

Household group	Total	Bumiputera	Chinese	Indian	Others
	Mean RM	Mean RM	Mean RM	Mean RM	Mean RM
Top 20%	12,159	10,666	15,254	13,127	9,741
Middle 40%	4,573	4,123	5,836	4,589	3,341
Bottom 40%	1,847	1,686	2,455	1,937	1,472

Source: Department of Statistics Malaysia. Household Income and Basic Amenities Survey Report 2012.

Ohmae's car income threshold category (professionals, technicians and associate professionals, clerical support workers and service and sales workers) have increased much more in percentage of the total workforce than other occupational groups (Malaysia Economic Monitor 2012).

Thus, the private car has become a dominant part of the modern consumption basket in Malaysia. We will add some observations among Malaysian middle class families to this statistical information. We have seen that many of these families have two cars, a more prestigious overseas made car and a national made one, and sometimes also motorbikes. Normally, there is a gender and generational division in families in the use of these vehicles. Often, the husband uses the foreign car to drive to work, for taking the family to shopping malls, restaurants and family occasions, while the housewife uses the national car and the older kids the motorbikes.

More middle class families can afford two cars because they have become two-income families, something that partly explains the success of smaller Perodua models. But two-income families do not represent a widespread phenomenon. Malaysian women have the lowest labour market participation rate (49 per cent in 2012) among Southeast Asian countries, compared to Singapore's 60 per cent and Thailand's 70 per cent (Hausmann *et al.* 2012). However, the low labour market participation rate hides the fact that many Malaysian women work in the flourishing informal sector and in this way contribute to family income generation and consumption (Malaysia Economic Monitor 2012; Nair 2012).

Tables 5.3 and 5.4 illustrate the high priority that cars have in Malaysian families. In July 2014 the total population in Malaysia was about 30 million. The number of people aged 25 to 65 was close to 15 million. The distribution of cars in urban areas is not far from the level of mobile phones and washing machines. In urban areas the percentage distribution of households having cars is 83.6 per cent while the percentage in rural areas is 62.7 per cent. This indicates, as already noted, that more families have more than one car. The two tables also indicate that more people from the bottom 40 per cent break through Ohmae's threshold and become car owners.

Table 5.4 shows that the number of registered cars and motorcycles in 2013 was nearly 22 million. The number of cars in this year amounts to more than one third of the population.

Table 5.3 Percentage distribution of households by items used urban/rural, Malaysia, 2012

Car		Motorcycle/Scooter		Mobile phone		Washing machine	
Urban	Rural	Urban	Rural	Urban	Rural	Urban	Rural
83.6%	62.7%	61.5%	77.6%	96.4%	91.6%	93.5%	82.9%

Source: Department of Statistics Malaysia, June 2013. Household Income and Basic Amenities Survey Report 2012.

Table 5.4 Number of motor vehicles registered by type, Malaysia, 2009 and 2013

Year	Cars	Motorcycles
2009	8,506,147	8,940,230
2013	10,535,575	11,087,878

Source: Department of Statistics Malaysia. Social Statistics Bulletin, Malaysia 2010 and 2014.

Numbers from Malaysia Economic Monitor (2015) underline the growth of private motor vehicle ownership. From 1997 to 2012 registered private motor vehicles had an average annual growth rate of 6.7 per cent. This number is well over three times the rate of population growth (2.0 per cent) and approximately 1.6 times the rate of growth of the economy as a whole (4.2 per cent). This expansion of motor vehicles gives Malaysia a person-to-car ratio of one to three. That is a high ratio, close to high-income countries (such as Denmark, which has a person-to-car ratio of one to 2.5 in 2015).

Proton and Perodua appear to have been left behind in the rapid growth of car ownership in recent years. They cannot live up to middle class consumers' more critical perception of consumer goods quality. The initial success of both Proton and Perodua in consumer demand has changed. Proton has for years been ranked at the very bottom end of the user-satisfaction scale. In a survey from 2010 of car owners of 14 car brands in Malaysia, Proton came as number 13 just ahead of the other 'national car', Perodua, at the very bottom of the scale (Athu-korala 2014, 11). Thus, low consumer satisfaction is another explanation for why non-national cars are now selling better than national ones (Sze 2015).

According to our modified Ohmae threshold categories people from the bottom 40 per cent should not afford a car. Still, they break through Ohmae's threshold, as noticed above, and become car owners. There are several explanations of this spread of car ownership (Mohamad and Kiggundu 2007; Fischer 2014). We will point at the easy access to car loans not only for the middle 40 per cent but also for the bottom 40 per cent. Many families are not only car or motorbike owners but also house or apartment owners. In 2012, 74.5 per cent of all households owned houses or apartments (Embong 2014). A considerable part of household income is spent on debt payment for cars and houses.

Easy-access private credit is the reason why household debt is soaring in recent years in Malaysia as in OECD countries (OECD 2014). According to Bank Negara Malaysia's annual reports 2013 and 2014, most of the private household debt is in residential properties but a large part is also in durables like cars and motorbikes (Bank Negara Malaysia 2013; 2014). Compared to other Asian countries Malaysia is in the forefront in terms of household debt to GDP. In 2013, Malaysia's household debt to GDP was 86 per cent while that of Singapore was 60 per cent, China 35 per cent and Indonesia 10 per cent (Malaysia Rating Corporation 2014).

An important reason why Malaysia is in the forefront in Asia in terms of household debt is not only due to easy access to loans in banks and credit institutions to purchase houses, apartments, cars and the like, but also because the government has provided loans to civil servants to buy cars (Mohamad and Kiggundu 2007). Bank Negara has not put restrictions on the growth in private consumption generated by debts (Bank Negara Malaysia 2013; 2014). This debt-generated consumption is a break with the saving culture that has been widespread in Asian countries. In the 1980s and 1990s, the gross national saving rate in East Asia and the Pacific was around 30 per cent (Loayza *et al.* 2000). The high saving rate reflected the emphasis that governments and households put on financial security and investment. The growing debt culture indicates the rise of a new consumption driven culture and politics that instigate people to purchase goods before having earned the money. The financial vulnerability that this new consumption behaviour creates for the Malaysian middle class and families in the bottom 4 per cent notwithstanding, the debt culture maintains a national car industry that is heavily dependent on domestic demand. It also maintains a system of automobility consisting not only of carmakers but also of infrastructure and housing development companies, as well as a huge leisure industry.

Until now the government has supported the private system of automobility. However, in the Eleventh Malaysia Plan 2016–2020 it focuses on the need for comprehensive and efficient public transport connectivity. This represents a new signal in traffic policy, but is up against many vested interests in the existing system built on private motor vehicles.

Conclusion

Our analysis has shown that the national car project has been conceived and planned to be an essential driver in Malaysia's transformation from a low income to a middle income and, in 2020, a high-income country. The middle class has played a crucial role in this transformation. Its huge demand for consumer goods, and especially durables like cars, has underpinned the development of a system of automobility which the government has favoured through its infrastructure and credit policy to give institutional support to the national car. The importance of the national car project is not limited to its role in Malaysia's industrialisation, but also encompasses questions of national pride and identity, especially for *Bumiputeras*, the ethnic majority, who have enjoyed job creation, skill upgrading and business privileges as vendors and suppliers. It has, however, been challenging to build a national flagship industry and keep the flag high as a newcomer in the competitive global car industry. Exports have been very limited, and government protection and subsidies have been necessary for sales on the domestic market.

The first stages in Proton Saga's cooperation with Mitsubishi Motor Corporation were hard trial periods. Bartu (1992) captures very precisely the initial problems, describing the assembly models as obsolete, and parts and components as second-class Mitsubishi. In addition to the partnership problems, the ethnic preference policy created problems because of its explicit objective to rely on *Bumiputeras* vendors, and not on ethnic Chinese vendors, who otherwise had long experience in the automobile supply industry. Many *Bumiputeras* who were appointed vendors had rent-seeking interests and much lower technical skill levels than vendors in Japanese car supply chains. Through the Malaysia-Japan Partnership Agreement, Japanese partners helped improve the skill level of *Bumiputera* vendors, and the skill formation improved in the national car project, although it has been up against a short-term skill upgrading tradition.

Although the first Proton Saga models were second-class vehicles, the car project succeeded in developing more robust and customised models and also its own engine and design in the course of the 1990s and 2000s. On the domestic market the project has been successful in terms of cars sold. Since 1985, Proton Saga's cumulative sales on the domestic market have been 3,500,000 cars. But its share of the domestic market has continually fallen, from 53 per cent in 2001 to below 20 per cent in 2014, overtaken by Perodua by 10 percentage points. In 2014, non-national brands were ahead of the two national brands. To catch up, Proton tries to renew models and production platforms in new partnerships, recently with Honda and then with Suzuki. An electrical prototype stage model is now being developed in partnership with Korean LG Electronics.

Can Proton win back the lost market share with these new partnership initiatives? It is difficult to answer this question, but our analysis has shown that Proton's future success is dependent on its ability to deliver high-quality and customised products. To achieve this, Proton depends on a leading car partner sharing technology, knowledge and production platforms. There are many vested interests in keeping Proton on track. Among them is the former Prime Minister Mahathir who has been the driving force in the national car project since day one. He has re-entered as chairman of the board of Proton, and works for the launch of a global small car as a market game-changer, and supports the strategy to enter cooperation with Indonesia in a national car project there. Mahathir believes Proton – with a modified model – could be the driving force behind an 'ASEAN car' with the help of a partly protected market in Indonesia and a potential of four million cars sold per year (FMT Reporters 2015). Other possible strategies could be to focus on export markets, or entering into a partnership with Chinese automakers for knowledge and technology transfer.

The middle class is the primary consumption agent on the Malaysian car market. Its consumption culture will be crucial for the traffic policy in the coming years, as indeed it has been in the past decades. The question remains whether policy makers will support public, collective transport, and limit traffic congestion and air pollution, or continue giving priority to private motor vehicles. Traffic congestion in the larger cities, especially Kuala Lumpur, has already reached terrible levels, but while the government is making plans for a new public transportation project, it simultaneously wants to stimulate sales for the two national car producers. The government is thus not interested in limiting private car transportation. Nevertheless, middle class preferences rather than government policies will decide future sales figures and the fate of Proton Saga and the national car project.

Note

1 Unlike several other authors we do not compare Malaysia's car production to Thailand's. In contrast to Malaysia, Thailand chose a strategy with an emphasis on letting foreign multinational carmakers build their own assembly lines and production platforms in the country and in this way included Thailand in their larger global production, export and value chains (Doner *et al.* 2004; Athukorala and Kohpaiboon 2010).

References

Abdulsomad, Kamaruding. 1999. Promoting Industrial and Technological Development Under Contrasting Industrial Policies: The Automobile Industries in Malaysia and Thailand. In *Industrial Technology Development In Malaysia: Industry and Firm Studies*, edited by Kwame Sundaram Jomo, Greg Felker and Rajah Rashia, 274–300. London: Routledge.

Alavi, Rokiah. 1996. *Industrialisation in Malaysia: Import substitution and Infant Industry Performance*. London: Routledge.

Associated Press News. 2015. Malaysia's Proton to Aid Indonesia with National Car Project. 6 February, http://neurope.eu/article/malaysias-proton-help-indonesia-study-feasibility-manufacturing-its-own-national-car/ (accessed 16 December 2015).

Athukorala, Prema-Chandra. 2014. Industrialisation through State-MNC Partnership: Lessons from the Malaysia's National Car project. *Malaysian Journal of Economic Studies* 51: 113–126.

Athukorala, Prema-Chandra and Archanun Kohpaiboon. 2010. Thailand in Global Automobile Networks. Geneva: World Trade Organization/International Trade Center.

Bank Negara Malaysia. 2013. Annual Report 2013. Kuala Lumpur: Bank Negara Malaysia.

Bank Negara Malaysia. 2014. Annual Report 2014. Kuala Lumpur: Bank Negara Malaysia.

Barter, Paul A. 2004. Transport, Urban Structure and Lock-in in the Kuala Lumpur Metropolitan Area. *International Development Planning Review* 26 (1): 1–24.

Bartu, Friedemann. 1992. *The Ugly Japanese: Nippon's Economic Empire in Asia*. Singapore: Longman Singapore Publishers.

Case, William 2005. New Reforms, Old Continuities, Tense Ambiguities. *Journal of Development Studies* 41 (2): 284–309.

Chin, James. 2015. The Cost of Malay Supremacy. *New York Times*, 27 August, www.nytimes.com/2015/08/28/opinion/the-costs-of-malay-supremacy.html?_r=0 (accessed 13 January 2016).

Chin, Joseph. 2008. Petronas Posts Record Profit. *The Star*, 15 July.

de Mooij, Marieke and Geert Hofstede. 2011. Cross-Cultural Consumer Behavior: A Review of Research Findings. *Journal of International Consumer Marketing* 23: 181–192.

Department of Statistics, Malaysia. 2013a. Household Income and Basic Amenities Survey Report 2012. Kuala Lumpur: Department of Statistics.

Department of Statistics, Malaysia. 2013b. Labour Force Survey Report. Kuala Lumpur: Department of Statistics.

Doner, Richard F., Gregory W. Noble and John Ravenhill. 2004. Production Networks in East Asia's Automobile Parts Industry. In *Global Production Networking and Technological Change in East Asia*, edited by Shahid Yusuf, M. Anjum Altaf and Kaoru Nabeshima, 159–208. Washington, DC: World Bank.

Economic Planning Unit. 2010. Tenth Malaysia Plan 2011–2015. Putrajaya, Malaysia: Economic Planning Unit, Prime Minister's Department.

Economic Planning Unit. 2015. Eleventh Malaysia Plan 2016–2020: Anchoring Growth on People. Putrajaya, Malaysia: Economic Planning Unit, Prime Minister's Department.

Embong, Abdul Rahman. 2014. The Middle Class in Malaysia: Market Expansion, Consumption and Vulnerabilities. In *Handbook of Contemporary Malaysia*, edited by Meredith Weiss, 177–188. Oxford: Taylor & Francis.

Fischer, Johan. 2014. Islamic Mobility: Car Culture in Modern Malaysia. *Journal of Consumer Culture*. Doi: 10.1177/1469540514531683.

Fleming, Daniel and Henrik Søborg. 2002. Dilemmas of a Proactive Human Resource Development Policy in Malaysia. *The European Journal of Development Research* 14 (1): 145–170.

Fleming, Daniel and Henrik Søborg. 2014. Are Emerging South-East Asian Economics Caught in a Middle-income Trap? Case: Malaysia. Paradoxes in Provision of Higher Skilled Labour. *Forum for Development Studies* 41 (1): 115–133.

FMT Reporters. 2015. Why Proton? Asks Indonesians 'Stunned' by National Car Deal. 9 February, www.freemalaysiatoday.com/category/nation/2015/02/09/why-proton-asks-indonesians-stunned-by-national-car-deal/ (accessed 13 January 2016).

Gasnier, Matt. 2013. Malaysia Full Year 2012: Record Year – Now with Brands Ranking. *Best Selling Cars Blog*, 11 March, http://bestsellingcarsblog.com/2013/03/malaysia-full-year-2012-record-year-but-no-more-info/ (accessed 13 January 2016).

Gereffi, Gary, John Humphrey and Timothy Sturgeon. 2005. The Governance of Global Value Chains. *Review of International Political Economy* 12 (1): 78–104.

Hans. 2015. A Look At Proton's Long History of MoUs That Never Came To Pass. Carlist.my, 17 June, www.carlist.my/news/look-protons-long-history-mous-never-came-pass/14600 (accessed 13 January 2016).

Hausmann, Ricardo, Laura D. Tyson and Saadia Zahedi. 2012. The Global Gender Gap Report. Geneva: World Economic Forum.

Johnson, Chalmers. 1982. *MITI and the Japanese Miracle: The Growth of Industrial Policy 1925–1975*. Stanford: Stanford University Press.

Jomo, Kwame Sundaram. 1994a. Introduction. In *Japan and Malaysian Development: In the Shadow of the Rising Sun*, edited by Kwame Sundaram Jomo, 1–17. London: Routledge.

Jomo, Kwame Sundaram. 1994b. The Proton Saga: Malaysian Car, Mitsubishi Gain. In *Japan and Malaysian Development: In the Shadow of the Rising Sun*, edited by Kwame Sundaram Jomo, 263–290. London: Routledge.

Kharas, Homi. 2010. The Emerging Middle Class in Developing Countries. OECD Development Centre, working paper no. 285. Paris: OECD.

Lee, Jonathan 2015. Proton to Sign ASEAN Car MoU with Indonesia Today? Paultan. org, 6 February, http://paultan.org/2015/02/06/proton-sign-asean-car-mou-indonesia-today/ (accessed 16 December 2015).

Lee, Kiong Hock and Shyamala Nagaraj. 2012. The Crisis in Education. In *Malaysia's Development Challenges: Graduating from the Middle*, edited by Hall Hill, Siew Yean Tham and Ragayah Haji Mat Zin, 213–232. London: Routledge.

Lim, Anthony. 2012. Proton and Honda Ink Collaboration Agreement. Paultan.org, 29 October, http://paultan.org/2012/10/29/proton-and-honda-ink-collaboration-agreement/ (accessed 13 January 2016).

Lim, Anthony. 2015. Proton ASEAN Car to be Rolled Out within 20 Months? Paultan. org, 2 October, http://paultan.org/2015/10/02/protonsaseancartoberolledoutwithin-20months/ (accessed 13 January 2016).

Loayza, Norman, Klaus Schmidt-Hebbel and Luis Servén. 2000. Saving in Developing Countries: An Overview. *The World Bank Economic Review* 14 (3): 393–414.

Mahidin, Mohd Uzir and Ramasamy Kanageswary. 2004. The Development of the Automobile Industry and the Road Ahead. *Journal of the Department of Statistics, Malaysia* 2: 1–32.

Malaysian Automotive Association. 2010. Annual Report. Kuala Lumpur: Malaysian Automotive Association.

Malaysian Development Authority (MIDA). 2004. The Automotive Industry in Malaysia. MIDA Working Paper. Kuala Lumpur: MIDA.

Malaysia Economic Monitor. April 2012. Modern Jobs. Bangkok: World Bank Office.

Malaysia Economic Monitor. 2014. Towards a Middle Class Society. Bangkok: World Bank Office.

Malaysia Economic Monitor. 2015. Transforming Urban Transport. Bangkok: World Bank Office.

Malaysia Rating Corporation Berhad. 2014. Malaysia: Loans and Household Debt – An Assessment. www.marc.com.my (accessed 13 January 2016).

Mohamad, Jamilah and Amin T. Kiggundu. 2007. The Rise of the Private Car in Kuala Lumpur, Malaysia: Assessing the Polity Options. *IATSS Research* 31 (1): 69–77.

Nair, Nevash. 2012. Increase in Demand for Tuition in Malaysia. *The Star*, 5 November.

Natsuda Kaoru, Noriyuki Segawa and John Thoburn. 2012. Globalisation and the Malaysian Automotive Industry: Industrial Nationalism, Liberalisation, and the Role of Japan. RCAPS working paper no. 1. Beppo City, Japan: Ritsumeikan Center for Asia Pacific Studies.

OECD. 2014. Fact Book 2014: Economic, Environmental and Social Statistics. Paris: OECD.

Ohmae, Kenichi. 1995. *The End of the Nation State: The Rise of Regional Economies.* New York: The Free Press.

Ravallion, Martin. 2010. The Developing Wold's Bulging (but Vulnerable) Middle Class. *World Development* 38 (4): 445–454.

Rosli, M. and Kari, F. 2008. Malaysia's national automotive policy and the performance of Proton's foreign and local vendors. *Asia Pacific Business Review.* 14 (1) 103–118.

Sadoi, Yuri. 1998. Skill Formation in Malaysia: The Case of Auto Parts Industry. *Southeast Asian Studies* 36 (3): 317–354.

Schmitz, Hubert. 2007. Reducing Complexity in Industrial Policy Debate. *Development Policy Review* 25 (4): 417–428.

Streeck, Wolfgang. 2012. Citizens as Customers: Considerations on the New Politics of Consumption. *New Left Review* 76: 27–44.

Sze, Gregory. 2015. Malaysian Automotive Association releases 2014 TIV. Paultan.org, 22 January, http://paultan.org/2015/01/22/maa-releases-2014-tiv-figures/ (accessed 13 January 2016).

Tan, Hong. 2001. Malaysia's HRDF: An Evaluation of Its Effects on Training and Productivity. Unpublished paper. Washington, DC: World Bank Institute.

Tan, Jeff. 2008. *Privatization in Malaysia: Regulation, Rent-seeking and Policy Failure.* London: Routledge.

Tan, Jonathan James. 2015. Proton Electric Car Still in a Prototype Stage – Parliament. Paultan.org, 29 May, http://paultan.org/2015/05/29/proton-electric-car-prototype-stage/ (accessed 13 January 2016).

Urry, John. 2004. The 'System' of Automobility. *Theory, Culture and Society* 21: (4/5): 25–39.

Wad, Peter and V. G. R. Chandran Govindaraju. 2011. Automotive Industry in Malaysia: An Assessment of its Development. *International Journal of Automotive Technology and Management* 11 (2): 152–171.

Part III

Contested car cultures

Consuming automobility

6 *Doi moi* on two and four wheels

Capitalist development and motorised mobility in Vietnam

Arve Hansen

Over the last decades bicycles have been substituted for motorbikes[1] at a remarkable pace in Vietnam. The whole country is now seemingly driving motorbikes, and statistics show that on average every Vietnamese household owns a motorised two-wheeler (GSO 2012). In the cities they are now ever-present, creating a constant soundscape of buzzing and honking. The frenzy of millions of motorbikes has become an icon of the new Vietnam that has been emerging so rapidly from the rubbles of war and extreme poverty. In the most recent decade, however, it has been the motorbike's turn to be challenged. In an increasingly affluent Vietnam, car ownership has seen a steep increase, particularly in urban areas. As the car arises as a strong competitor in terms of comfort, status, and scarce road space, transport in Vietnam seems set for another transition.

The radical changes of Vietnamese streetscapes are part of a larger process of socio-economic transformations in the country since the onset of the economic reforms known as *doi moi*[2] in 1986. Put briefly, the reforms consisted of a range of policies breaking with the former planned economy, such as decollectivising agriculture, allowing private economic initiatives and private accumulation and, crucially, opening up Vietnam's economy to regional and global markets (see for example Hansen 2015a; Masina 2006; Van Arkadie and Mallon 2003; Fforde and De Vylder 1996). Following the reforms Vietnam had one of the fastest-growing economies in the world in the 1990s and 2000s (Malesky *et al.* 2011), and the World Bank (2013) now considers the country a 'development success story'.

This chapter considers how the rapid motorisation of Vietnam's streets can be understood in relation to the multi-scalar development processes associated with *doi moi*. Furthermore, the chapter asks what the case of cars and motorbikes can tell us about Vietnam's development trajectory both in terms of industrial aspirations and socio-economic changes. Taking Vietnam's capital city Hanoi as a starting point, the chapter analyses the escalation of consumption of private vehicles following reforms through macro-scale political-economic changes as well as everyday mobility practices. The findings are based on 'motorbike ethnography' in Hanoi (Hansen 2016b), combining mobile participant observation with interviews with car and motorbike owners, policy makers, retailers and manufacturers.

The chapter starts by analysing Vietnam and Hanoi's 'motorbike revolution' before moving on to the subsequent rapid emergence of automobility. It then considers the status hierarchy of vehicles in Hanoi, and argues that the role of cars as 'positional goods' has depended on significant changes in the communist regime's attitude towards consumer goods. The chapter then argues that the motorisation of Hanoi's streetscapes can be seen as a physical manifestation of Vietnam's transition to capitalism.

A city on two wheels[3]

Hanoi used to be famous for its tranquillity and the many bicycles in the streets. Bicycles were first imported during French colonial times (Arnold and Dewald 2011), but later played a central role in the independence wars against both French and US forces. After independence, they remained vital to mobility, something that the estimated 600,000 bicycles in Hanoi in 1981 bear witness of (Koh 2006). Indeed, bicycles dominated transport in the 1990s, and as late as 2005 one third of non-walking trips in the city were carried out on a bicycle (World Bank 2014). Still today, young Vietnamese girls on bicycles donning *ao dais*[4] represent a national symbol. As I elaborate below, the bicycle has played a vital role in Hanoi and Vietnam's transport trajectories, although motorbikes have now almost rendered their non-motorised siblings obsolete as a means of transportation.

Motorbikes were certainly present in Hanoi before *doi moi*. According to Koh (2006) there were already more than 50,000 of them in 1981. Many of these came from what used to be South Vietnam (where they often originally entered from France), and many were imports from the Soviet Union. Still, however, owning a motorbike was far from common. Together with the dominance of bicycles, the early motorbikes nevertheless contributed towards firmly embedding scripts for two-wheeled mobility in the social and material fabric of Hanoi (Hansen 2015b). In the 1990s, the already visible popularity of motorbikes also made them part of development strategies for a government with high ambitions for industrialisation.

The motorbike revolution

Industrialisation has in different ways been central to Vietnam's development strategies since independence (Beresford 1988, 2008). With little available capital, however, *doi moi* gradually opened up for foreign investments. Influenced by the East Asian developmental states, the Vietnamese government attempted to combine state control and foreign capital to develop domestic industries (Masina 2006). For the motorcycle industry the policies consisted of import substitution, with high tariffs on imports combined with licences for foreign manufacturers to produce motorcycles in Vietnam. The intention behind import substitution was to develop domestic manufacturing capacity through cooperation with foreign manufacturers, but the protective policies also saw the socialist government give big Japanese capital almost monopoly on motorbikes in Vietnam. East Asian motorcycle manufacturers saw the potential for a huge market, and particularly Japanese, but also Taiwanese, firms started producing vehicles in the country in the mid-1990s (Fujita 2013a). This increased the availability of motorbikes, and the two-wheeler in many ways became the very symbol of development and reforms in Vietnam (Truitt 2008). Particularly Honda became a dominant player in 'democratising' motorbike ownership. Honda was so central to the diffusion of motorbikes in Vietnam, and models such as the Honda Wave so popular, that *Xe Hon Da*[5] became a common way to refer to motorbikes in general, something that is still visible in many parts of the country. By the late 1990s Honda enjoyed a 67 per cent market share (Fujita 2013a), but this was also when the real 'motorbike revolution' started.

As Rigg (2012) discusses extensively, development processes are often significantly less planned than they appear to be in the development literature and in the rhetoric of states. What has come to be known as the 'China shock' is a good example of such 'unplanned development'. While the Honda Dream became the symbol of Vietnamese aspirations, the prices for Japanese motorbikes were still too high for most Vietnamese consumers. This meant a market opportunity for low-cost motorbikes, and around the start of the millennium copies of Japanese motorbikes started pouring across the border from Vietnam's giant neighbour to the north, China. To circumvent import laws these motorbikes were often transported as knockdown kits to be assembled by a rapidly increasing number of Vietnamese entrepreneurs (Fujita 2013a, 2013b). This made available inexpensive (but usually relatively low quality) motorbikes, and nationwide the annual sales of motorbikes more than tripled from 500,000 in 1999 to 1.7 million in 2000 (Hansen 2016a). At the same time, Honda's share of the market dropped from 67 per cent in 1998 to 12 per cent in 2001. But, as Fujita (2013a) contends, the China shock made Japanese manufacturers start placing larger parts of the manufacturing process in Vietnam, as well as developing models designed for the Vietnamese market. This in turn led to affordable but high quality motorbikes and in combination with a tightening of import regulations by the government, Honda Vietnam managed to reclaim the market and again become the dominant player. Meanwhile, Chinese motorbikes have almost disappeared from Vietnamese cities, but still represent a large share of the motorbike population in rural areas (Fujita 2013b).

Vietnam now has a substantial, yet mostly foreign owned, motorbike industry. The extraordinary consumption of motorbikes cannot be understood without these large-scale changes in provision and the political economy of development. Nevertheless, a focus on economic development cannot really tell us *why* so many Vietnamese started driving motorbikes. The relationship between consumption and production is much debated, but it is clear that supply does not necessarily create its own demand. Rather, as Warde (2005) argues, the effect of production on consumption is mediated through the nexus of social practices. Thus, in order to better understand the motorbike revolution, I shift the analytical focus from top-down to bottom-up, and consider the many pillars of Hanoian everyday mobility practices.

Hanoi and the 'system of moto-mobility'

Vehicles are first and foremost used in order to participate in other social practices. In other words, spatial mobility is rarely a goal in itself. In Hanoi, *doi moi* in many ways radically altered everyday life, with new forms of housing and employment, rapid urbanisation, and new leisure activities. In the heydays of socialism, urban planning in Hanoi was strongly influenced by the Soviet Union, with the state constructing so-called 'microrayons' designed to let inhabitants fulfil all their daily needs within a short distance (see Logan 2000). With *doi moi* the state monopoly on production of urban housing was abandoned (Logan 2000; Hoai Anh Tran 2015), and through mostly private initiatives a rapid expansion of suburbs started in the early 1990s (Drummond 2012). These are examples of new developments that were enabled by, but also required, improved mobility.

In Hanoi in the early reform years, bus services were in a sorry state, the old tramway from the times of French Indochina was removed, and the popular *xe lam* ('tuktuk') was banned from the streets (Thanh Nien News 2012). Meanwhile, as commuting distances increased and bicycling became a much riskier undertaking in the increasingly motorised streetscapes, the role of bicycles started to diminish. Furthermore, the common practice of parking (and even driving) motorbikes on pavements, as well as the range of businesses operating from pavements, often crowd out pedestrians. Leather *et al.* (2011) find that even though trip lengths often could make walking and cycling convenient ways of getting around town, the poor infrastructure of Hanoi makes these little tempting options. In other words, Hanoi's motorscapes and infrastructure take on agency in co-shaping mobility practices towards motorised vehicles.

Both infrastructure and regional economic integration thus created favourable conditions for moto-mobility, and the motorbike became the 'must-have' consumer object of post-*doi moi* Hanoi. The motorbike was in many ways the perfect next step from the bicycle. It is not very different from it, and is almost as easy to operate. The main difference is that it is a whole lot faster, and allows its driver to cover much greater distances than on a bicycle. As Truitt (2008, 5) has put it:

> Unlike bicycles, motorbikes promise effortless mobility or, rather, mobility that relies on fossil fuel rather than human exertion. A motorbike user enjoys mobility without physical exertion, accelerating with a twist of the handle and braking with a slight tap on the foot pedal.

Motorbikes could follow in the tyre-prints of the bicycle, something that was reinforced by the specific physical and economic spatialities of Hanoi. Significant parts of the city's built infrastructure are dominated by narrow roads and complex networks of small alleys (*ngo* or *ngach* in Vietnamese) that have developed in a dialectical relationship with the dominance of non-motorised and motorised two-wheelers. Hanoi's geography of consumption has also followed the two-wheeled development, and cafes, shops and other businesses are placed along streets with parking space only for two-wheelers. Many shopping practices, such as purchasing fruit and vegetables from street vendors, are carried out without ever leaving the vehicle.

In this context, the motorbike provides a rather unique sense of mobility. Motorbikes can go almost anywhere, and can usually be driven right to the front door of any service or business. Back home, the motorbike often follows its owner inside the house, and at night time is frequently parked in the living room. The possibility of relatively quickly moving from door to door all over the densely populated city almost becomes an addiction, as moto-mobility becomes firmly embedded and embodied in the habits and practices of urban life (Hansen 2015c).

The motorbike is now absolutely vital to everyday life in Hanoi, and represents around 85 per cent of total traffic, while bicycles have diminished to around 2 per cent.[6] I interviewed a young girl who reflected upon the role of the motorbike in her everyday life. She told me that throughout her 21 years in Hanoi she had only once ridden a bus inside the city. She used the motorbike whenever she moved around the city, and argued that this was indeed the only option available: 'It's convenient for me, I think [...] It's my only choice, right. I cannot walk around Hanoi, I cannot drive a car, I don't have one and I can't, so yeah, motorbike is like the only choice' (interview, November 2013). This reflects the lock-in of transport consumption that is usually associated with cars (e.g. Urry 2004). When infrastructure and everyday practices are organised around a particular form of transport, this becomes the 'only choice'.

The changes and continuations of mobility practices and consumption and retail geographies on the local scale, together with the national and regional-scale changes in trade networks, have co-created what I term a 'system of moto-mobility' (see Hansen 2016b). Influenced by Urry's (2004) 'system of automobility' this term reflects the fact that consumption of motorbikes is driven by much more than individual decisions or 'needs'. The larger material, social and symbolic frames in place contribute towards the continuation and strengthening of particular patterns of human behaviour and human-technology interactions. In other words, moto-mobility is manifested and reinforced through socio-material aspects ranging from regional and global trade networks to corner repair shops and traditional wet markets in narrow alleyways. The system of moto-mobility is not necessarily a new phenomenon per se, but is rather a somewhat different version of what research on automobilities has analysed concerning the role of the car in mature capitalist countries. The dynamics of the motorbike are different, but related to those of cars; the motorbike is still a predominantly private means of performing practices of mobility, of getting from A to B, of connecting the different socialities of everyday life. The future of this 'system', however, is uncertain.

The motorbike revolution represented a significant transport transition in Vietnam and Hanoi. A new transition is however underway, as cars are competing with motorbikes at all levels, from national industrial aspirations to everyday mobility practices.

Driving development?[7]

Due partly to the complete dominance of motorbikes, there has been little room for private cars in the streets of Hanoi. Although in transport research the term 'motorisation rate' is normally used to measure car ownership, it is clear from the above discussion that Hanoi (and Vietnam) is highly motorised although few own a car. Car ownership has been restricted by government tax policies, and cars are very expensive to acquire and use compared to two-wheelers. The high taxes on cars in the context of poor public transportation networks have indeed rather unintentionally further favoured motorbikes. This could be changing. To the dismay of foreign motorcycle manufacturers, there is now much talk of the Vietnamese government planning on imposing restrictions on motorbike ownership. This can be seen in a 2013 adjustment to the 'Vietnam Road Transport Development Scheme to 2020 and orientation towards 2030', which states that the government aims to:

> Reduce the growth in quantity of motorbikes using administrative, economic and technical measures in order to limit the quantity of motorbikes nationwide; motorbikes are [to be] *primarily used in rural areas and the areas without public passenger transport; there will be 36 million motorbikes by 2020.*
> (Prime Minister of Vietnam 2013, n.p., italics added)

The same report states that public transport is expected to meet 25 per cent of the demand for transport in Hanoi. While not stating it explicitly, and indeed only expecting a modest increase in car ownership, this shows that the doors are opening for the car. It also indicates the changing attitudes towards motorbikes. Increasingly, two-wheelers are seen as a necessary evil, as dirty and dangerous, whereas cars present an image of progress, modernity and industrialisation.

In other countries with widespread use of motorbikes, such as Thailand, the dominance of two-wheelers seems to have represented a transitional phase, whereas car ownership has increased significantly as incomes have risen (Jakapong and Chumnong 2010). Vietnam's Ministry of Industry and Trade (MOIT 2013) makes it clear that this transition is also expected in Vietnam. Crucially, the Vietnamese government aims to meet this transition with the supply of domestically manufactured cars, as indeed has been accomplished in Thailand (see Thoburn and Natsuda in this volume for an overview of the Thai auto industry).

The regional and global economic integration following *doi moi* made cars available for import, and the Vietnamese government has targeted the automobile industry to become a 'spearhead industry', in other words to reap the potential of automobile industrialisation that has been so important in other late-industrialisers (see discussion by Hansen and Nielsen in this volume). As put by Vietnam's Ministry of Industry and Trade in a draft for a new automobile master plan:

> That the automobile industry contributes not only to the amelioration of the quality of the labour force, but also to the development of industry, to the economy and to the society is an obvious fact recognised by most countries which have developed automobile industries.
>
> (MOIT 2013, 5, translated from Vietnamese)

In a context where policy makers fear the so-called 'middle-income trap', the auto industry is presented as a possible saviour on the golden road towards becoming a high-income country.

Until the mid-1990s, the only auto manufacturing taking place in Vietnam was represented by the producer of military vehicles Hoa Binh. After *doi moi*, and similar to the experience of the motorcycle industry, the Vietnamese government realised they would not be able to develop a car industry without foreign capital. While the dream of developing a national car brand was abandoned, the doors were opened for foreign investors, first as joint ventures with Vietnamese state-owned companies (Sturgeon 1998). The industry is now largely represented by foreign auto giants, but the expected positive spillover effect to other industries and the rest of the economy have firmly placed the auto industry at centre stage of Vietnam's manufacturing aspirations.

However, the development of the auto industry has overall been a failure, with little technological spill-over, low local contents ratios and largely disappointing sales figures. Furthermore, as a vivid example of Vietnam's problems of inter-ministerial coordination (Hansen 2015a), the Ministry of Industry and Trade has met opposition from the Ministry of Transportation and the Ministry of Finance. The latter two ministries fear the impact of cars on traffic as well as the loss of tax revenues if reducing overall taxation levels. Thus, Vietnam is currently in the situation of pushing for automobile industrialisation but simultaneously restricting the main market for cars produced in the country. But the biggest challenge could yet be ahead of the Vietnamese auto industry. It is currently protected behind significant tariff walls. By 2018, however, due to the ASEAN Free Trade Agreement (AFTA), Vietnam will have to remove all tariffs on imports from the rest of Southeast Asia, including more successful automobile producing countries such as Thailand and Indonesia. This could mean the end to Vietnam's auto industry dreams, but at the same time could lead to cheaper cars for Vietnamese consumers.

The sales of motorbikes have slowed down since 2011, and there is now much talk in Vietnamese media of the motorbike market being saturated (see for example Thanh Nien News 2014a; Tuoi Tre News 2014). At the same time, although still far behind two-wheelers in sales numbers, the presence of cars has rapidly increased. Nationally, the number of four-wheelers on Vietnamese roads has been estimated to have grown tenfold between 1996 and 2014, reaching approximately two million (National Traffic Safety Committee, cited in Thanh Nien News 2014b). While Vietnam still has a low car ownership ratio (at 21 per 1000 people, OICA 2014), this is expected to change. APERC (2013) predicts the number of cars nationally to reach up to four million by 2020, while Vietnam's Ministry of Industry and Trade (MOIT 2013) projects 11 to 17 million cars on Vietnamese roads by 2030. As with motorbikes, increased regional economic integration has played and will play a crucial role in these changes. But again, changes in provision cannot provide the full picture of this transition, and I thus return to the streets of Hanoi.

Emerging automobility in Hanoi

In Hanoi, cars are certainly making an impact, and have since the mid-2000s become a much more common sight. According to the World Bank (2014), the number of cars in the streets of Hanoi has been growing by an annual rate of over 20 per cent from the mid-2000s, reaching around 200,000 vehicles in 2012. In central Hanoi cars are moving around very slowly, usually surrounded by swarms of motorbikes. Hanoi's built infrastructure furthermore makes the car in many ways highly inconvenient and inflexible. Cars cannot access the networks of alleyways in the capital, cannot easily be stopped alongside the road to allow their driver to shop or sit down for a coffee or tea, and obviously cannot be parked inside the living room. Parking is indeed a chronic nightmare for car-owners in Hanoi.[8] The car thus disrupts and changes the mobility of its drivers and passengers away from many of the practices otherwise associated with Hanoian everyday life (Hansen 2015b).

At the same time, however, a car brings along a new set of benefits. The allure of the car is often related to mundane categories such as cleanliness, comfort, health and safety. Although highly convenient for getting around town quickly, compared to cars driving a motorbike is hot in the very high summer temperatures and wet in the frequent and often sudden Hanoi rain. A car furthermore makes it possible to get through the many floods in Hanoi unscathed, and to relatively safely bring along family and friends in the rather dangerous traffic. The sociality of driving and 'passengering' in a car is also different from a motorbike. While a motorbike has allowed for new forms of intimacy for young couples (Truitt 2008), the car provides a private capsule for social interaction. All of these aspects of private automobility were well captured by a young businessman in Hanoi:

> When I drive a car, the wind doesn't hit my face. I can listen to music and audio books. I can listen to my mobile, avoid noises. I can avoid the rain. I can feel the cool air through the air conditioner. I can avoid the flood in Hanoi. My shoes are always dry. If I feel sleepy, I can stop and park the car along the roadside and sleep for a while. Inside the car, I can put many things, and if I want to have a coffee inside the car I can drink it. Moreover, I can talk with my girlfriend in the car. I can talk with her in a low

voice. On the motorbike, both of us have to talk really loud. I can drive faster than on the motorbike. It is very pleasant driving the car.

(Interview, May 2013, translated from Vietnamese)

Simultaneously, a car allows its driver and passengers to stay pale[9] and clean. As a young Hanoian businesswoman owning both a car and a motorbike told me: 'It's more convenient to be inside the car. Because it's clean and, you know, [on a motorbike] after coming back home my face will be black because of the dust' (interview, March 2013, translated from Vietnamese).

Interestingly, a car is also seen as the most healthy transport option in Hanoi's streets. Indeed, concern for health was one of the most important reasons for acquiring a four-wheeler, according to my car-owning informants. In a rather paradoxical relationship to the pollution from cars, many middle-class Hanoians see the car as a way of protecting themselves and their family from the often poisonous air of the city (Hansen 2016a). In other words the car disallows some of the old practices of two-wheelers, but allows the overall practice of mobility to be performed in a safer, cleaner and 'healthier' fashion more in line with the comforts and expectations of a middle-class lifestyle.

The popularity of cars does not, however, mean that motorbikes are disappearing. Very few get rid of their motorbikes when they purchase a car. Many of my informants would choose between car, motorbike or sometimes taxi, to get around, depending on the goal of the trip. If going to the local wet market, bicycles or motorbikes were used; if going to the new supermarkets for bulk shopping (a rather new practice in Hanoi) a car could be used as these new spaces of consumption are designed to accommodate four-wheelers. If moving around downtown Hanoi the motorbike is usually used, at least if only one or two persons are going together. If taking the family around, or going for longer trips, perhaps outside the city, the car is the preferred option. Still, the agency of the car is highly visible in urban planning, with gated or semi-gated 'New Urban Areas' being developed on the outskirts of the city (Hansen 2015b). These New Urban Areas diverge significantly from the older parts of Hanoi. Instead of the low and narrow houses characteristic of old Hanoi, they have high-rise buildings. And instead of local wet markets, they have modern supermarkets and often large and luxurious shopping malls. And, crucially, instead of narrow streets, these areas have highways with several lanes and parking facilities to accommodate cars (Hoai Anh Tran 2015). In other words, the expectation of car ownership is being built into the infrastructure and consumption geography of the new Hanoi.

Alongside the car's entry to the streets, the symbolic value attached to motorbikes has been diminishing. Not long ago the perhaps most powerful sign of modernity and development in Vietnam (Truitt 2008), the motorbike has for the middle class largely been relegated to an everyday commodity (Earl 2014). Meanwhile, the private car has overtaken the top position in the status hierarchy of goods, and emerged as not only a development goal for national industry but also a mobile personal development goal in the streets. While Vietnam's millions of motorbikes were emblematic of the rapid changes following market reforms, the new position of the car arguably reflects an even deeper transition to capitalism.

Capitalism on wheels[10]

With rapid economic growth, living standards have improved dramatically in Vietnam during the last decades. As in any capitalist transition, however, this has also involved increasing social inequalities (see for example the contributions in Taylor 2004). Particularly those with political connections have been able to accumulate significant wealth since *doi moi*, and class differences have been rapidly increasing. The new economic reality has made possible the emergence of a middle class, not seen in (North) Vietnam since the days of French colonialism (see Bélanger *et al.* 2012). At the same time, the social and indeed political meanings of consumer goods have changed radically. As Vann (2012) argues, in a country still ruled by a communist party that is involved in most parts of the economy, and with little freedom of speech or media, the strongest sense of liberty *doi moi* has brought along comes in the shape of consumption. Thus, the well-off parts of the population are able to purchase and display goods that would be judged as bourgeois excess not long ago. This of course makes perfect sense. While a planned economy usually focuses on producing and delivering *enough* goods to people, a capitalist economy fundamentally depends on growth, and thus on increasing levels of consumption (see discussion in Wilhite and Hansen 2015).

The capitalist transition has not only opened for high consumption, it has altered social hierarchies. At least there is more room for alternatives to the strict hierarchies of the communist party. Along with this a change in modes of social distinction has emerged. We know much about the ways in which goods are used both to display and acquire social positions, most famously through the work of Veblen (2005) and Bourdieu (1984). Veblen used the concept of conspicuous consumption to explain the purchase of luxury goods for the display of economic power in a new socio-economic context where inherited social positions were losing their monopoly on hierarchically structuring society. This speaks well to the situation in Vietnam after *doi moi*, which has led to what Nguyen-Marshall *et al.* (2012) have referred to in their book title as 'the reinvention of distinction'.

Whether you are successful or not in the market economy is one of the main social classifiers of the new Vietnam, and consumption is used to display and entrench 'success'. And there is currently no better way to display success than to drive a car, or at least to own a car. According to many of my informants, it is now common for wealthy people to acquire a car even if they have no intention of using it. They purchase it, park it in front of their houses, and then use their motorbikes to get around the city. These examples show that a sense of pragmatic mobility prevails in Hanoi. They also show that the car as a material object designed for mobility can be physically immobile while still providing significant social benefits to its owner.

Usually, however, cars are also physically in use. They are now visible all over Hanoi, also in the parts where streets are so narrow that a car causes instant havoc. The fact that it can move around in turn makes it more important for social performance than a house. As put by a young businessman in Hanoi: 'the car is the best symbol of success. You can rent an apartment, but you have to own your car' (interview, March 2013). In the business environment, this takes on a more practical side. Businessmen in Hanoi today use their car to show actual or potential business partners that they are successful businessmen. I interviewed one young Hanoian businessman who had recently sold his practical family car and bought a more expensive and less practical model. He told me: 'If I have a meeting or appointment with [a] customer I have to go by car'. When I asked why he said 'Because ... you know ... if I go by car maybe my image is better with the customer'. He said if he had already known the contact for a long time he could still use his motorbike (which he used frequently), but if needing to make an impression he had to drive his car. But not any car would do. 'It should be nice; usually it should be [an] expensive car. Like you know the cost is maybe more than 50,000 US Dollar' (interview, April 2013). The statements by these young businessmen were confirmed in several interviews. What they are discussing is a form of conspicuous consumption, but perhaps more accurately they are explaining how they use their cars in strategies of distinction. The car is used as an object to define their position as successful businessmen. At least the car *presents* them socially as successful. There are many stories in Hanoi today of ambitious young men who acquire big loans, often in the informal economy and at extreme interest rates, to purchase a car, hoping the vehicle will aid them in their business endeavours.

But distinction is tricky, and the practice of flaunting expensive cars is frowned upon by the educated part of the elite in Hanoi, according to whom this type of behaviour belongs to the 'new rich'.[11] As an older and apparently highly successful businessman with strong connections to the old communist hierarchy told me, this is something rich peasants do. Of course you will have a car (he did not; he would usually take taxis everywhere), but you would not try to 'show off' with it. This is seen as vulgar public display of wealth (interview, October 2013). After years of socialist rule in Vietnam, there is however no clear group of 'old rich' in the conventional sense. There are, however, those that have grown up in the corridors of socialist power. They may not themselves even be members of the communist party, but they have in various ways been privileged due to either their own or their parents' political connections. This often involves higher education and a certain know-how when it comes to behaving among the rich and powerful. The market economy now produces a range of formal and informal ways of acquiring significant amounts of money. As put in an interview by a young Vietnamese anthropologist: 'The transition of Vietnam makes many people suddenly become rich with money falling from the sky but not from their effort and capability' (interview, May 2013). Or in the words of a marketer for a large, foreign auto company in Hanoi:

Demand is very high on cars now. We usually make [a] joke: Vietnam is a very poor country but we have the best and the most beautiful cars in the world. People are very poor but they have a lot of money.

(Interview, October 2013)

Importantly, as Bourdieu (1984) has explained in detail, in processes of distinction consumption is simultaneously used to define social classes and *defined by* social classes. In other words, certain goods and certain behaviour become embedded in the expectations of belonging to particular strata of society. In Hanoi, while still an elusive dream for most people, owning a car has become normalised as part of being (upper) middle class. Thus, many relatively wealthy businessmen have explained to me that the car does not really work as a status symbol, since 'everyone has one now'. With 21 cars per 1000 people this is mildly put an overstatement, but this just serves to make the point clearer.

Buy a car, build a house, get a wife

While the car is already becoming unremarkable for the better off in Vietnam, it seems to have achieved a position as a 'must-have' object, a dream towards which many Vietnamese now aspire. Indeed, when explaining the position of the car in Vietnam today, many of my informants referred to a traditional Vietnamese proverb. According to this there are three things a man should strive to achieve in life: to buy a buffalo, build a house and get a wife. In the new, more affluent and more capitalist Vietnam, a young man should still build a house and get a wife. But he can forget about the old buffalo. In order to be successful he now needs to purchase a car.

Conclusion

I started this chapter by asking how the boom in consumption of private vehicles can be understood in relation to the multi-scalar development processes of *doi moi*, as well as what cars and motorbikes can tell us about Vietnam's development trajectory. From a macro-economic perspective, global and regional economic integration has been crucial for both the motorbike revolution and the emergence of automobility in Hanoi and Vietnam. The manufacturing of vehicles can be seen as examples of the successes and failures of Vietnam's economic development strategies: successes in terms of attracting foreign direct investment and developing low and medium-tech industries, and so far failures in escaping the 'middle-income trap' and develop high-tech industrial capacities (see Masina 2015).

Nevertheless, *doi moi* has radically increased the availability of consumer goods such as private vehicles, and this chapter has shown how the 'motorbike revolution' in Vietnam can to a certain extent be understood as an outcome of a combination of intentional industrial policies and unintentional outcomes of these. Particularly Chinese manufacturers played a crucial role in driving down prices on motorbikes and thus 'democratising' ownership, although formally Japanese manufacturers have been the key players in the development of Vietnam's motorcycle industry. For cars the picture is less clear, although *doi moi* has also made cars more widely available. In policy moves that are detrimental to the attempts to develop a domestic automobile industry, however, the Vietnamese government has limited car ownership through very high taxes and fees, in turn unintentionally favouring motorbike ownership. This has made cars very expensive and accessible only to the relatively wealthy. But there are signs that the policies are changing. Due to requirements from AFTA, Vietnam will have to remove restrictions on imported cars by 2018, which could lead to an influx of imported cars from other Southeast Asian countries.

The extraordinary consumption of motorbikes and now the emergence of cars cannot be understood without the transformations in the systems of provision for vehicles. From a closed planned economy dependent on imports from the Soviet bloc, with *doi moi* Vietnam opened the gates to global and regional capitalism. Nevertheless, although economic theories predict increased consumption of cars alongside economic growth (Medlock and Soligo 2002), production determinism cannot explain the extent to which people started using motorbikes, and now cars, to perform mobility. As Sheller and Urry (2006, 210) remind us: 'Mobility is always located and materialised, and occurs through mobilisations of locality and rearrangements of the materiality of places'. *Doi moi* involved much more than macro-economic processes. Reforms have created a more affluent, and more mobile, Vietnam. This is a Vietnam where more and more people can both access and afford goods providing new comforts and luxuries, and also one where consumer goods can be used to display success in the market economy. It is, however, also a more unequal society, where the differences between the haves and have-nots represent a stark contrast to the socialist ideals of the country. While the millions of motorbikes in Vietnam are physical manifestations of the very rapid improvements in material living standards in the country over the last decades, cars represent a new round of transformations and, I argue, a deeper transition to capitalism.

Although the extent to which Vietnam has transitioned to capitalism is still being discussed (Hansen 2015a), it is hard to argue against the presence of global capitalism in the streets of Vietnam's cities. As is typical for contemporary capitalism and indeed for Vietnam's development experience in general, the cars on the roads in Vietnam are manufactured by big actors from more mature capitalist economies. They originate in countries such as Japan, South Korea, France, Germany and the US, and can in many ways be seen as 'global capitalism on wheels'. Even if manufactured within Vietnamese borders, usually the majority of the parts used for assembling the vehicles are imported (Hansen 2016a).[12] Simultaneously, these icons of global capitalism have symptomatically become the ultimate symbol of personal success in the nominally socialist country.

Writing around the time when car consumption started taking off in Vietnam, Truitt (2008, 16) concluded that 'as the lighter, more flexible, but more exposed motorbike is pushed to the side of the road, the privately owned car may come to define the aspirations of the middle class in Ho Chi Minh City'. At least for Hanoi, her predictions were right on target. Just as Volti (2008, 1001) observes that 'the spirits of Henry Ford and Alfred Sloan have prevailed over those of Mao Zedong and Mahatma Gandhi', the same can be said about Ho Chi Minh's preaching of modesty and frugality. The car is a powerful representation of success in today's Vietnam, and the motorbike will certainly have a strong competitor in the years to come. As car ownership becomes increasingly normalised, Vietnam's cities may possibly see a projection of their own futures in the gridlocked streets of other large Southeast Asian cities, such as Jakarta, Manila and Bangkok.

Notes

1 As is common practice in Vietnam, I use the term motorbike to refer to most two-wheelers, although I use 'motorcycle' when discussing industrial developments. Most motorbikes in Vietnam range between 50 and 150 CC and are relatively small in size. The fully automatic versions would elsewhere usually be known as scooters.
2 *Doi moi* literally translates as 'change towards something new', but is usually translated as 'renovation' both inside and outside Vietnam.
3 The following section draws on Hansen (2015b).
4 *Ao dai* is the Vietnamese 'traditional' costume, consisting of a tight-fitting silk tunic worn over pants. The contemporary version emerged as a French-Vietnamese hybrid during French colonial times (see Leshkowich 2003).
5 *Xe* is the classifier for vehicles in Vietnamese. *Xe may* is the word for motorbike.
6 Sample surveys in Hanoi traffic conducted by the World Bank (2014) in 2012 found that two-wheeled transport together represented 85.8 per cent of total traffic. Of this, motorbikes represented 96.8 per cent, bicycles 2.6 per cent and electric scooters 0.6 per cent.
7 The following section draws on Hansen (2016a).
8 Available parking space in the capital has been calculated to be able to accommodate 10 per cent of the total number of cars (Hanoi People Committee 2011).
9 Aiming to stay pale, particularly among women, is a strong cultural trait in Vietnam, as in many other Asian cultures (see Hansen *et al.*, 2016). The motorbike exposes you to the sun, and Vietnamese girls and women go a long way to cover their bodies with additional jackets, skirts and facemasks to escape the sun. This hassle is avoided in a car.
10 Parts of this section draw on Hansen (2016b).
11 In Vietnamese the Sino-Vietnamese term *trọc phú* is used, *trọc* meaning stupid, uneducated or impolite, and *phú* meaning rich.
12 Nevertheless, as part of a wider trend in Vietnam of seeing anything produced in the country as of dubious quality, many prospective car owners are looking for fully imported models, despite much higher costs.

References

APERC. 2013. *APEC Energy Demand and Supply Outlook* (5th edition). Tokyo: Asia Pacific Energy Research Centre.

Arnold, David and Eric DeWald. 2011. Cycles of Empowerment? The Bicycle and Everyday Technology in Colonial India and Vietnam. *Comparative Studies in Society and History* 53 (4): 971–996.

Bélanger, Danièle, Lisa B. Welch Drummond and Van Nguyen-Marshall. 2012. Introduction: Who Are the Urban Middle Class in Vietnam? In *The Reinvention of Distinction: Modernity and the Middle Class in Urban Vietnam*, edited by Van Nguyen-Marshall, Lisa B. Welch Drummond and Danièle Bélanger, 1–17. Dordrecht: Springer.

Beresford, Melanie. 1988. Issues in Economic Unification: Overcoming the Legacy of Separation. In *Postwar Vietnam: Dilemmas in Socialist Development*, edited by David G. Marr and Christine P. White, 95–110. Ithaca: Cornell Southeast Asia Program.

Beresford, Melanie. 2008. Doi Moi in Review: The Challenges of Building Market Socialism in Vietnam. *Journal of Contemporary Asia* 38 (2): 221–243.

Bourdieu, Pierre. 1984. *Distinction: A Social Critique of the Judgement of Taste*. London: Routledge & Kegan Paul.

Drummond, Lisa B. Welch. 2012. Middle Class Landscapes in a Transforming City: Hanoi in the 21st Century. In *The Reinvention of Distinction: Modernity and the Middle Class in Urban Vietnam*, edited by Van Nguyen-Marshall, Lisa B. Welch Drummond and Danièle Bélanger, 79–93. Dordrecht: Springer.

Earl, Catherine. 2014. *Vietnam's New Middle Classes: Gender, Career, City*. Copenhagen: NIAS Press.

Fforde, Adam and Stefan De Vylder. 1996. *From Plan to Market: The Economic Transition in Vietnam*. Boulder, Colorado: Westview Press.

Fujita, Mai. 2013a. Does China's Economic Rise Help or Hinder the Development of its Neighbours? IDS Evidence Report. UK: Institute of Development Studies.

Fujita, Mai. 2013b. The Rise of Local Assemblers in the Vietnamese Motorcycle Industry: The Dynamics and Diversity of Industrial Organization. In *Vietnam's Economic Entities in Transition*, edited by Shozo Sakata, 146–166. Basingstoke: Palgrave Macmillan.

GSO (General Statistics Office of Vietnam). 2012. Household Living Standard Survey 2012. Hanoi: Statistical Publishing House.

Hanoi People Committee. 2011. Tong hop ve ha tang GTVT, so lieu phuong tien trong khu vuc vanh dai III [Overview of transport infrastructure and data of vehicles in the ring road III area]. Hanoi People Committee: Hanoi.

Hansen, Arve. 2015a. The Best of Both Worlds? The Power and Pitfalls of Vietnam's Development Model. In *Emerging Economies and Challenges to Sustainability: Theories, Strategies, Local Realities*, edited by Arve Hansen and Ulrikke Wethal, 92–105. London: Routledge.

Hansen, Arve. 2015b. Transport in Transition: *Doi moi* and the Consumption of Cars and Motorbikes in Hanoi. *Journal of Consumer Culture*. Doi: 10.1177/1469540515602301.

Hansen, Arve. 2015c. Motorbike madness? Development and Two-Wheeled Mobility in Hanoi. *Asia in Focus* 2: 5–15.

Hansen, Arve. 2016a. Driving Development? The Problems and Promises of the Car in Vietnam. *Journal of Contemporary Asia*. Doi: 10.1080/00472336.2016.1151916.

Hansen, Arve. 2016b. Hanoi on Wheels: Emerging Automobility in the Land of the Motorbike. *Mobilities*. Doi: 10.1080/17450101.2016.1156425.

Hansen, Arve, Kenneth Bo Nielsen and Harold Wilhite. 2016. Staying Cool, Looking Good, Moving Around: Consumption, Sustainability and the 'Rise of the South'. *Forum for Development Studies*. Doi: 10.1080/08039410.2015.1134640.

Hoai Anh Tran. 2015. Urban Spaces Production in Transition: The Cases of the New Urban Areas of Hanoi. *Urban Policy and Research* 33 (1): 79–97.

Jakapong Pongthanaisawan and Chumnong Sorapipatana. 2010. Relationship between Level of Economic Development and Motorcycle and car Ownerships and their Impacts on Fuel Consumption and Greenhouse Gas Emission in Thailand. *Renewable and Sustainable Energy Reviews* 14 (9): 2966–2975.

Koh, David W. H. 2006. *Wards of Hanoi*. Singapore: Institute of Southeast Asian Studies.

Leather, James, Herbert Fabian, Sudir Gota and Mejia Alvin. 2011. Walkability and Pedestrian Facilities in Asian Cities: State and Issues. ADB Sustainable Development Working Paper Series. Manila: Asian Development Bank.

Leshkowich, Ann Marie. 2003. The Ao Dai Goes Global: How International Influences and Female Entrepreneurs Have Shaped Vietnam's National Costume. In *Re-orienting fashion: The Globalization of Asian dress*, edited by Sandra Niessen, Ann Marie Leshkowich and Carla Jones, 79–115. Oxford: Berg.

Logan, William S. 2000. *Hanoi: Biography of a City*. Singapore: Select Publishing.

Malesky, Edmund, Regina Abrami and Yu Zheng. 2011. Institutions and Inequality in Single-Party Regimes: A Comparative Analysis of Vietnam and China. *Comparative Politics* 43 (4): 401–419.

Masina, Pietro. 2006. *Vietnam's development strategies*. New York: Routledge.

Masina, Pietro. 2015. Miracles or Uneven Development? Asia in the Contemporary World Economy. In *Emerging Economies and Challenges to Sustainability: Theories, Strategies, Local Realities*, edited by Arve Hansen and Ulrikke Wethal, 53–64. London: Routledge.

Medlock, Kenneth B. and Ronald Soligo. 2002. Car Ownership and Economic Development with Forecasts to the Year 2015. *Journal of Transport Economics and Policy* 36 (2): 163–188.

MOIT (Vietnam Ministry of Industry and Trade). 2013. Quy hoach phat trien cong nghiep o to Viet Nam den nam 2020, tam nhin den nam 2030 [Vietnam Automotive Industry Development Master Plan to 2020, with Vision to 2030]. Hanoi: Ministry of Industry and Trade, Socialist Republic of Vietnam.

Nguyen-Marshall, Van, Lisa B. Welch Drummond and Danièle Bélanger, (eds). 2012. *The Reinvention of Distinction: Modernity and the Middle Class in Urban Vietnam*. Dordrecht: Springer.

OICA. 2014. World Vehicles in Use. www.oica.net/wp-content/uploads//total-inuse-2013.pdf.

Prime Minister of Vietnam. 2013. Approving the Adjustment on Vietnam Road Transport Development Scheme to 2020 and Orientation Towards 2030. Decision No. 356/QD-TTg. Hanoi: Socialist Republic of Vietnam.

Rigg, Jonathan. 2012. *Unplanned Development: Tracking Change in South-East Asia*. London: Zed Books.

Sheller, Mimi and John Urry. 2006. The New Mobilities Paradigm. *Environment and Planning A* 38 (2): 207–226.

Sturgeon, Timothy J. 1998. *The Automotive Industry in Vietnam: Prospects for Development in a Globalizing Economy*. Hanoi: Development Strategy Institute, Ministry of Planning and Investment, Socialist Republic of Vietnam.

Taylor, Philip, (ed.). 2004. *Social Inequality in Vietnam and the Challenges to Reform*. Singapore: Institute of Southeast Asian Studies.

Thanh Nien News. 2012. Hanoi Wants to Bring Back Tuk-Tuks after Eliminating Them. http://thanhniennews.com/society/hanoi-wants-to-bring-back-tuktuks-after-eliminating-them-5355.html.

Thanh Nien News. 2014a. Vietnam Motorbike Market Slump to Continue. www.thanhniennews.com/business/vietnam-motorbike-market-slump-to-continue-23874.html.

Thanh Nien News. 2014b. Vietnam Sees Faster-than-expected Growth of Motorbikes. http://thanhniennews.com/society/vietnam-sees-fasterthanexpected-growth-of-motorbikes-24223.html.

Truitt, Allison. 2008. On the Back of a Motorbike: Middle-class Mobility in Ho Chi Minh City, Vietnam. *American Ethnologist* 35: 3–19.

Tuoi Tre News. 2014. Motorbike Market Almost Reaches Saturation in Vietnam: Insiders. http://tuoitrenews.vn/business/18144/motorbike-market-almost-reached-saturation-in-vietnam-insiders.

Urry, John. 2004. The 'System' of Automobility. *Theory, Culture & Society* 21(4/5): 25–39.

Van Arkadie, Brian and Raymond Mallon. 2003. *Viet Nam: A transition tiger?* Canberra: ANU Press and Asia Pacific Press.

Vann, Elisabeth F. 2012. Afterword: Consumption and Middle-Class Subjectivity in Vietnam. In *The Reinvention of Distinction: Modernity and the Middle Class in Urban Vietnam*, edited by Van Nguyen-Marshall, Lisa B. Welch Drummond and Danièle Bélanger, 157–170. Dordrecht: Springer.

Veblen, Thorstein. 2005 (1899). *The Theory of the Leisure Class: An Economic Study of Institutions*. Delhi: Aakar Books.

Volti, Rudi. 2008. A Car for the Great Asian Multitude. *Technology and Culture* 49: 995–1001.

Warde, Alan. 2005. Consumption and Theories of Practice. *Journal of Consumer Culture* 5: 131–153.

Wilhite, Harold and Arve Hansen. 2015. Reflections on the Meta-practice of Capitalism and its Capacity for Sustaining a low energy transformation. In *Sociologie de l'énergie: Gouvernance et pratiques sociales*, edited by Christine Zelem and Christoph Beslay, 35–40. Paris: CNRS Editions.

World Bank. 2013. Vietnam Overview. www.worldbank.org/en/country/vietnam/overview.

World Bank. 2014. Motorization and Urban Transport in East Asia: Motorcycle, Motor Scooter & Motorbike Ownership & Use in Hanoi. Technical Report No. 1: Context and Scoping. Hanoi: World Bank.

7 Transport and mobility

The Filipino *via crucis*

Rolando Talampas

At his presidential inaugural address in 2010, Benigno Simeon C. Aguino (popularly known as 'PNoy') proclaimed his anti-'*wangwang*' (sirens used by government vehicles) promise, declaring that the days of 'blaring, much-abused sirens' were over, while also signalling his administration's campaign against corruption and the 'mind-set of entitlement' regarding road use (Interaksiyon. com 2011). Indeed, from then on only emergency service vehicles would be allowed to hurriedly plough through traffic while the rest of the public would be left to cope with each passing traffic jam as best they could. But so far, the Metro Manila Development Authority, the state agency in charge of traffic management in the National Capital Region (NCR, also called Metropolitan Manila, or Metro Manila for short), has been unable to address the mounting traffic congestion problems in the Philippines' largest urban centre, leading some (Herrera 2015; see also White 2015) to question if PNoy's six-year term that was set to end in 2016 has been successful. For example, the persistent '*tukod*' (stalled traffic) at the historical EDSA (Epifanio delos Santos Avenue, named after a Filipino historian, a 24-kilometre north-south circumferential road previously named Highway 54), the site of the 1986 People Power Revolution, shows just how difficult it is for people to get to their destination, especially at peak hours.

While EDSA traffic may thus be slow, or even often at a complete standstill during rush hours, the Philippine economy is said to be one of fastest growing in the world (Robinson 2015) at about 6 to 7 per cent annually. And to many, mobility now seems to be less of a problem than before insofar as a large number of Filipinos increasingly move about, or even migrate out of the country: About ten million Filipinos live or work abroad in more than a hundred different countries to earn money for their children's education, shelter, health, and consumption; farmers abandon farm lands (to the detriment of agriculture) and head for the cities, while low-cost air carriers and new cars – and air-conditioned buses ferried across island destinations on board roll-on-roll-off vessels – provide new means for greater circulation and movement (Philippine Statistics Authority n.d.). Yet such new forms of mobility remain unavailable to many ordinary Filipinos, who still use the Pasig River ferry along the heavily silted and stinking waterway that divides Manila north and south. Manila's urban poor develop small plyboard carts with small bearing wheels to move passengers along the old railroad tracks in the city, and the remaining, and often ageing, farmers convert Chinese-made hand tractors into three-wheeled vehicles (called *kuliglig*, literally cricket) often treading dangerously along the national highway.

In light of this it is timely to consider mobility in the country's metropolis as a pressing issue that warrants closer scrutiny. Up to now, legitimate concerns about the urban transport mess have been raised in a few studies, although in very different ways. One study connects urban transport woes to the colonial legacy and claims that it was the entry of the automobile that, especially in the colonial city of Manila, led to 'profound changes in the formation of modern societies and the very idea of modernity' (Pante 2014, 855). Another study, by Chiu and Shioji (2006), chronicles the way in which the *calesa's* (a horse-drawn coach) cultural appeal facilitated the shift that led to the enthronement of the jeepney as the 'king of the road' in post-war Philippines, visible in the jeepney driver and operator's fascination with metal horse figures as decorative, symbolic reminder of old-fangled transport animal. Last, there are several reports prepared by the think tank, the Philippine Institute of Development Studies (PIDS), that seek, in part, to critique how government failure in the fields of urban and transport planning has produced a situation where the country lags behind many of its neighbouring Asian countries (Manasan and Mercado 1999; Aldaba 2013; Navarro 2014; Ofreneo 2015). In contrast, in this chapter I discuss Filipino mobility in the context of Metro Manila with particular reference to the specificities of the contemporary transportation situation. I argue that while transportation is a public good, mobility has become a private and personalised pursuit. This discrepancy poses a barrier to development, one that is sustained not only by the lack of concern for public welfare, but also by the transformation of the urban and rural economy. In spite of civil society promotion of the principles of 'inclusive mobility' (Romero 2015; see also Fernando 1998) – most of which are already covered by law and, presumably, by common standards of morality – and its calls for behavioural change, the state's inability to provide basic public goods, and to respond appropriately to the traffic situation (Santiago 2014) may well, I suggest, frustrate popular expectations for even modest improvements of current conditions. Metaphorically speaking, urban mobility in Manila today is not unlike the *via crucis* (the way of the Cross), the 'path of suffering' associated with Christ; the deterioration of the traffic situation is too obvious to miss, and people who have been in Manila long enough to remember how easy it once was to move about can hardly be blamed for moving out as soon as they can. Metro Manila reportedly has more vehicles per kilometre of road than Singapore and more people per square kilometre than Tokyo; with 16 cities under its coverage, Metro Manila's transport system relies on more than 400 private bus companies covering more than 800 routes. In fact, about 80 per cent of the vehicles in Metro Manila are privately owned; there are about 35,000 jeepneys; 6,000 utility vehicles (UVs), and 200,000 tricycles and pedicabs in the NCR (UP Forum 2015). While tricycles and pedicabs are confined to local routes of about five kilometres per trip, many of the other vehicles run on six circumferential roads and ten radial roads, a good number of which are said to be 'incomplete' or in poor condition.

This chapter seeks to historicise and chronologise key changes in the trajectory of jeepney, tricycle and car transportation, and to weave the changes into a narrative of the quest for mobility by different segments of the urban population. Transport modes are adopted by people as they locate themselves and their circumstances within a given set of conditions, and no matter how much they may try to become masters of their own mobility they always have to contend with factors beyond their control. How they do so in Metro Manila is the main concern of this chapter. I begin by offering a brief historical overview of transport modes in Manila and its environs; this is followed by an account of the reign of the jeepney in the post-war years, and the gradual emergence of many of Manila's current mobility troubles. The subsequent sections look first at the triumph of the tricycle and the factors that led to it, and then at the quest for automobility via car ownership and its concomitant contribution to the present transport congestion.

Historical overview

Animal-drawn carts and various water crafts brought pre-colonial Filipinos and their goods to their destinations. While the various small communities across the more than 7,100 islands had built their homes in clusters of small villages called *barangays* by rivers or the seaside, the Spanish colonial administrators who ruled the Philippines from the sixteenth to the late nineteenth centuries forced people to cluster around churches and town halls and deliberately limited construction of roads in political-religious and commercial centres.[1] Not until November 1892 was the first railway network opened, running from Manila to Dagupan, about 215 kilometres north of Manila.

At the turn of the twentieth century, the Americans had replaced the Spanish, and intensified road-building. They introduced the automobile and, with electricity now available, introduced the electric street car, called *tranvia*, in Manila. The *tranvia* replaced the four-line 1889 system that had used horses and steam engines. Still, most natives relied on horse-drawn coaches going by local names such as *calesas*, *caromatas*, or *caretelas*. Along the Pasig River and the coast of the Manila Bay, where many boatmen also lived with their families, people also used small sailing boats called *cascoes*, *lorchas* and *gabarras* (barges).

The introduction of motorisation in transport also meant modernisation. Modern transport workers were represented by the for-hire car drivers who were paid daily wages. In contrast to the *cocheros* (drivers of horse-drawn carriages), who were seen by the Americans as involved in a pre-modern form of transportation (Pante 2012; 2013), car drivers were moving up the social ladder due to better incomes. Cars, therefore, became an important facet of transportation in the colonial city. Outside Manila, the colonial government wanted more 'farm-to-market' roads to connect with the rural economy, although it had doubts about the utility of railway development – and even more so about air services – to agricultural producers (Porter 1939, 288).

World War II practically destroyed almost all the pre-war infrastructure and killed many animals used for transport. As Japan surrendered unconditionally in 1945, the subsequent war damage payments ensured that roads were among the priority rehabilitation projects (Schein 1951). The Philippine Planning Commission was tasked to make a plan for the basic road infrastructure in the city, which included major thoroughfare plans consisting of the previously mentioned ten radial and six circumferential roads (Morichi and Acharya 2013, 26). Tellingly, the plan excluded the building of railways.

In the 1950s, the Philippines remained largely agricultural, while the import substitution strategy favoured manufacturing and other industries in anticipation of the decline of US assistance by 1954. This period thus saw the introduction of economic protectionist measures via tariffs, a preference for domestic industries that used up foreign reserves, and strict foreign exchange controls, among others. These resulted in low state support for agriculture and an equally low agricultural contribution to the economy. For that reason, transport and mobility in rural areas remained backward.

The jeepney years and Manila's troubles

The Filipino jeepney rose from the ashes of World War II when Manila was one of the most devastated post-war cities. Being a US colony, military jeeps were already used in the Philippines before Japan invaded, and when they returned, the Americans brought many more with them. The limited six-to-eight-capacity *auto calesa* (called AC) used in the immediate post-war period was a converted wartime jeep, and people used it much as they would a horse-drawn *calesa*, only one equipped with a motor (Chiu 2008). Unwilling to bring the military jeeps with them back to the US when they left again, the American military thus provided the occasion for Filipinos to use the jeep to address the severe post-war transportation problems: Unable to import cars due to poor foreign exchange conditions in the 1950s, Filipino entrepreneurs converted the jeeps of the US Army into a vehicle that came to be known as the jeepney. This new vehicle was not only crowned the 'king of the road' as its numbers rose; it was also a celebrated 'national car'.

Different versions of the genesis of the jeepney exist, and different people are credited with the invention, depending on the criteria one adopts. According to an anonymous 'auto historian', it was the *calesa* painter Anastacio Francisco who operated a shop that in 1951 built bodies for jeepneys that allowed more passengers. Painting a *calesa* consisted of finishing lacquer-like work on the coach and adorning it with floral or vine decorations to go with embossed brass designs. The more famous Leonardo Sarao, another *calesa* painter, is, however, credited with rolling out the first commercially produced jeepney. But the same 'auto historian' maintains that 'the earliest passenger jeepney is said to have been conceived, built, and driven in 1945 by Clodualdo Delfino, a musician-entertainer who needed to make a living immediately after liberation'. 'Sarao', 'Francisco', and a few other names would later become strongly and popularly associated with the jeepney. Throughout the 1950s and 1960s, the jeepney used surplus military engines and thick galvanised iron (GI) sheets for bodies; metal horse figures adorned their hoods; and they all ran on petrol fuel. Beginning in the 1970s, all public utility jeepneys started running on second-hand diesel fuel engines, mostly from Japan, as the government subsidised diesel.

A Philippine labour export policy mandated in 1974 in the light of the Middle Eastern oil and world maritime trade boom caused many prospective job applicants to head for Manila for document processing, something which may have contributed to significant additions to the city's population. The income of many of these eventual migrants to the Middle East was ploughed back into Manila's economy and parts of it were invested in new jeepney units. Tellingly, it became fairly noticeable in the 1970s and 1980s that the mudguards of some jeepneys proclaimed the source of the investments through phrases such as 'Katas ng Saudi' or 'Katas ng Barko', which literally translates into 'sweat from Saudi Arabia' and 'sweat from ship'.

Already emerging in the enlarged city landscape were signs of a pervasive non-readiness of local leaders to deal with urban development planning, something which was clearly visible in the multiplication of informal settlers; residential lot developments being sold without roads and utilities; the proliferation of residential and commercial structures along highways; and roads congested with vehicular traffic (Navarro 2014, 11–12). Up to the time when Ferdinand Marcos fled the country in 1986, Marcos' wife Imelda presided over the affairs of the Manila Metropolitan Area. She famously promised to build what she called the 'city of man', one that focused on 'human settlements' with little regard for mobility. As Manasan and Mercado (1999, 12) argue, 'these ad-hoc arrangements were found to be inadequate in addressing the complex problems of the metropolis'. In hindsight, what the Marcoses and their technocrats – wielding authoritarian power – could have done was to strategically introduce more rational road and transport projects (Navarro 2014, 13, 17–18).

The post-Marcos years saw more public utility jeepneys hit the road all across the country, their numbers eventually totalling around half a million. But in 1995, the government stopped issuing jeepney franchises and the current remaining 160,000 jeepneys are now the target of a government phase-out plan. Dancel (2015) summarises the fate of the jeepney thus: 'It remained loud and gaudy. That went towards making it an icon. But assembled like the motor vehicle equivalent of Frankenstein, it also broke down often. That made it impractical in the long run'. Having now become 'less like an icon and more like a dinosaur', the jeepney is threatened by the entry of more efficient and comfortable utility vehicles. Whereas jeepney franchises specified routes – the violation of which would lead to heavy fines or, more commonly, bribes to traffic enforcers – utility vehicles load passengers at one terminal and seek to cut travel time as much as possible by choosing alternative routes to their destination, and by making as many trips as possible per day. Taking a utility vehicle (earlier called 'FX' after the Toyota model 'Tamaraw FX', now called 'UV Express') which moves faster and is more flexible can thus alleviate mobility woes for people going to and/or from work or school. In effect, these utility vehicles have become a new, modern airconditioned jeepney or perhaps even a big-capacity taxi charging a small fare. UV sales rates are on the rise, and unable to face the competition, Sarao Motors, that was synonymous with the jeepney, closed shop in 2000.

Triumph of the tricycle?

An even more affordable option is the tricycle, also called a motor-taxi. Tricycles are typically an urban phenomenon and it is basically a motorcycle with a passenger sidecar attached to accommodate, by law, a maximum of four passengers, including the driver (Congress of the Philippines n.d.). But in practice, tricycles often carry more than four. They are basically confined to roads not devoted to jeepneys and buses and are prohibited by law on national highways.

The tricycle's predecessor was the pedicab, which in all likelihood came into existence before the Japanese invasion, as attested to by photos that can be found on the internet. In the pre-war years, the pedicab serviced short-distance travel in Quiapo and downtown Manila, and queued in wait for passengers by a bridge that connects Manila north and south. The entry of the Japanese motorcycle in the Philippines in the 1950s (see Guillen 2004, 30) added more power to the pedicabs and ended the days of quiet, gas-free and smokeless ferrying of passengers. Later called the tricycle, this vehicle now provides employment on a large scale to people across the region, even if one study reports that the tricycle drivers' incomes have been negatively affected by the entry of cheap motorcycles (Malit 2010).

While there were less than three million (combined private and for hire) tricycles in 2008, the number had grown to more than four million about five years later (see Table 7.1). More than half a million were registered by local government regulatory offices in the NCR in 2008 and probably more operate without formal accreditation.[2] Low capital requirement, low maintenance costs and high returns on investment encourage their proliferation (Roschlau 1985; Urban Partnerships Foundation 2006, 6–7). As such, the Philippines has become a 'tricycle country' where people rely on this vehicle for their everyday transport. Although the law specifies what a tricycle should look like and how many passengers it can carry, the tricycle has been fashioned to adapt to different terrains, clientele and utility (see e.g. Guillen and Ishida 2004, 58 for the 'side', 'center' and 'open' cab types), and overloading and so-called 'top loading' practices (where usually three or four small children, or a couple of adults, ride atop the sidecar) outside the NCR are common. Cabanatuan City, some 100 kilometres north of Manila, takes pride in being the 'Tricycle Capital of the Philippines'. Here, tricycle assembly is a key industry, and dealers are known to treat their customers/audience to raffle draws and scantily clad girls dancing to modern pop music.

Table 7.1 Registered land vehicles in the Philippines, 2007–2012

Item	2007	2008	2009	2010	2011	2012
Private	**4,558,727**	**4,908,332**	**5,216,646**	**5,631,377**	**6,096,423**	**6,417,809**
Cars	700,384	713,175	732,659	759,683	788,372	808,968
Utility vehicles	1,534,634	1,535,003	1,609,698	1,707,705	1,764,865	1,821,527
Buses	6,696	6,184	7,045	7,753	8,769	5,653
Trucks	255,522	269,367	281,282	288,427	298,789	308,644
Motorcycle/Tricycles	2,039,850	2,360,304	2,559,997	2,841,646	3,206,255	3,440,777
Trailers	21,641	24,299	25,965	26,163	29,373	32,240
For hire	**887,023**	**899,211**	**931,048**	**934,176**	**970,946**	**969,784**
Cars	37,648	35,342	39,812	41,787	33,131	36,426
Utility vehicles	215,585	215,929	217,967	217,338	229,330	220,114
Buses	23,142	23,032	25,519	26,566	25,262	27,298
Trucks	16,919	17,941	21,435	21,373	21,786	23,867
Motorcycle/Tricycles	591,254	604,238	623,663	624,078	658,466	658,675
Trailers	2,475	2,729	2,652	3,034	2,971	3,404

Source: Philippine Statistics Authority, 2014 (www.nscb.gov.ph/secstat/d_trans.asp).

In Metro Manila, tricycle sidecars are colour-coded, numbered and stamped with 'Tricycle Operators and Drivers Association' (TODA) membership. TODA regulates tricycle operations at the street level by maintaining terminals and basically collecting daily dues. TODA membership does not, however, restrict operations to specified routes as so-called 'special trips' can be negotiated by passengers to a non-TODA route terminal destination. One huge TODA terminal is located at the corner of Commonwealth Avenue and Batasan (legislature) Road in Quezon City. In this terminal, passengers are typically headed for government offices such as the House of Representatives, the Civil Service Commission, or the Department of Social Welfare and Development, or for the many residential communities (both rich and poor) that surround these offices. Even gated communities in the area allow tricycles to ferry non-residents or domestic servants. Tricycle drivers are often residents of the same areas of their tricycle operation and park their vehicles in front of their house. They refill their vehicles via neighbourhood resellers of Coca-Cola bottled petrol, sometimes with 2T oil additive for the remaining two-stroke, 125 cc Yamaha, Kawasaki or Suzuki engines (while the 'Clean Air Act' has illegalised these two-stroke motorcycles, Shell has developed the 2T oil additive and thus saved tricycles from being phased out).

The triumph of the tricycle can easily be seen in their increasing numbers over the years. From 2007 to 2012, the combined number of motorcycles and tricycles increased from about 2 million to just short of 3.5 million (see Table 7.1). It is highly possible, according to anecdotal accounts from overseas workers, that some tricycle purchases were intended to provide employment for relatives left behind. Thus, the affordable tricycle resurrects hope for the less educated rural migrants, or provides income augmentation for the under-employed (RBAP n.d.; Viola 2007, 16). But there is a dark side to working as a tricycle driver as well insofar as they have been described as vitamin C-deficient (Su and Kayali 2008), HIV/AIDS-vulnerable (Morisky 2005), and drug/crime-implicated (e.g. Taruc 2015). Most tricycle drivers inhabit spaces of squalid conditions that are often threatened with demolition and/or relocation. And a recent proposal to replace tricycles with the battery-powered 'e-trikes' will pose an additional threat to the tricycle and its driver.

While millions of Filipinos thus use the tricycle every day, some have developed a negative attitude towards the tricycle as they acquire other means of transportation. While they may blame the tricycle for the many gridlocked streets, the desire to live a middle-class life in an urban setting akin to those found in 'developed' countries marginalises the tricycle, something which is reinforced by, among others, national road building programmes that design tricycles out of local existence. And there are already street signs in some parts of Metro Manila – such as the Makati Central Business District and at some university campuses – that tell tricycles to operate elsewhere. Some local legislation also depicts tricycles as sources of danger to the commuting public, and clean air campaigners want the last two-stroke engines of this, 'the poor man's' form of mobility, removed. The tricycle and its drivers may thus soon face a future marked by poverty. Yet while this middle-class dream of a modernising city and a modernised form of mobility has many takers, it is more likely that only genuine development gains experienced by those people who struggle to move out of poverty will convince the broader public that the days of the tricycle are numbered.

Cars for caring

While many Filipinos still have to find a successful way to move out of poverty so as to aspire for new and alternative means of mobility, an increasing number of Filipinos already own private cars, something which is also an indicator of economic success. This is especially the case for people working in the expanding service sector, the only sector that has grown consistently since the mid-1980s (Mitra 2013). There are indications that the service sector will continue to be the country's primary contributor to annual productivity growth, something which is sure to benefit service sector workers, many of whom are also car owners – either of 'pre-loved' or, increasingly so, brand new vehicles. In a six-country (China, Japan, Thailand, Vietnam, Indonesia and the Philippines) study, Filipino car buyers highlight valuing qualities such as 'richness, luxury, superiority and "coolness"', as well as affective elements such as 'comfort, excitement and relaxation' (Tan Van *et al.* 2014, 38–39). And Filipino car owners are said to be the 'fifth highest globally who view a car as an important symbol of the success they have achieved in life', according to A. C. Nielsen (cited in Tan Van *et al.* 2014). By owning a car they wish to 'demonstrate their improving social status' (Rivera 2014).

First introduced in the early 1900s, cars were initially (US colonial) government-acquired. 'The influx of American-made cars', writes Pante (2014, 859), 'especially after the Ford Model T came out in 1908, led to a rapid increase in for-hire cars'. The Americans improved the highways and motor transportation and after three decades there were already 52,000 cars in the country (Porter 1939, 287). While this number may have increased somewhat by 1941, when Japan invaded the Philippines, most cars were either destroyed or seized by the Japanese military.

An import ban controlled the entry of completely built-up car units in the 1950s. This reportedly boosted car parts manufacturing and assembly using imported 'kits' (Takacs 1994, 128). While there is hardly any available evidence of just how many cars there were during this period, extant photos from the 1960s collection of the University of Wisconsin-Milwaukee show clean, wide, spacious roads in Manila with only a small number of cars such as the Chevy Bel-air 1958, Simca 1961–1962, Toyopet 1960s, VW Beetle 1960s, or the early 1960s Mercedes Benz 220. In the 1960s, owning a Mercedes Benz car gave rich Filipinos status and elegance; but even riding a taxi – the Mercedes Benz was part of the Manila taxi fleet at the time – would achieve more or less the same.

In the early 1970s, the Volkswagen assembler in the Philippines conceived of the '*sakbayan*', a native national car (Ofreneo 2015, 1) akin to Malaysia's Proton (see Fleming and Søborg, this volume). But as it were, Japanese cars simply flooded the market and became more popular among those who could afford them. Also, the global oil shocks made the US-produced Fords, Chryslers and Chevrolets expensive to drive because of their fuel inefficiency. At the time, car gear boxes, knocked-down car units and the like were assembled in export processing zones. A strike among the Ford plant workers who earned a meagre US$1.50 a day in 1980 forced the company to close down its Mariveles, Bataan export processing zone (Holland 1980), if only for a while. An export policy enunciated in the 1980s envisioned that car manufacturing would bring in more foreign exchange for the country, but the number of (mainly Japanese) cars in Metro Manila continued to rise, from 218,964 in 1980 to 410,814 in 1995. Strikingly, car-owning households on average owned more than one car (Manasan and Mercado 1999).

In 1999, President Joseph Estrada inaugurated the Metro Manila Railway Transit (MRT) from North Avenue station in North Avenue, Quezon, to Buendia station in Makati. From then on, people going to Makati did not need to drive their cars from Quezon City as the MRT made it very convenient and easy to reach the Makati Central Business District. But in spite of this, the number of cars in Manila continued to go up. One possible explanation for this continued rise is the start, in 1998, of the operations of companies based at the Subic Freeport importing so-called 'surplus' cars from Japan. Sold at bargain prices, these surplus cars totalled 10,234 in 2005 (Japan Customs cited in Chiu 2011). More ports in Luzon and elsewhere in the country subsequently began importing not only 'surplus' Japanese cars, but also Korean and other foreign cars, many of which eventually found their way to Metro Manila. To check this, then President Gloria Arroyo issued Executive Order 156 in December 2002, thus banning surplus car imports except at Subic. Subic, of course, then became the exclusive entry point of more and more surplus vehicles, including luxury vehicles, even if the effectiveness of the ban was challenged by Port Irene in Cagayan province, where the business of converting and registering expensive right-hand drive imports continued until 2014.

Brand new car sales reportedly reached 288,609 units in 2015 (Magkilat 2016), with Toyota, Mitsubishi, Hyundai, Ford and Isuzu ostensibly expanding their dealership throughout the country (Sevilla-Mendoza 2015). Cars, dealers maintain, have now become affordable, thus boosting sales (PNA 2013). But in addition to the enhanced ease of availability facilitated by the increase in show-rooms and outlets, the booming car sales may also be the result of a variety of other influences such as privately organised car shows, vintage car exhibits, media coverage and exposure, more accessory dealers, and other forms of private entrepreneurship. In domestic life, and where families can afford it, children are taught early on to appreciate diecast Ferrari and Lamborghini toy cars and bump cars. It even happens that car-owning families fraudulently alter their underage children's birthdates for them to secure a driving licence to drive the family car, thus eliminating the need to hire a driver. The country's rich and famous – people such as the businessman Manny Pangilinan, boxer/congressman Manny

Pacquiao and TV host Willie Revillame – display their car collections for others to admire and dream of. While their luxury cars certainly match their status, others who dream of following in their footsteps may simply settle for auctioned cars in the 'pre-loved' car market, or bank on winning one in raffle games sponsored by malls, banks, cellular phone companies or supermarkets.

In many ways, the Filipino quest for automobility has gone beyond meeting basic needs. This can be seen in how 'the rich and the reckless' – the rich kids, so to speak, some of whom are gifted a car by their parents – engage in dangerous drag racing in specified locations, such as the stretch of Macapagal Avenue in Pasay City. Challenges to go and race are made by eyeball contact, or are arranged by gambling-inclined youngsters, who, in a manner reminiscent of the movie *The Fast and the Furious*, may even wage their girlfriends as the prize. More worrisome, and now also increasingly caught on the ubiquitous closed circuit TV (CCTV) cameras, road rage incidents resulting from simple traffic altercations have involved men with guns settling their differences or arguments (Ramos 2012, 20). And, of course, with more cars on the road there is an increase in car related traffic accidents. In 2006, 27 per cent of all traffic accidents in Metro Manila involved cars, followed by motorcycles (20.7) and jeepneys (19.2) (NSCB 2007). In 2014, a whopping 90,258 road accidents occurred in Metro Manila, averaging a full 248 accidents per day, according to the Road Crash Statistics Report of the Metropolitan Manila Development (cited in Medina 2015). The presence of cars in traffic accidents is very likely to increase during the years ahead, and the sense of achievement, entitlement, success, and social status that is associated with owning and driving a car is not likely to be replaced by a heightened sense of civic duty or civility in traffic any time soon.

Concluding remarks

Transportation in the Philippines comes in many forms, and different categories of people engaged in different forms of livelihood will seek to fulfil their need for mobility in different ways. From horses or even *carabaos*, to animal-drawn carriages, jeepneys and *auto calesas*, to tricycles and cars, people from all layers of society make their way, across land or water, through the difficult, daily grind of Metro Manila's metaphorical *via crucis*. Evolving from the original precolonial settlement by the mouth of a river, to a colonial city, to a war-ravaged entrepot and government centre, to a bustling metropolis and the nerve centre of national affairs, Metro Manila epitomises the many contradictions and contestations of contemporary Filipino mobility. In the quest for mobility, people in Metro Manila resort to the jeepney, the tricycle and cars, each of which at different moments in history laid claims to scarce space on the city's roads. Never really designed to augment, supplement or compete with each other, these vehicles moved people not only physically but also socially. They ferried workmen and women to their jobs, brought kids to school, or crowned one's exertions with a visible badge of accomplishment. Yet the present-day crisis – especially on Metro Manila's main thoroughfares – signals a paralysis not only of mobility, but more importantly also of the capacity to think constructively about the crisis: Many studies have been carried out and plans drawn up to alleviate the trials and tribulations of travel, but they have historically never come to fruition. Centralised traffic management under a metropolitan agency from the 1980s to the present seems unable to harmonise the transport and traffic environment connecting the sixteen component cities.

Notes

1 The legacy of the narrow cobblestone roads can still be seen in heritage towns such as Vigan, about 400 kilometres north of Manila.
2 The 'motortricyboat', a variant of this illegally operating tricycle on Manila's streets, is basically pedicab powered by the engines usually strapped to small fishing boats, leading some to suspect that the motortricyboats were probably first used in coastal cities such as Davao in Mindanao.

References

Aldaba, Rafaelita. 2013. Can the Philippine Auto Industry Survive Smuggling? PIDS policy note no. 2013–05. http://dirp4.pids.gov.ph/ris/pn/pidspn1305.pdf (accessed 31 December 2015).

Chiu, Candy Lim. 2011. Used Car: What's The Use? A Philippine Experience of Japan Surplus Vehicles. *Oxford Journal: An International Journal of Business & Economics* 6 (1).

Chiu, Candy Lim and Hiromi Shioji. 2006. PUJ versus AUV: Rivalry of Development and Survival In and Out of the Road – The Case of Transport Industry in Metro Manila Philippines. 6th Global Conference on Business and Economics. www.gcbe.us/6th_GCBE/data/PUJ%20versus%20AUV%20Rivalry%20of%20Development%20and%20Survival%20In%20and%20Out%20of%20the%20Road%20The%20Case%20of%20Transport%20I.doc (accessed 16 January 2016).

Chiu, Imes. 2008. *The Evolution from Horse to Automobile: A Comparative International Study.* New York: Cambria Press.

Congress of the Philippines. n.d. House Bill No 1911. www.congress.gov.ph/download/basic_16/HB01911.pdf (accessed 2 January 2016).

Dancel, Raul. 2015. Special Feature: End of the Road for Manila's Jeepneys. *Asia News Network,* 8 December, www.asianews.network/content/special-feature-end-road-manilas-jeepneys-5034 (accessed 1 January 2016).

Fernando, Priyanthi. 1998. Gender and Rural Transport. *Gender, Technology and Development* 2 (1): 63–80.

Guillen, Marie Danielle. 2004. A Study on Development of Local Public Transport Policy: The Case of Tricycles and 'Habal-habal' in Davao City, Philippines. MA thesis, University of Tsukuba.

Guillen, Marie Danielle and Haruo Ishida. 2004. Motorcycle-Propelled Public Transport and Local Policy Development – The Case of 'Tricycles' and 'Habal-habal' in Davao City Philippines. *IATSS Research* 28 (1): 56–66.

Herrera, Ernesto. 2015. 'Wangwang' Alive and Well. *Manila Times,* 27 April, www.manilatimes.net/wangwang-alive-and-well/179023/ (accessed 1 January 2016).

Holland, Joe. 1980. Scrambling for a Foothold. *New Internationalist,* 1 April, http://newint.org/features/1980/04/01/trade-unions/ (accessed 25 December 2015).

InterAksyon.com. 2011. PNoy Vows to Stop 'Wang-Wang' Culture. 25 July, www.inter aksyon.com/article/9270/pnoy-vows-to-stop-wang-wang-culture (accessed 2 January 2016).

Magkilat, Bernie. 2016. Car Sales Jump 23% in 2015-CAMPI. *Manila Bulletin*, 12 January, www.mb.com.ph/car-sales-jump-23-in-2015-campi/ (accessed 16 January 2016).

Malit, Froilan, Jr. 2010. Globalization and its Impact on Tricycle Drivers in the Philippine Informal Economy. *Journal of Labor and Industrial Relations* 30 (1/2): 210–218.

Manasan, Rosario G. and Ruben G. Mercado. 1999. Governance and Urban Development: Case Study of Metro Manila. PIDS discussion paper series no. 99–03. http://dirp3.pids.gov.ph/ris/pdf/pidsdps9903.pdf (accessed 25 December 2015).

Medina, Marielle. 2015. Did you Know: 2014 Road Accidents in Metro Manila. *Philippine Daily Inquirer*, 12 May, http://newsinfo.inquirer.net/690709/did-you-know-2014-road-accidents-in-metro-manila (accessed 22 February 2016).

Mitra, Raja Mikael. 2013. Leveraging Service Sector Growth in the Philippines. ADB economics working paper series no. 366. www.adb.org/sites/default/files/publication/30385/ewp-366.pdf (accessed 5 January 2016).

Morichi, Shigeru and Shurya Raj Acharya, (eds). 2013. *Transport Development in Asian Megacities: A New Perspective*. London: Springer.

Morisky, Donald. 2005. HIV/AIDS Prevention among the Male Population: Results of a Peer Education Program for Taxicab and Tricycle Drivers in the Philippines. *Health Education Behavior* 32 (1): 57–68.

National Statistics Coordination Board (NSCB). 2007. On Average, 41 Traffic Accidents Per Day Occurred in the Country in 2006. www.nscb.gov.ph/factsheet/pdf07/fs5_16.asp (accessed 2 January 2016).

Navarro, Adoracion. 2014. Scrutinizing Urbanization Challenges in the Philippines through the Infrastructure Lens. PIDS discussion paper series no. 2014–2037. http://dirp3.pids.gov.ph/webportal/CDN/PUBLICATIONS/pidsdps1437.pdf (accessed 15 December 2015).

Ofreneo, Rene. 2015. Auto and Car Parts Production: Can the Philippines Catch Up with Asia? ERIA discussion paper series. www.eria.org/ERIA-DP-2015-09.pdf (accessed 1 January 2016).

Pante, Michael D. 2012. The Cocheros of American-occupied Manila: Representations and Persistence. *Philippine Studies* 60 (4): 429–462.

Pante, Michael D. 2014. Mobility and Modernity in the Urban Transport Systems of Colonial Manila and Singapore. *Journal of Social History* 47 (4): 855–877.

Philippine Statistics Authority. n.d. Local Travel and Tourism. https://psa.gov.ph/tags/local-travel-and-tourism (accessed 2 January 2016).

Philippine Statistics Authority. 2014. Rail, Water, Land and Air Transportation Statistics 2003–2012. www.nscb.gov.ph/secstat/d_trans.asp (accessed 11 May 2016).

PNA. 2013. More Filipinos Can Now Afford to Buy Brand New Cars. 13 July, www.interaksyon.com/motoring/more-filipinos-can-now-afford-to-buy-brand-new-cars (accessed 26 December 2015).

Porter, Catherine. 1939. Philippines Improving Transportation Facilities. *Far Eastern Survey* 8 (24): 287–288.

Ramos, Glen. 2012. The Ruthless Act of Road Rage. *Health Beat* 73: 17–20.

Rivera, Danessa. 2014. Filipino Middle Class to Grow Auto Industry in Two Years – Nielsen Survey. GMA *News*, 24 April, www.gmanetwork.com/news/story/358219/money/economy/filipino-middle-class-to-grow-auto-industry-in-two-years-nielsen-survey (accessed 29 December 2015).

Robinson, Josh. 2015. The 20 Fastest-Growing Economies This Year: China Tops the List, According to Economists Surveyed by Bloomberg. *Bloomberg*, 25 February, www.bloomberg.com/news/articles/2015-02-25/the-20-fastest-growing-economies-this-year (accessed 2 January 2016).

Romero, Segundo. 2015. Traffic and inclusive Mobility. *Rappler*, 14 October, www.rappler.com/thought-leaders/109135-traffic-inclusive-mobility (accessed 1 January 2015).

Roschlau, Michael W. 1985. Provincial Public Transport. *Philippine Studies* 33 (4): 431–458.

Rural Bankers Association of the Philippines (RBAP). n.d. Tricycle Operators Get Green Light. http://files.archive.rbapmabs.org/dvds/project-management/04success/04success_docs/IVB-MABSWinners/IVB-18-TricycleOpsGreenLight.pdf (accessed 28 December 2015).

Santiago, Rene. 2014. Ending Metro Manila Traffic Woes. *Philippine Daily Inquirer*, 14 September, http://opinion.inquirer.net/78446/ending-metro-manila-traffic-woes (accessed 13 January 2016).

Schein, Ernest. 1951. War Damage Compensation through Rehabilitation: The Philippine War Damage Commission. *Law and Contemporary Problems* 16 (3): 519–542.

Sevilla-Mendoza, Aida. 2015. Who Sold the Most Cars in PH in 2014? *Philippine Daily Inquirer*, 4 February, http://motioncars.inquirer.net/34671/who-sold-the-most-cars-in-ph-in-2014 (accessed 27 December 2015).

Su, Glenn and Sara Kayali. 2008. Blood Vitamin C Levels of Motorized Tricycle Drivers in Paranaque, Philippines. *Industrial Health* 4: 389–392.

Takacs, Wendy. 1994. Domestic Content and Compensatory Export Requirements: Protection of the Motor Vehicle Industry in the Philippines. *The World Bank Economic Review* 8 (1): 127–149.

Tan Van, Hong, Kasem Choocharukul and Satoshi Fujii. 2014. The Effect of Attitudes Toward Cars and Public Transportation on Behavioral Intention in Commuting Mode Choice – A Comparison across Six Asian Countries. *Transportation Research Part A: Policy and Practice* 69: 36–44.

Taruc, Paolo. 2015. Tricycles: As Iconic as Jeepneys and Just as Problematic. CNN Philippines, 25 March, http://cnnphilippines.com/news/2015/03/16/Tricycles-As-Iconic-As-Jeepneys.html (accessed 25 December 2015).

Urban Partnerships Foundation. 2006. Chapter 7: Urban Transport. www.ombudsman.gov.ph/UNDP4/wp-content/uploads/2012/12/Chap-07.-Urban-Transport-30Nov06-UPF.pdf (accessed 25 December 2015).

Viola, Michael. 2007. The Filipinization of Critical Pedagogy: Widening the Scope of Critical Educational Theory. *Journal for Critical Education Policy Studies* 7 (1): 16.

White, Lynn III. 2015. *Philippine Politics: Possibilities and Problems in a Localist Democracy*. New York: Routledge.

8 The shared road

Cars, pedestrians and bicyclists in Japan

Joshua Hotaka Roth

Within the Asian context, the Japanese automobile industry developed earlier than other countries, establishing itself by the 1930s primarily as the supplier of trucks for the Japanese military. The era of mass automobility, when private cars became affordable to an expanding middle class, began in the 1960s. In the last 20 years, the numbers of registered automobiles has hardly changed, and the numbers of newly licensed drivers has actually been on the wane. Much like the US, Canada and many European countries, we can say that Japan is a 'mature' automobile society. Given this status, it is curious that a large part of the road infrastructure in Japanese urban and suburban neighbourhoods does not appear to be dedicated exclusively to cars. On these roads, cars must share spaces with pedestrians and bicycles. Perhaps this explains the fact that more than 50 per cent of traffic deaths in Japan involve pedestrians and bicyclists, a startling proportion in relation to, for example, the US figure of just 16 per cent (IRTAD 2015, 20). These figures appear to support urban planners' contention that separating modes of transport has safety benefits, insofar as many Japanese neighbourhood streets are often shared between different modes of transportation. In this chapter, however, we will explore the possibility of an alternative understanding of 'the shared road'. For one thing, while pedestrian and cyclist deaths comprise a large proportion of total traffic fatalities in Japan, total fatalities there are quite low compared to the US, and much more in line with Western Europe.

The highest ever number of traffic fatalities in Japan was recorded in 1970, early in the era of mass automobility, at 16,765. Despite the large increases in the number of cars on the roads and miles driven in subsequent decades, traffic fatalities fell to 4,838 by 2014 (Naikakufu 2015, 1).[1] The substantial decline in overall traffic deaths certainly has to do with several key developments: safety technologies (air bags, anti-lock brakes), traffic safety law (seat belt requirements, speed limits, harsher drunk driving penalties), and better road infrastructure (better sight lines, guard rails, kerbs, etc.). If we examine the decline more carefully, however, we see that perhaps culture too can help explain the decline, especially at certain moments in the history of driving.

The decline took place primarily in two periods, from 1970 to 1975, and from 2002 to 2014. The recent declines may be explained primarily by improvements in safety technology, increased efficacy of emergency response, and a steep decline in the numbers of young drivers (Naikakufu 2015, 4). The decline in the 1970s, however, occurred at a time when the large numbers of new drivers were becoming more seasoned and acculturated to the reality of roads shared with pedestrians and bicycles. It was a time of traffic safety campaigns and a discourse on driving manners (Roth 2012).

Such different factors purportedly contributing to the decline in fatalities, of course, need to be considered relationally. Some economists would argue, for instance, that safety features in cars actually *reduce* the incentive to drive carefully and thus work at cross purposes with efforts to cultivate safe driving habits. One suggests that if we really wanted to cultivate safe driving habits, we would dispense with the seat belts and air bags, and replace them with a metal stake mounted to the steering wheel pointed at the heart of the driver (Landsburg 1993). Indeed, while driving fatalities declined following the adoption of air bags as standard in most Japanese cars, total accidents and injuries increased for several years (Naikakufu 2015, 1).

A similar paradoxical relationship potentially exists between infrastructure and driving habits. Could it be that those roads that are the most well-equipped with guardrails and pavements separating modes of transportation in fact lead to more dangerous driving behaviour, while infrastructure that is less dedicated to car traffic is actually safer? This chapter grapples with this question. In doing so, I will give special consideration to infrastructure, and the paradox in the Japanese case of a decline in both accidents and fatalities precisely where infrastructure has been least modified, and where cars must share the road with bicycles, pedestrians, and other modes of transportation. Specifically, this chapter explores the question of whether the shared street, often viewed as inherently dangerous and an under-developed form of infrastructure, may actually have had a positive impact on Japanese driving behaviour.

The pre-war start of the automobile industry and the post-war rise of mass automobility

In the first half of the twentieth century, before a mass market for automobiles had developed, it was the military that ensured demand for the fledgling auto industry. In 1918, the Act to Aid the Production of Military Vehicles was passed by the Diet, stipulating that the military would requisition vehicles from local manufacturers (Odaka *et al.* 1988, 22). Ford and GM built plants in Japan in the late 1920s, but the Automobile Industry Act of 1936 required they source parts from Japanese parts makers, and limited overall annual production at the Ford plant to 12,350 units, and the GM plant to 9,470. Local parts manufacturers had made great strides by the time Ford and GM were forced out of Japan in 1939 (ibid., 35). Toyota, which had started out as a manufacturer of automated textile looms, became viable in the automotive sector at this time, and Nissan established itself as foreign competition was excluded (Togo 1993). But the structure of the Japanese auto industry continued to be marked by the earlier start of parts makers. By the 1980s, 81 per cent of the net sales value of finished automobiles in Japan went to subcontractors, compared to 61 per cent in the US and 59 per cent in Germany (ibid., 54).

Early technology transfer was an important part of the growth of the Japanese automobile industry, even as it demonstrated early innovations. Some technology was acquired overseas, as when Nissan imported an entire production line in the late 1930s (ibid., 35). Other technology came through domestic sources. In Japan, military arsenals played a key role in diffusing advanced technology necessary for car manufacturing. This is comparable to the US, where the auto industry first formed in the Connecticut River valley, where gun manufacturers were located in the late nineteenth century and the most skilled work force and advanced machine tools were concentrated. In Japan, the Osaka Arsenal provided forging dies, blueprints and technical advice to several firms involved in early automobile production, including Kwaishinsha which was starting the first line of Datsuns in 1918 (ibid., 26–27).

The mantle of the 'king of industries', a breeding ground for innovations that have revolutionised production processes in all areas of manufacturing, shifted decisively from the gun industry to the automobile industry as Ford's large-scale implementation of the assembly line in the early twentieth century ushered in the era of mass production (Womack et al. 1990). Half a century later, the set of innovations that constituted what is called 'lean production' gave the Japanese auto industry an advantage even as these innovations have been adopted in other countries and transformed manufacturing processes worldwide (ibid.). Many Japanese workers experienced the kind of deskilling that comes with mass production as manufacturing processes are broken down into ever-smaller parts (Kamata 1982; Kumazawa 1996; Roth 2002), but the post-war Japanese compact between labour and management, guaranteeing the stability of lifetime employment in exchange for company unions aligned with the interests of the firm (Gordon 1985), empowered some workers in large firms to become problem solvers within the context of assembly line production, contributing to continuous improvement (kaizen) of efficiency and quality control (Womack et al. 1990; Nonaka 1995; Cole 1989). Lean production also involved just-in-time sourcing of component parts, innovations that integrated car design with manufacturing and customer relations (Womack et al. 1990).

While the automobile industry got off to a relatively early start in Japan compared to other Asian countries, mass automobility did not really get underway until the 1960s, when rising wages and lower costs made personal cars affordable for an expanding middle class. Personal car ownership skyrocketed from just 364,000 in 1960, to 6,559,000 in 1970, to 21,293,000 in 1980.[2] Roads that had been dominated by trucks and buses in 1960 came to be filled with personal automobiles (see Figure 8.1). Along with the increase in personal automobiles, there was an increase in paved roads from under 30,000 kilometres in 1960, to 187,000 kilometres in 1970, and 510,000 kilometres in 1980.

Leading up to the 1964 Tokyo Olympics, a new highway system, along with the bullet train, garnered much attention. But most of the newly paved roads

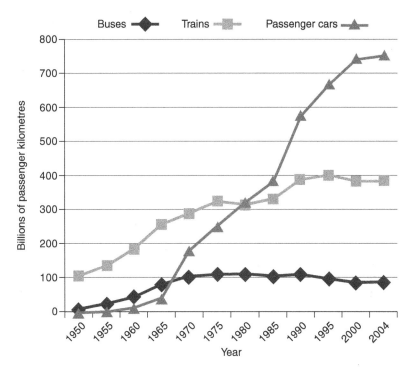

Figure 8.1 Passenger kilometres (in billions) on buses, trains and passenger cars in Japan (source: Ministry of Internal Affairs and Communications, Statistics Bureau, retrieved from www.stat.go.jp/english/data/chouki/12.htm, last accessed 10 January 2016).

were in fact narrow, pre-existing neighbourhood roads. Mass automobility came onto the scene after urban areas were already densely built up, and significantly after a very extensive urban and suburban rail system had already been in place. Certain suburbs were eventually designed with cars in mind, but many suburban neighbourhoods had been pioneered much earlier by the railroad companies, which ensured ridership and profits by establishing department stores at their terminals in city centres, tourist sites at the other end of the line, and lots of suburban residential housing in between (Sand 2005, 132–161). Japanese streets tended to be narrow, and cities had limited power to broaden them for cars. To a great extent, cars were newcomers that had to adapt to pre-existing spaces that they would share with other modes of transport.

Separating modes of transport

In November 2010, a massive construction project was completed to elevate a 13 kilometre stretch of the Chuo line, the busiest commuter train line from Tokyo centre through the dense sprawl of the western suburbs. Train crossings along this stretch were known as the 'crossings that do not open' (*akazu no fumikiri*). During the morning rush between 8 and 9 a.m. as many as 25 trains pass most points in each direction along the Chuo line – almost one every minute with the two directions combined! The 30 seconds or so between trains was not long enough to allow the barriers to open. For an hour or more at a stretch, black and yellow striped bars would remain lowered across the road by the tracks, and flashing red warning lights and alternating warning bells would sound, as cars backed up impatiently for long awaited and very brief openings to cross. Plans have been made for further extension of 'vertical intersections' (*rittai kousa*) along the Chuo line. Japan Railways claims that the elimination of rail crossings has not only eased traffic congestion, but also contributed to local development and unified neighbourhoods previously divided. Rail crossings do not involve a simultaneous sharing of space by trains, cars, bicycles and pedestrians. The space of crossing is temporally organised so trains have exclusive use when the crossings are closed, and are barred when the crossings are open to other kinds of traffic. Yet the space of crossings can be considered as shared, even if temporally organised. The move to vertical intersections means that trains gain more fully dedicated paths, separate from the rest of traffic.

Many urban planners advocate dedicated paths for different modes of transport, not just trains, in order to reduce accidents as well as congestion. In addition to the vertical intersections for rail and automobiles, numerous pedestrian overpasses also allow the separation of pedestrians and automobiles along large roads. Pavements with elevated curbs and sometimes guardrails have become standard in the city centre. Yet such moves to separate modes of transport go against the grain of the long-standing character of Japanese streets. Several dozen rail lines radiate like spokes from the central loop line in Tokyo, and while many are elevated near the centre, railway crossings remain commonplace throughout the city. Furthermore, different modes of transport continue to share the large majority of neighbourhood streets, many of which sport nothing more than a white line along their edges to distinguish between car lanes and the pedestrian zone. There are almost no bicycle lanes in Tokyo, although bicycles are used daily by many as a means of commuting to train stations, or to go about daily activities such as shopping or taking children to day care. Alongside the limited efforts to separate modes of transport, government agencies spearheaded by the police have made concerted efforts to enhance traffic safety by focusing on driving behaviour. Some automakers contributed to the driving safety campaigns with public service advertisements such as the one by Toyota described in the following section.

Is your driving becoming a dangerous gamble?

In 1980, Dentsu, the largest advertising agency in Japan, produced a public service announcement for Toyota that emphasised the risks involved in driving. It opens with a close-up of a middle-aged man, a red scarf wrapped around his head, a revolver in his hands. He spins the cartridge and points the gun to his temple. The narrator asks 'is your driving becoming a dangerous gamble?' (*anata no unten wa kiken na kake ni natteimasenka?*) The scene cuts to the front view out of a car windshield driving along a narrow street. As was typical in many urban neighbourhoods, five or six foot high cinderblock walls flush to the street obstruct views around corners. As the car approaches one blind intersection the narrator intones the driver's thoughts: 'probably nothing will jump out in front of me' (*tabun tobidasanai darouka*). Cut to the man with the gun to his head. Eyes tightly shut, click, he pulls the trigger. A blank. Cut to the front view out of windshield as car approaches next blind intersection. The narrator intones again 'probably nothing will jump out in front...' Cut to man with revolver to head. Click, again a blank. The narrator asks again, 'has your driving becoming something of a gamble?' Cut to the front view out of windshield as car approaches next blind intersection. Suddenly, a soccer ball rolls out onto the street and tyres screech. Cut to a close up of an adorable three or four-year-old boy, red scarf wrapped around his head, looking plaintively into the camera. The narrator asks, 'if he jumped out in front of your car, are you certain you would be able to stop?' (*moshi tobidashitara anatawa kanarazu tomaremasuka?*)

Toyota's public service announcements about the dangers of driving contrasted sharply with its typical commercials that emphasised the attractive dimensions of cars – their speed, elegance, reliability and efficiency. In such commercials, cars become an indispensable means of realising middle class respectability, freedom and individuality, romance and sexuality. Such images were threatened, however, by the grim reality of traffic accidents and fatalities that spiked in the early 1970s, roughly a decade into the era of mass automobility in Japan. Toyota's public service announcements aligned the company and its cars on the side of safety. While they focused on danger, injury and death, these announcements were not depicted as inherent to the car or the inadequacies of the road infrastructure. Rather, all the blame for accidents was placed on the driver.

One cannot fault Toyota for focusing attention on the driver. As opposed to trains, planes and ships, piloted by highly trained corporate employees whose movement is centrally coordinated, the system of automobility involves millions of relatively autonomous, unsupervised, human drivers sharing the roads with more vulnerable pedestrians, bicyclists and children at play. Without sufficient raised pavements, dedicated bike lanes and playgrounds to separate those who are more vulnerable from relatively heavy and fast moving cars, the onus of ensuring safety on the roads resolved on the driver.

The dangers of shared roads, especially in Japan and other Asian contexts with high population densities, are apparent in the proportion of traffic fatalities represented by pedestrians and bicyclists. An international comparison shows that these categories comprised well over 50 per cent of all traffic fatalities in Japan, far higher than in any Western European country (IRTAD 2015, 20). The only country that comes close is Korea. Pedestrian fatalities have been a major part of all traffic fatalities in Japan for decades.

The overall traffic fatality rate in Japan, however, has declined dramatically in recent decades, as it has in most developed countries. The decline in fatalities has taken place even as Japan's streets continue largely to be shared, and raises the question of whether the shared street is inherently dangerous. Indeed, there is some evidence that the shared street can help reduce accidents. Holland's successful *woonerf* (living street) experiments, where pavements are lowered to street level, and all traffic lights and stop signs are removed, suggests that the shared street does not necessarily lead to greater fatalities. With pedestrians on pavements, and bicycles in their own lanes, drivers of cars gain a licence to speed. Tom Vanderbilt, in his book on traffic, quotes Dutch traffic engineer Hans Monderman as saying 'when you have the feeling that at this moment a child could drop in front of my car, you slow down' (Vanderbilt 2008, 193). The shared street can inculcate careful attention among drivers, and this can lead to lower fatality and accident rates (Vanderbilt 2008, 186–203). The fatality rate per capita for pedestrians is lower where drivers expect to see them, in cities such as New York (Vanderbilt 2008, 85–86). One study shows that as the overall distance ridden by bicyclists in The Netherlands increased in the 1980s and 1990s, there was a substantial decline in fatalities per distance ridden (Jacobsen 2003, 208).

To what degree has the shared street shaped the distinctive characteristics of Japanese driver behaviour positively? As one friend told me as we wound our way through some narrow alleys in his neighbourhood where children were playing in the middle of the street, cars did not have a privileged place on these roads. Rather, he felt cars just occasionally borrowed them from their actual owners – local residents on foot or bicycle.

We should not rush to characterise Japan as a country of the shared road in contrast to America's open road. Even within Japan, the shared road contrasts with the dream of the open road promoted in many car advertisements. And yet even as many Japanese pursue the dream of the open road on highways and country roads, the infrastructural inertia of many of the urban neighbourhoods where most Japanese live has contributed to the evolution of a driving culture that takes for granted the presence of pedestrians and bicyclists.

Sharing the road

In any country context, people using a variety of modes of transportation share the roads. But they can share in different ways. The idea of sharing can encompass a range of behaviour. At one end, we have the mere co-presence of multiple parties on the road. At the other end, these parties act with some consideration for each other, with understandings of when someone should give way to another. In certain countries drivers give way to slower moving non-motorised transport, but in many others people driving larger vehicles assume that they have priority (Notar 2012). In some countries most drivers change lanes with care, signalling their intentions to other drivers, while in others drivers will freely move to fill any empty spaces that present themselves in the road ahead of them, shifting lanes frequently, at times achieving a kind of efficient flow of traffic, at times causing accidents or terrible traffic jams as intersections get blocked.

Japanese drivers in recent decades tend to practice what might be called 'considerate' driving. And yet for many years they have had trouble sharing the road in this way, as seen in the rash of traffic accidents that began in the late nineteenth century when the first cars were introduced to Japan (Sasaki 2009, 176–178). The first Japanese traffic fatality involving a car occurred on 26 October 1905, when a five-year-old girl was run over in Osaka (Sasaki 2009, 180). It was not long before a manual for the use and care of cars was drawn up by one of the only auto manufacturers in the country at the time, the Tokyo Automobile Company (*Tokyo Jidosha Seisaku Sho*), which built cars and supplied them to other businesses along with trained drivers (Sasaki 2009, 196). At the time, the government had not established any licensing requirement, and there were no insurance policies to cover accidents involving automobiles.

The Tokyo driving manual was written in 1909, and included 105 points covering such things as appropriate handling of petrol, tyre pressures and issues related to the engine. More than half of the manual related to driving, with a number of points that covered the necessity of sharing the road with other forms of transport. Eight points were specifically about encounters with horse-drawn carriages and the ease with which horses are spooked by car horns, several about the need to be on the lookout for reckless rickshaws darting about oblivious to cars, the dangers of hand carts emerging from side streets, and other scenarios involving drivers and pedestrians (Sasaki 2009, 201–202).

Despite some of these early efforts to educate drivers and shape their behaviour, by the mid-twentieth century, Japanese roads had become quite dangerous, with infamous 'kamikaze taxis' and a generally wild style of driving that some Japanese judged unfavourably compared to the mature styles they found more prevalent in other countries (JAF News 1967). It is clear that automobile drivers assumed a kind of privilege and priority over other objects on the roads.

It was around the time that traffic fatalities hit an all-time high that a popular discourse on driving manners emerged in car magazines that critiqued aggressive and showy driving, and promoted the virtues of considerate and calm driving. Many car companies took part in this new discourse on driving manners, as they had an interest in forestalling a negative critique of cars in general. 'Mutual giving way' (*yuzuri-ai*) was a key term in this manners discourse as was 'heartfelt driving'. In the 'calm driving pledge' promoted by the Japan Automobile Federation in 1969, people were urged to 'hang their hearts' (*kokoro-gakete*) on the 'heart-held principle' (*kokoro-gamae*) of 'peaceful heart driving' (*anshin-unten*) (Roth 2012).

The manners discourse was part of a wider effort to 'harmonise' cars and humans (*kuruma to ningen no chowa*), to achieve a renewed sense of what would be necessary for heavy and potentially fast moving cars to share the roads with slow moving and unprotected pedestrians and other vulnerable objects (*Kuruma no techo* 1970). Efforts at harmonisation included new licensing requirements, driver education programmes, moral suasion of safety campaigns, and finally infrastructure design that started to separate some of the most vulnerable populations (children) from the onslaught of automobile traffic. Dedicated playgrounds were constructed, and school commute routes (*tsugakuro*) were established with the intent of maximising safety (Roth 2011).

Moral suasion: achievements and limits

The dramatic decline in fatalities in recent decades suggests that cars and humans have been 'harmonised' to a great degree, and this is reflected in the way many Japanese drive. It is not uncommon in Japan for two cars driving in opposite directions on alleys to have to stop when they reach each other because these alleys are often too narrow for two cars to get by each other easily. Drivers frequently have to lower their windows and pull their side view mirrors flush with their cars in order to squeeze past each other. Sometimes, even that is not enough and one driver must back up to a slightly wider point on the road to let the other car get by. The other driver will often hold up one hand as a sign of appreciation and bow his head slightly, or tap lightly twice on the horn as he passes. On highways, drivers will readily allow others to merge or shift lanes in front of them, and those let in will flash their blinkers twice to indicate their appreciation.

But the drivers of two cars unable to get past each other on a narrow alley may not always be able to decide readily who will back up. Sharing does not come easily to everyone. Men may have more trouble giving way than women, and some women feel resentful that men expect them to give way, or suggest that they do not know how to back up (Roth 2014). And occasionally cars will push their way a little too fast down streets near train stations crowded with pedestrians, and drive past bicycles as if they were not on the road at all.

It is clear that there are some limits to the efficacy of moral suasion – attempts by government authorities as well as non-governmental organisations to persuade individuals to drive responsibly. Looking at a couple of examples of actual drivers will give some sense of the limits but also the achievements of moral suasion.

Haruto and Mieko

Two or three times per week, Haruto takes Mieko for a drive. Mieko is 86 years old. Haruto is her 40-something adopted son, an unmarried graduate of an elite private university in Tokyo. Sitting in the passenger seat, Mieko notes with some irritation how slowly Haruto takes any corner, almost coming to a standstill in intersections to be sure that his way is clear of pedestrians, cyclists or other cars. I have ridden with Haruto on numerous occasions, and every time I have noted the extreme care with which he drives. He has never had a speeding ticket. He understands the speed limit literally and always drives below it.

Mieko often sits with their beautiful Shiba dog in the back seats of their Toyota Porte, a boxy car that Haruto selected because its sliding passenger side door makes it easy for Mieko to get in and out. Driving in the congested western suburbs of Tokyo can be irritating for Haruto, but the two of them enjoy themselves once they are on the highways and country roads outside of the city. Mieko gave up driving when she was about 80 years old, roughly the time when Haruto, then 39 years old, was adopted and moved in with her. She first got her licence in 1957 when she started teaching public elementary schools in Tokyo's western suburbs. Mieko admitted to having had her share of speeding tickets, but insisted that she never got into an accident.

Kōji

Kōji, married but childless, is a 40-something dropout of another elite private university in Tokyo. He too claims never to have had an accident, although he loves driving his sports car at high speeds on the highway. He has received more than his share of speeding tickets – dozens, in fact – and has had his licence suspended for several months multiple times. On three different occasions he was caught driving with a suspended licence, which led to his licence being revoked. Each time, he had to wait a full year before becoming eligible to apply for a new licence. In the past, Kōji was sometimes caught by the white motorcycle police (*shirobai*), but now tickets are sent to him in the post, generated by the radar guns and cameras positioned alongside many highways.

Kōji thinks uniform speed limits on highways are stupid, arguing that people should drive at speeds at which they are comfortable – speeds that will vary considerably according to ability. He argues that radar guns and speed limits are appropriate for neighbourhood streets. Those are the ones where there is real danger of kids running out in front of cars, and where limited sight lines can lead to bad collisions with other vehicles. Kōji insists that he has always driven within his capacity to control the vehicle, but acknowledges that public roads can present unforeseen dangers.

Kōji and Haruto agree that driving involves some degree of danger and of pleasure. Yet the source of pleasure is very different for them. For Kōji, it is speed and the sense of mastery as he pushes himself close to his limits. While Kōji claims to drive within his abilities, it seems to some degree that pleasure for him comes from courting danger, from the vertigo (*illinyx*) of speed, and the competitive thrill (*agon*) of racing with other like-minded drivers that he occasionally encounters on the road.[3]

For Haruto, pleasure is not as apparent in his driving experience as is a kind of anxiety about its dangers. In addition to his cautious driving style, the stickers on the back of his car indicate that driving is a serious business for him, not a game. On one yellow sticker bold black lettering states 'TAKE CARE TO MAINTAIN SAFE FOLLOWING DISTANCE' (*shakan kyori chuui*). Two other smaller stickers indicate that the car is equipped with a driving camera and an anti-collision sensor. In applying the small stickers to the car, Haruto projects a positive self-identity as a safety conscious person. Even if Haruto does not experience pleasure in the act of driving itself, he seems to derive a kind of pleasure, or at least satisfaction, in having performed all the research necessary to maximise safety. His pleasure derives in constructing a self-identity as a practical, considerate and informed driver, capable of making decisions for the benefit of others as well as himself.

Japanese traffic safety experts may look upon Haruto as the ultimate positive outcome of long-standing efforts to instil a safety consciousness considered essential for the harmonisation of varied forms of transport sharing Japan's narrow roads. Yet few are as obsessively devoted to safety as is Haruto. He represents one extreme in a spectrum of attitudes towards driving.

Kōji, on the other hand, represents the recalcitrant subject of traffic regulation, a testament to the limits of moral suasion. While he is more recalcitrant than the average Japanese driver, many drivers have a positive estimation of their own driving ability (optimistic bias), similar to Kōji, and will regularly drive over the speed limit. While there is some indication that the optimistic bias (about one's own abilities) may not be as prevalent in Japan and other 'collectivist' cultures when compared to the US and European contexts, the tendency may just be muted rather than non-existent.[4]

But for all of Kōji's scorn for traffic regulation, the distinction he makes between driving on highways and on neighbourhood roads suggests that he has absorbed some of the emphasis on safety in the moral suasion campaigns. He recognises the particular kinds of dangers involved when sharing space with pedestrians and bicycles, and adjusts his driving accordingly. However, Kōji's moderation on neighbourhood roads is shaped not by moral suasion alone, but the felt danger of speeding on narrow roads shared with others. Which brings us back to the question of infrastructure.

Road classifications

The Ministry of Land, Infrastructure, Transport and Tourism (MLIT) classifies roads according to administrative jurisdiction, but also in a way that corresponds broadly to Kōji's distinction between highways and neighbourhood roads. At one end, there is the high-speed national auto way (*kōsoku jidōsha koku-dō*). In 2012 the network of these stretched 9,268 kilometres all over Japan. These roads are for the exclusive use of motorised vehicles that can maintain high speeds. In the past, smaller vehicles like the K-cars (engines limited to 660cc) were not allowed on these roads, but improvements to these cars have made them eligible. These roads generally have two lanes of traffic in either direction, separated by a median, and with limited access except through on and off ramps. Next, there are the general national roads (*ippan koku-dō*). In 2012, these roads spanned 67,427 kilometres. These may be one or two lanes in either direction, generally without a dividing median, and with traffic lights at intersections. The next category is similar to the general national roads except that the jurisdiction lies at different prefectural and municipal levels (*todofuken-dō*). These roads extended 142,409 kilometres. Finally, there is the category of the village and town roads (*shichoson-dō*), which correspond more closely to neighbourhood roads, although they may contain the greatest variation in widths, speed limits and other restrictions. These roads cover 1,054,517 kilometres (MLIT 2014).

In a different publication dealing with accident prevention, MLIT usefully groups the first three categories above (high-speed national auto ways, general national roads and prefectural and municipal roads) under the heading of arterial roads (*kansen dōro*), and some subset of village and town roads under the heading of neighbourhood roads (*seikatsu dōro*, lit. daily living roads). The key distinction is between those roads where the speed of traffic means that the roads are for the exclusive use of automobiles, as opposed to those roads that are shared with pedestrians and bicyclists (MLIT 2015a).

Clearly, Japan's roads are not all shared, and if they had their way, many urban planners would try to separate modes of transport on local roads too, widening them and creating separate lanes for cars and bicycles as well as raised pavements for pedestrians. The pace of these transformations has picked up ahead of the 2020 Tokyo Olympics. And yet the narrowness of streets in many older districts means that the large majority of urban streets will not accommodate raised pavements as long as property owners are not willing to give up a metre or two of their land abutting the road. Given the small plot sizes to begin with, such concessions are generally unlikely. And even when some property owners agree to give up some land allowing the road to be widened for a stretch, others are unwilling to give anything up when requested by city authorities for no monetary compensation, and the road will suddenly narrow again.

Japanese urban planners know that densely built urban neighbourhoods are vulnerable to the spread of fire in the case of earthquakes, and this, more than a desire to build pavements, is a primary reason for efforts to widen some roads. After the Tokyo earthquake of 1923 that destroyed much of the city in fires, the new architectural standards law stipulated a minimum width of four metres for newly constructed roads (barely wide enough for two compact cars to squeeze past each other), as well as fire resistant facades for wooden houses. Even narrower alleys that pre-existed the new law were grandfathered in, however, and continued to pose a fire risk. Bureaucrats planned wider streets at half-kilometre intervals along which zoning would allow taller concrete buildings to be built, serving as a kind of fire line that could at least contain fires from spreading from one neighbourhood to another (Sorenson 2002, 124–131).

In Tokyo, this kind of planning was done for those old downtown (*shitamachi*) neighbourhoods such as Sumida-ku in the eastern part of the city that were largely destroyed in the 1923 Tokyo earthquake, and burnt down again with the fire bombings of 1945. It was also planned for the suburbs expanding westward in the post-war period. Large sections of the city in between the old downtown and the western suburbs, however, have remained a jumble of narrow alleys, including the neighbourhood of Higashi Matsubara, Setagaya Ward, which will be discussed below.

As noted above, the total kilometre expanse of high-speed roads exclusively for the use of automobiles is a fraction of that of village and town roads, much of which are shared with pedestrians and bicycles. While there has been some effort to separate modes of transport, infrastructural constraints make it difficult to achieve.

Identifying danger spots

Analysis of traffic accident data on arterial roads (*kansen dōro*) from 2007 through to 2010 led bureaucrats in the Ministry of Land and Transportation to identify 12,650 'high accident locations' (*kiken kasho*). Of these, 3,490 locations accounted for 69 per cent of accidents, and became the focus of concerted ameliorative efforts (MLIT 2015a). Measures included the lengthening right turn lanes when cars cut in front of oncoming traffic,[5] creation of pavements protected by guard rails, reducing the speed of left turn lanes by making them less like gradually curving highway exits, and creating a dividing median between lanes of oncoming traffic. Signage was also improved to warn of sharp curves and various collision dangers (ibid.).

In addition to arterial roads, MLIT bureaucrats analysed accidents along neighbourhood roads (*seikatsu dōro*) and have promoted 'safe walking areas' (*hōkōsha anshin eria*) – zones where pedestrians and bicyclists would have priority over cars. They have done so with the standard arsenal of traffic calming techniques such as textured road surfaces at regular intervals, chicanes (shallow left-right turns in the road), and the use of white lines and plastic traffic pylons to narrow car lanes (ibid.).

On neighbourhood roads, the Ministry of Education in 2012 had already begun a review of school commute routes (*tsugakuro*) to identify danger locations (*kiken kasho*). In Iwata City in Shizuoka Prefecture, the board of education asked people at each school to come up with a list of the top five danger locations along the commute routes for their students. Each school turned to the children's associations (*kodomo-kai*) in the school district, which are made up of the parents of school-aged children in a given neighbourhood. Children's associations are responsible for determining gathering points for groups of children who walk together to school in the morning. The children's association will also determine the school routes themselves in their neighbourhoods, and thus are an important source of information about danger spots. These associations may report to the schools directly, but can also send their requests to the local neighbourhood association (*jichikai*), which may relay them to the local school, the local board of education (*kyōiku iinkai*) and the Division of Roads and Rivers (*dōro kasen ka*) at city hall. Representatives from various administrative units including the police will do inspections and prioritise those spots that they find the most dangerous and that fall within the budget allocated for road work in a given year.[6]

Examples of the kinds of requests for action on dangerous spots and responses by the authorities suggest how people are thinking about shared and divided spaces. At the Iwata City Hall, I was shown a fat binder with a collection of papers – one page from each of the city's 23 elementary schools with a list of five danger spots each. Included were explanations of the dangers involved, requests for action, printouts from Google maps of specific locations, as well as photographs of these danger spots supplied by those making the request. Bureaucrats scribbled in brief assessments based on their reviews of the sites.

Members of one children's association made a request that a short bridge over a culvert be widened to better accommodate a school commute route. There was no guardrail or concrete divider separating the pedestrian path from car traffic on this bridge. When two cars going in opposite directions crossed the bridge, there was almost no room at all for pedestrians. The cost of widening the bridge, however, was deemed too great to meet this request. In this case, the solution was to divert the school commute route toward another bridge a block away. That bridge did not have a raised pavement or guardrail separating pedestrians from car traffic either, but it was somewhat wider than the other bridge, wide enough to warrant a white line (*hakusen*) along one side to indicate the pedestrian zone.

In another case, a request was made to divert the school commute route in order to avoid one particular house whose resident had threatened or shouted at numerous children. In response, the route, which had followed a raised pavement separate from car traffic, was diverted to a street with no pavement.

School commute routes from various neighbourhoods start to converge as they approach a school. The block or two adjacent to a school may actually be closed to car traffic between seven and eight in the morning for the safety of students. But such a closure generally is applied to a very limited area, for a limited period of time. Exceptions are granted to residents on restricted blocks, who are issued special permission slips from city hall to place on their dashboard if they need to drive from their homes when their road is otherwise closed to car traffic. Few Japanese elementary schools have pavements or guardrails separating pedestrians from car traffic. For most of the day, those streets around schools are shared just like most other neighbourhood streets.

Recently, city planners have taken some innovative approaches to slowing traffic around schools. The white lines on the road in front of one school in Iwata City were adjusted to widen the pedestrian zones on both sides of the street. These zones were painted green, the colour generally used in Japan for school commute routes. In addition, the white line that had run down the centre of the street was removed, creating a single, wide lane for cars going in both directions to negotiate, prompting drivers to slow down and drive with greater care.

While some planners advocate separating modes of transport, and putting in hard barriers to ensure the protection of the more vulnerable travellers in certain locations, the decisions made about danger spots discussed above suggest several reasons why few pavements and bicycle paths have been built. In addition to financial and space constraints, parents, teachers, administrators and local government officials who determine and adjust school commute routes seem to share a conviction that shared spaces can be made to work, that they are not inherently dangerous.

White lines

Roads on which pedestrian and car traffic is separated by a white line are shared to a greater degree than are roads where guardrails or concrete curbs perform this function. And yet the white line can act as a symbolic divider that gives drivers some sense of privilege compared to roads without any such markings. One retiree in Yokohama, Matsushita-san, with whom I have exchanged numerous emails, explained that white lines defined a road as a 'car road' (*shadō*). He was particularly galled that the city had painted the white line on what was his private property. Forty-five years ago, the road was a 'farm road' (*nōdō*) just four metres wide. When a nursery school opened nearby, property owners along this road agreed to set back their lots one metre, allowing the road to be widened so children could walk along it more safely. Small metal plates implanted in the asphalt indicated the old property boundaries. Once the road was widened, however, the city painted the white lines past the metal plates, onto what had been private property. The widened road, with its clearly demarcated car lane, became busy with cars and trucks, including dump trucks and even tractor-trailers. Matsushita-san commented that since the widening, local residents faced the possibility of being run over on their own property. Needless to say, all of this undermined the initial goal of making the road safer for kindergarteners walking to and from school.

A couple of years ago, when the Division of Public Works was repaving the road, Matsushita-san petitioned them not to repaint the white lines where they had been. He said they should be painted along the old property line, arguing that it was a neighbourhood road, a 'daily living road' (*seikatsu dōro*). After an extended period of deliberation, the city asked Matsushita-san to allow the white line to encroach on his property again, but not quite as much as before. In the end, the car lane was narrowed by about ten inches, which may not be sufficient to keep the trucks off the road, but Matsushita appreciated the added space along the sides. He says that it gives him a greater sense of security when he's out on a walk.

Conclusion

Kōji drives me along the Kan-nana-douri (#7 loop line), one of the relatively old arterial routes that skirts around the centre of Tokyo, and follows the navigation system's voice command to make a left turn down a small alley. Kōji is taking me back to my lodgings in the Higashi Matsubara neighbourhood after we spend the day at the old motorcycle racetrack in Funabashi City, 30 minutes to the east of Tokyo. The small alley is a quintessential 'daily living street', so narrow that Kōji thinks it must be a one way, but it is not. He slows down to a pace just a little faster than a vigorous walk. It is at a pace that, if a small boy were to jump out in front of the car at one of the many blind alleys, Kōji probably would have enough time to stop and avoid hitting him. In this neighbourhood, it is probably the bicycles, especially those with electrical assist motors, that pose the greatest danger to pedestrians. It is quite a change from the Kan-nana ring route, two lanes in each direction divided by a short concrete median, and especially the Shuto-kosoku metropolitan highway along which we were speeding just a few minutes earlier, where Kōji would tailgate other cars, waiting for opportunities to swerve into the next lane and pass. An aggressive driver on highways, the 'daily living road' in Higashi Matsubara tamed him, or maybe we can say that Kōji has acculturated to the overall driving context, and modulates between different modes of driving elicited by different roads.

Some of the neighbourhood roads had white lines painted along them, but many did not. And even on the main road by one of the local train stations, where a line of cars would wait patiently for the railroad crossing to open, the cars would proceed slowly along behind pedestrians and bicycles, knowing that there was no use in honking or gunning their engines, that here the white lines did not really give them the priority it did in other locations. In one instance I observed a group of nursery school children being socialised to the shared road with some guidance from teachers. They had gathered by one railroad crossing, waiting for the train to go by. As the crossing opened, the teachers ushered the children across the tracks single file, as cars that had been waiting on the other side crossed in the opposite direction. Other cyclists and pedestrians scurried across as the bells started ringing, lights flashing, and the crossing closed once again and children exclaimed 'another train!' One might say that drivers are simultaneously socialised when encountering groups of children on the street, to drive in a manner that ensures a degree of safety.

It would be mistaken to think that the shared road in itself leads to cautious driving behaviour, just as it would be mistaken to assume that shared roads are more dangerous than roads on which different modes of transport are separated. Early proponent of the shared road, Hans Monderman, is aware that it comes with a learning curve. Initially, there are real dangers to the shared road. But when people told him that they felt unsafe on them, he responded that it is precisely this felt danger that makes people cautious. In fact, Monderman writes, 'I hope that some small accidents happen, as part of the learning process of society' (Vanderbilt 2008, 199).

It seems that many Japanese have learned how to drive on narrow roads more cautiously than they did in 1970. Although 'daily living roads' constitute roughly 85 per cent of Japanese road distances, just 34 per cent of traffic fatalities take place on them. Meanwhile, 'arterial roads' constitute 15 per cent of all roads in Japan, and yet 66 per cent of traffic fatalities occur on them (MLIT 2015b). Reducing fatal accidents on these two different kinds of roads will take different approaches. Even as the culture of the shared road has developed somewhat organically in Japan based in part on infrastructural constraints, there is little consensus among planners about whether sharing or separating spaces is the better strategy for neighbourhood streets. Planners could help further foster a culture of careful driving on neighbourhood roads by more clearly presenting the 'daily living streets' as shared spaces, distinct from those higher speed roads that are exclusively for the use of cars.

Notes

1 The 1970 figure of 16,765 was based on reported deaths within 24 hours of accidents, while the 2014 figure was based on deaths that occurred within 30 days of the accident resulting from injuries. We may assume that the 1970 figure would have been somewhat higher if the 30 day standard had been used at that time.
2 Ministry of Internal Affairs and Communications, Statistics Bureau, retrieved from www.stat.go.jp/english/data/chouki/12.htm, last accessed 10 January 2016.
3 Vertigo and competition describe two of the four basic types of games according to Roger Callois's (1961) typology. The other two types of games are chance (alea), and mimicry (mimesis).
4 See Kahneman and Lovallo (1993) on optimistic bias.
5 In Japan, people drive on the left side of the road, so right turns involve crossing lanes of oncoming traffic. When a line of cars wanting to turn left gets too long it can extend into the lane of cars wanting to go straight, increasing the chance of rear end collisions.
6 This information based on interviews conducted at Iwata City Hall in Shizuoka Prefecture. Division names and procedures may vary slightly from one city to another, but the range of administrative units involved, and the active participation of local residents is quite similar throughout Japan.

References

Callois, Roger. 1961. *Man, Play, and Games*. New York: Free Press of Glencoe.
Cole, Robert E. 1989. *Strategies for Learning: Small Group Activities in American, Japanese, and Swedish Industry*. Berkeley: University of California Press.
Gordon, Andrew. 1985. *The Evolution of Labor Relations in Japan: Heavy Industry, 1853–1955*. Cambridge, MA: Council on East Asian Studies, Harvard University.
IRTAD. 2015. Road Safety Annual Report 2015. Paris: International Transport Forum.
Jacobsen, P. L. 2003. Safety in Numbers: More Walkers and Bicyclists, Safer Walking and Bicycling. *Injury Prevention* 9: 205–209.
JAF (Japan Automobile Federation) News. 1967. 5 (11): 8–9.
Kahneman, Daniel, and Dan Lovallo. 1993. Timid Choices and Bold Forecasts: A Cognitive Perspective of Risk Taking. *Management Science* 39 (1): 17–31.
Kamata, Satoshi. 1982. *Japan in the Passing Lane: An Insider's Account of Life in a Japanese Auto Factory*. New York: Pantheon Books.
Kumazawa, Makoto. 1996. *Portraits of the Japanese Workplace: Labor Movements, Workers, and Managers*. Boulder, CO: Westview Press.
Kuruma no techo. 1970. No. 83: 37–40.
Landsburg, Steven E. 1993. *The Armchair Economist: Economics and Everyday Life*. New York: The Free Press.
MLIT (Ministry of Land, Infrastructure, Transportation and Tourism). 2014. Dōro toukei nenpou 2014 [Annual statistical tables on roads]. www.mlit.go.jp/road/ir/ir-data/tokei-nen/2014/nenpo02.html (last accessed 29 June 2015).

MLIT. 2015a. Kōtsū jiko taisaku no torikumi [Measures responding to traffic accidents]. www.mlit.go.jp/road/road/traffic/sesaku/torikumi.html#2-2-1 (last accessed 29 June 2015).

MLIT. 2015b. Kōtsū jiko no genjō [Current situation of traffic accidents]. www.mlit.go.jp/road/road/traffic/sesaku/genjyo.html (last accessed 29 June 2015).

Naikakufu. 2015. Heisei 27 Kōtsū anzen hakusho [White paper on traffic safety]. www8.cao.go.jp/koutu/taisaku/h27kou_haku/pdf/gaiyo/1-1-1-1.pdf (last accessed 6 October 2015).

Nonaka, Izumi. 1995. The Recent History of Managing for Quality in Japan. In *A History of Managing for Quality*, edited by J. M. Juran, 517–552. Milwaukee, WI: ASQC Quality Press.

Notar, Beth E. 2012. My Father is Li Gang! Power and Transgressive Mobility in Contemporary China. Paper presented at the American Anthropological Association Annual Meetings in San Francisco, November.

Odaka, Kōnosuke, Keinosuke Ono, and Fumihiko Adachi. 1988. *The Automobile Industry in Japan: A Study of Ancillary Firm Development.* Tokyo, Japan: Kinokuniya Co.

Roth, Joshua H. 2002. *Brokered Homeland: Japanese Brazilian Migrants in Japan.* Ithaca, NY: Cornell University Press.

Roth, Joshua H. 2011. Harmonizing Cars and Humans in Japan's Era of Mass Automobility. *The Asia-Pacific Journal* 9 (45): 1–13.

Roth, Joshua H. 2012. Heartfelt Driving: Discourses on Manners, Safety, and Emotions in Japan's Era of Mass Motorization. *Journal of Asian Studies* 71 (1): 171–192.

Roth, Joshua H. 2014. Is Female to Male as Lightweight Cars are to Sports Cars? Gender Metaphors and Cognitive Schemas in Recessionary Japan. In *Vehicles of Moral Imagination*, edited by David Lipset and Richard Handler, 88–110. New York: Berghahn Books.

Sand, Jordan. 2005. *House and Home in Modern Japan: Architecture, Domestic Space, and Bourgeois Culture: 1880–1930.* Cambridge, MA: Harvard University Asia Center.

Sasaki, Isao. 2009. *Nihon jidōsya shi II: Nihon no jidōsya kanren sangyō no tanjō to hatten* [Japan Automobile History II: The Birth and Development of Japanese Automobile Related Industries]. Tokyo: Miki Shobō.

Sorensen, André. 2002. *The Making of Urban Japan: Cities and Planning from Edo to the Twenty-First Century.* London: Routledge.

Togo, Yukisaka. 1993. *Against All Odds: The Story of the Toyota Motor Corporation and the Family that Created It.* New York: St. Martin's Press.

Vanderbilt, Tom. 2008. *Traffic: Why We Drive the Way We Do (and What It Says About Us).* New York: Knopf.

Womack, James P., Daniel T. Jones and Daniel Roos. 1990. *The Machine That Changed the World.* New York: Rawson Associates.

9 Car crazy

The rise of car culture in China

Beth E. Notar

The word 'car' in Mandarin, *qiche*, literally 'vapour vehicle', comes from the word *che*, 'cart' or 'chariot'. The traditional Chinese character 車 looks like a cart, as seen from above, without its horse or ox, and *qi*, the word for 'vapour', contains the water symbol to the left 汽. These 'vapour vehicles' (some early autos were actually steam powered) first appeared in China in the early twentieth century. A Hungarian man reportedly imported the first car to Shanghai in 1901 (Dikötter 2006, 90), although a Shanghai Urban Planning Exhibition Centre photograph shows the first car in Shanghai in 1903. In 1902, Commander Yuan Shikai (later president), gave the Empress Dowager Cixi a Benz in Beijing (Dikötter 2006, 90). Photographs from the 1930s in the Shanghai Urban Planning Exhibition Centre show dozens of cars parked along the Bund, and by the 1940s satirical cartoons, such as Zhang Leping's, which featured the homeless orphan boy San Mao, show the difficulties of trying to cross a busy street through car traffic (Zhang 1948).

In the early twentieth century, cars in China, as elsewhere, were only for the elites who could afford them. Yet by the 1920s, as in the US and Germany (Seiler 2008; Sachs 1992), there arose a dream of mass automobility. In 1922, China's Nationalist founding father, Sun Yat-sen (Sun Zhongshan), called forth the modernist dream of 'one car per every man' (Sun 1929, 219).

Sun's dream of mass automobility, however, was deferred. After Chinese Communist victory in 1949 and the establishment of the People's Republic of China, private cars were banned. Ironically, although the Communists had used images of cars as symbols to critique Nationalist corruption, after victory, only high-ranking Communist Party and government officials had access to chauffeur-driven cars (Notar 2014). By the 1980s, 50 to 80 per cent of Chinese urbanites commuted by bicycle (Gaubatz 1999, 43–44). However, after China designated the auto industry as one of the 'key pillars' of the economy in 1991 (CAE 2003), Chinese auto production and consumption has grown exponentially. By 2009, China became both the world's largest car market and world's largest producer of cars and vehicles (*China Daily* 2013).

This chapter describes China's urban transformation from cities once dominated by bicycles – from the 1950s to the 1990s – to cities now dominated by cars. In the context of China's rise to become the second largest economy in the world, its auto industry has been designated as one of the key 'pillar' industries (CAE 2003, 1; Chu 2011), and millions of new drivers are now 'hitting the road' each year (Conover 2006; Gerth 2010, 2016; Zhang 2009). As China embraces this 'system of automobility' (Urry 2004), or what Catherine Lutz calls the 'car system' – 'the complex that includes the quasi-private and embodied technology of the car, governance practices, changed time-space conceptions, and landscapes of affordance to the car' (Lutz 2014, 232) – new vehicle sales have surpassed those in the US (*China Daily* 2009). With millions of new drivers, it is perhaps not surprising that traffic accidents have become the leading cause of death for people under 45 (*China Daily* 2011).

How did this shift from a society characterised by bicycle mobility to one characterised by automobility occur? What are the implications of this new system for ideas about space and place, and mobility and status? As an anthropologist of China I am asking, what does it *mean* for a society to transform itself from one dominated by walking, biking and taking public transport – to one dominated by automobiles? What does it mean to have millions of new vehicles and millions of new drivers enter the landscape in the span of a few years?

Below I provide some background on the political and economic factors that have shaped China's transformation from a society of bicycle mobility to one characterised by automobility. Then I provide a brief overview of auto production and consumption. Next, I discuss some of the profound changes in urban space, place and public health before examining some of the less obvious temporal transformations: in addition to spending time stuck in traffic jams, elites as well as a new middle class in China are spending time doing things they never did before: going car and car decoration shopping, going on road trips, and even going drag racing.

China's reform era transformations

In 1986, during my second year studying abroad in China, the Flying Pigeon (Fei Ge) bicycle factory sold a record three million bicycles. Twelve years later, in 1998, the company sold only 200,000. That year, it fired most of its 7,000 workers and moved to a smaller factory (Rocks 2004).

After China's paramount revolutionary-era ruler, Mao Zedong, died in 1976, and Deng Xiaoping (formerly purged by Mao) came to power in 1978, China's Communist Party decided to depart from its more 'leftist' policies and follow a path of 'reform and opening' (*gaige kaifang*). This meant implementing market reforms and 'opening' to foreign trade and direct investment. As part of these reforms, China began to move away from its centralised, planned economy. Communes were disbanded, many state-run factories were closed, and college graduates were no longer guaranteed jobs. Instead, the country began to move toward a system where foreign companies could set up joint ventures, private businesses such as shops and restaurants were allowed to open, and graduates would have to compete for jobs. Whereas previously the system had emphasised collectivism and worked by allocation, the system started to highlight individualism and began to work in part through market competition and consumption.

In 1978, the year that Deng Xiaoping came to power, Beijing Auto Works contacted the American Motors Corporation, and a delegation from the Ministry of Machine Building went to Germany to speak with Volkswagen (Anderson 2012, 55–56). In his memoir of 30 years reporting on the auto industry in China, Li Anding describes how between 1978 and 1982, there was political wrangling over whether or not China should produce sedans for private consumption, since they were seen as 'bourgeois'. It was not until June 1982, when Deng Xiaoping personally gave the 'green light', that sedan production went into gear (Li 2011, 17–18). At first very slowly and then very quickly this led to Chinese central or local state owned enterprises establishing 'joint ventures' with foreign auto manufacturers, as well as independent Chinese auto companies starting their own factories.

Production

Vehicles were first produced in China in the north-eastern city of Changchun. Changchun had been the Japanese capital of Manchuria, named 'New Capital' (Mandarin Xinjing; Japanese Shinkyoo). The Communists located the First Auto Works (FAW) there at the site of a former Japanese military encampment (Buck 2000, 89). Ground for the factory was broken in 1953, and, along with Soviet technical assistance, FAW produced the first mid-weight 'Liberation' (Jiefang) trucks in 1956. 'Eastern Wind' (Dongfeng) sedans, as well as 'Red Flag' (Hongqi) limousines reserved for high-ranking government and party officials, started to roll off the assembly line in 1958 (Anderson 2012, 54; FAW 2015). In 1958, an auto factory in Shanghai started to produce 'Phoenix' (Fenghuang) brand sedans (Anderson 2012, 54; Harwitt 1995, 17–18).

The 'Second Auto Works' opened in 1969 in Wuhan, in Hubei province and manufactured mostly trucks (Dongfeng Motor Corporation 2015). However, during the Cultural Revolution, production ceased until 1975 (Anderson 2012, 55). After 1992, Second Auto Works changed its name to Dongfeng, and now manufactures mostly passenger cars (Dongfeng Motor Corporation 2015).

Between 1958 and 1978, approximately only 600 passenger cars per year were manufactured in China, either for use by officials or for use as taxis (Anderson 2012, 55). However, with the start of the reform era in 1978, Chinese factories and cities began to negotiate joint ventures with foreign automakers to produce passenger cars. Beijing Auto Works had begun manufacturing 'jeeps' in the 1950s with Soviet technical assistance and in 1978 they approached the American Motors Corporation (later bought out by Chrysler and then by Daimler), owner of Jeep; a joint venture was established in 1984 (Anderson 2012, 55; Mann 1989, 37–42). Also in 1978, the Chinese Machine Building Minister arrived unexpectedly with a delegation at the Volkswagen factory in Wolfsburg, West Germany to inquire into establishing a joint venture (Anderson 2012, 56; Posth 2008, 4–5).

Although purchase of private passenger cars was technically legalised in 1984, it was not until 1991 that auto production and consumption were promoted by the State Planning Commission. In a formal 'Automotive Industry

Policy' the auto industry was designated to be a 'pillar industry' of the Chinese economy (Anderson 2012, 64–65; CAE 2003). Before entry into the World Trade Organisation, it was anticipated that China would have to reduce tariffs on imported cars. Therefore, China started to actively develop both joint ventures as well as independent automakers (Gerth 2010, 2016).

In the early years of the development of the auto industry, tension existed between central government officials, who sought control, and local Communist Party and government officials, who were seeking to establish their own companies. For example, China consultant G. E. Anderson describes how, despite a 1988 and 1994 central government moratorium on the establishment of new car factories – production was to be limited to the 'big three' – First Auto Works, Second Auto Works (later called Dongfeng Motor Corporation) and Shanghai Auto, and the 'little three' – Beijing-Jeep, Guangzhou-Peugeot, and Tianjin Auto – the Communist Party Secretary of Wuhu, Anhui province, Zhan Xialai, started the Chery (Qirui) auto company by recruiting an engineer, Yin Tongyao, away from the First Auto Works-Volkswagen joint venture. At first Chery just started to manufacture engines with an old assembly line bought from Ford in the UK. Then Yin obtained plans for how to manufacture a Jetta from a Spanish subsidiary of VW. The first Chery car was produced in 1999. However, since Chery did not yet have central government permission to manufacture cars, the cars could not get licence plates, and therefore were only driven locally. When the central government discovered this, they forced Chery to give a 20 per cent stake of the company to the Shanghai Automotive Industry Corporation (SAIC) (Anderson 2012, 3–5, 62–67). Later, after Chery had become 'one of China's largest exporters of automobiles', it received central government support (Anderson 2012, 5).

By 2015, half of the ten largest automakers in China were joint ventures, and half were independent Chinese companies. Their joint venture, Fortune 500 ranking and 2014 profits are listed in Table 9.1.

Consumption

Vehicle sales are divided into passenger cars (*chengren che*) and commercial vehicles (*shangyong che*) (which includes buses, trucks and vans, although, in the countryside, commercial vehicles such as trucks and minivans are often used to transport passengers who hitch rides).

In 2013, China broke the world record for the most passenger cars sold in any one country in one year – more than 20 million (Kennedy 2014). The best-selling passenger cars in China over the past three years are listed in Table 9.2.

Chinese-foreign joint venture companies dominate the market in terms of sedan sales but independent Chinese companies such as Great Wall (Changcheng) are starting to capture some of the SUV markets. Amongst the joint ventures, FAW-VW (Volkswagen), Shanghai-VW and SAIC-GM, three of the earliest joint ventures in China, dominate. In addition, we notice the dearth of Japanese models. Although auto company representatives from Japan

Table 9.1 The ten largest automakers in China with their joint venture, Fortune 500 ranking and 2014 profits

1 Shanghai Auto (SAIC Motor)
Joint ventures with VW and GM
#60 Fortune 500, US$4.54 billion

2 First Auto Works, Changchun, Jilin province
Joint venture with Volkswagen-Audi
#107 Fortune 500, US$4.248 billion

3 Dongfeng Motor Group, Wuhan, Hubei province
Joint ventures with Honda and Kia
#109 Fortune 500, US$1.6 billion

4 Beijing Automotive Group
(Originally joint venture with AMC-Jeep, then Chrysler, then Daimler, then
    Cerberus, then Hyundai)
#207 Fortune 500, US$819 million

5 Guangzhou Automobile Industry Group, with production not in Guangzhou but in
    Chongqing
(Originally a joint venture with PSA Peugeot-Citroën)
#362 Fortune 500, US$284 million

6 Zhejiang Geely Holding Group, Hangzhou
#477 Fortune 500, US$275 million

7 Chang'an located in Guangzhou
Joint venture with Ford
Not listed

8 Chery (Qirui), Wuhu, Anhui province
Not listed

9 BYD (Build Your Dreams), Shenzhen
Not listed

10 Great Wall, Baoding, Hebei province
Not listed

Source: adapted from Zhang 2009; Dunne 2011; Anderson 2012; Fortune 2015.

came to China as early as 1977 (Li 2011, 5) and although Chinese officials tried early on to recruit Toyota to establish a joint venture, Toyota was unwilling to agree to the terms of technology transfer which the Chinese requested (Anderson 2012, 131). However, Japan has shipped thousands of (often used) cars into mainland China 'through the back door' via Hong Kong (Dunne 2011, 25, 48). I also found in my interviews with middle-aged professionals in China that there existed lingering resentment from the War with Japan (1937–1945), and that if people were going to buy a joint-venture car they would prefer to purchase a German or American make. In the future, this may no longer matter for a younger generation of Chinese consumers.

Shanghai-GM's Wuling Hongguan MPV had astonishing sales in 2014: 750,000 vehicles. These are seven-seat 'family vehicles' which retail at a base

Table 9.2 2014 Top ten best selling passenger cars in China (including SUVs and MPVs/
multipurpose vehicles)

Rank	Model	# sold
1	SAIC-GM Wuling (MPV)	750,000
2	Chang'an Ford Focus	391,800
3	Shanghai VW Landa	372,000
4	Great Wall Haval H6 (SUV)	315,900
5	Shanghai-VW Santana	307,300
6	Dongfeng Nissan Sylphy	300,100
7	FAW-VW Sagitar	300,100
8	FAW-VW Jetta	297,000
9	SAIC-GM Buick Excelle	293,100
10	SAIC-GM Chevrolet Cruze	266,000

Source: adapted from *China Daily*, 20 January 2015.

list price of RMB 43,800 (US$7,163) (*China Daily* 2015). Seven seats are just right for the current urban Chinese family: a single child, parents and two sets of grandparents (although Chinese urbanites are now allowed to have a second child).

Electric and hybrid car sales in China grew from 38,163 in 2014 to 136,733 in 2015 in total (22,258 electric only in 2014 to 87,531 electric only in 2015) (Young 2015). There is evidence that the Chinese government is working to promote electric vehicles (EVs), electric scooters and electric bicycles (EV-2s). For example, there are state subsidies, incentives for reduced licence plate and registration fees, and the growth of the Shenzhen-based company BYD (*Biyadi*, Build Your Dreams), which produces electric batteries and cars (Gerth 2016). Beijing currently limits licence plates for petrol powered cars to 20,000 per month, but there are no such limits for EVs. Similarly, Shanghai waives registration fees for EVs (Edelstein 2015). Still, this is only a tiny fraction of car sales in China, and the lowest price hybrid EVs, the Geely EK-2 and the BYD hybrid 'Shang' have a base retail price of RMB 100,000 RMB and RMB 139,800 (US$15,424 and 21,563), similarly priced to the best-selling Shanghai-VW Lavida Longyi (base list price of RMB 112,900/US$17,414), although double the best-selling SAIC-GM Baojun and Wuling 'family vehicles'.

As might be expected, China's used car market has been growing as well. In 2014, over 6.05 million vehicles were traded, up 16.3 per cent from 2013. The majority (58 per cent) were sedans, accounting for 3.51 million vehicles, but SUVs, of which 200,000 were traded, are the fastest growing market, up 25 per cent from 2013. In addition to on-site used car dealers, used e-commerce is growing with auction websites such as www.youxinpai.com and www.cheyipai. com, or consignment websites such as www.guazi.com or www.souche.com (PRNewswire 2015).

In addition, China has had the fastest-growing luxury car market in the world. BMW sales in China jumped 62 per cent in 2011, and BMW has been opening a dealership there almost daily (Doig 2012). Lamborghini sales have 'skyrocketed' 150 per cent (Li 2011). From the first to the third quarters of 2015, all German luxury cars sales in China outstripped those in the US, although Audi sales, the car of choice for Chinese officialdom, while still far ahead of those in the US, dropped slightly from 2014 to 2015 (see Table 9.3).

China's motorcycle production and consumption has had a parallel and similarly meteoric rise. China is the largest producer of motorcycles: 23 million were manufactured in 2013 (Vanderklippe 2014). However, over 200 Chinese cities currently have bans or restrictions on motorcycles (Nesbitt 2014), presumably to both give preference to cars and to try to manage traffic congestion.

As the history of the rise of car cultures has shown, cars do not simply enter a landscape, they radically transform it (e.g. Baldwin 1999; Brilliant 1989; Seiler 2008). A huge infrastructure is needed to support a society dedicated to automobility. There not only have to be places to refuel cars, places to purchase and repair cars, but also places to drive them and park them. In *Personal Cars and China*, the authors note: 'The impact of the automotive industry on society is unlike that of any other industry. The automobile is not just a technology or mode of transportation: it is a fundamental determinant of the entire economy' (CAE 2003, 7). What does it mean for people in Beijing and other Chinese cities to drive a car instead of ride a bicycle? What are the implications of this for China? Below I briefly examine three consequences: the transformation of urban and rural space and place, the negative impact on public health and increased mortality.

Impacts of automobility

City streets in China – once dominated by bicycles – have been rebuilt to accommodate cars. This has meant the demolition and reconstruction of the old urban centres of most Chinese cities (often done with low-cost immigrant labour) – to create highways, ring roads and overpasses (Zhang 2006; Zhang 2009). This has happened in other times and places, such as urban planner Robert Moses' New York in the 1950s, but the speed and scale of the transformation of Chinese cities is unprecedented (Zhang 2006). It would be as if *most* of the old neighbourhoods of Boston, New York and Washington, DC were

Table 9.3 German luxury car sales, China and US compared, January to September 2015

Make	China rank	# sold	% change	US rank	# sold	% change
Audi	1	414,411	−0.3	3	147,403	+12.5
BMW	2	342,683	+2.0	1	294,930	+6.9
Mercedes Benz	3	266,287	+30.9	2	249,890	+7.2
Porsche	4	44,240	+36.0	4	39,300	+11.0
Total		1,067,621			731,523	

Source: Bekker (2015).

demolished and rebuilt within ten years, along with those of Chicago, Atlanta, Dallas, Houston, Phoenix, Denver, Seattle and San Francisco.

When I return to Beijing, there is little about the city that I recognise from my student days except for the area around the Forbidden City and Tian'anmen Square, with its familiar portrait of Chairman Mao. A few years ago, when a friend told me to meet her at a coffee shop, I had no idea that I was next to Haidian Road where I used to bike as a student, until she told me. There was nothing I could see anywhere that I remembered.

During the Mao years, under the 'work unit' (*danwei*) system of urban planning, a city dweller was allocated housing according to where he or she worked, usually somewhere nearby the factory, school or office.[1] In the reform era, many people no longer live in work unit housing. Moreover, since old urban neighbourhoods have been demolished to make room for new roads and new construction, people have had to relocate to the suburbs.[2] This detachment of residency from work units (Gaubatz 1999, 33), as well as the growth of the suburbs, has led to a perceived 'need' for car transport (Gerth 2010, 23–24), at least until, or if ever, public transport fully connects the suburbs.

But it is not just within Chinese cities that new car-friendly roads have been built. Thomas Campanella, in *The Concrete Dragon*, writes that 'into the late 1980s, China's highway system consisted of less than 200 miles of modern high-speed, limited-access motorway', but 'by 2006 the National Trunk Highway System spanned 25,480 miles making it second in length only to that of the American interstates' (Campanella 2010, 222). In other words, in just 20 years, China has developed a national highway system that rivals that of the US.

Yet, we could say that China is *returning* to Sun Yat-sen's 1922 dream of 'one car per every man' or person (Sun 1929, 219). In the 1920s, China already had started to embark on the road to an automobile society. In the early twentieth century, as elites in China began to purchase private automobiles (and as metropolitan areas began to use public buses for the masses), new urban roads were constructed. For example in 1935, the southwestern city of Kunming (about which I will say more below), in order to make room for the growing number of automobiles there, demolished over 2,000 homes (Dikkoter 2006, 82). One could say that this was a harbinger of future auto-related urban destruction beginning in the mid-1990s and continuing to the present.

As one might envision, the public health consequences of shifting from a bicycle society to an auto-mobile society have been huge. In 2007, China overtook the US as the biggest emitter of carbon dioxide (Vidal and Adams 2007), and since then air quality of major Chinese cities has deteriorated. On 28 February 2015, the investigative reporter Chai Jing posted her documentary, 'Under the Dome' (*Qiongding zhi xia*) on the *People's Daily* website. The documentary takes the form of a TED talk with lecture, slides and video clips showing pollution in Chinese cities, interviews in industrial towns and personal fears for her daughter's health. The site received approximately 150 million visits in three days, until it was blocked by censors in advance of the National People's Congress meetings (see Mufson 2015), although it is still available on YouTube, with English subtitles. In July 2015, a non-profit organisation called Berkeley Earth posted a paper on their website documenting some of the negative health consequences of air pollution in China. The authors argue that approximately 1.6 million deaths in China each year, or over 4,000 deaths per day, are attributable to air pollution (Rohde and Muller 2015). Elites in Beijing and other cities have begun to invest in expensive air filters for their cars and offices (Wong 2013).

As people bike less and drive more – and participate in the kind of consumption practices that have gone along with car culture, such as going to a MacDonald's drive-through for fast food – obesity in China has been on the rise (Bruno 2012). In 1985, I never saw a normal Chinese person (someone who was not an official) who was overweight. Now it is not uncommon to see extremely overweight children. Similarly, Peter Hessler, in his book *Country Driving*, documents how a rural family outside Beijing who buys a car starts to lead a more sedentary lifestyle, with adverse health consequences.

Most disturbingly, a shift to an automobile society has severely impacted mortality. According to a recent *China Daily* (2011) report: 'Traffic accidents are the leading cause of death for people age 45 and younger in China'. While data on traffic fatalities is disputed, according to the medical journal *The Lancet*, between 81,000 and 221,000 people now die in traffic accidents in China each year (Alcorn 2011).

Given the negative consequences of a shift to an automobile society – urban demolition and displacement, decreased air quality, increased obesity, increased traffic fatalities – we might ask what is the *appeal* of cars?

Cars are not just cars

As anthropologists have long pointed out, things are not just things. Things take on special symbolic significance depending on who uses them and how (e.g. Appadurai 1990 [1986]). Moreover, cars are a special kind of thing, one that Pierre Lemonnier has called a 'strategic object' which communicates '*key values or fundamental characteristics of particular social relations*' (2012, 12; italics in original).

One theme that emerges in historical and literary analyses of cars in China is a tension between viewing cars as either negative symbols of elitism and foreign influence or as a means to modern mobility and individual freedom (e.g. Barmé 2002; Lee 1999; Lu 1999; Sun 1929). Yet neither of these grand narratives, one more 'socialist', one more 'capitalist', seems to fit neatly with the meanings of car use in China.

During the Mao years, while political elites lacked disproportionate purchasing power and while available consumer goods were limited (Davis 2000), elites *were* allocated preferential access to goods and services based on rank. One of the ways in which political rank was clearly manifested was through who had access to which kind of vehicle (Barmé 2002, 180). Now, political elites are no longer the only ones to have access to cars. Since 1994, businessmen, entrepreneurs and even professors are now buying, or hoping to buy cars. The old system of status distinction (Bourdieu 1984) is giving way to a new system, but this system is still in flux. While cars, along with homes, may be thought of as one of the primary forms of what Thorstein Veblen (1998) termed 'conspicuous consumption', it would be a mistake to assume that car consumption and use in China will necessarily follow American, European or Japanese patterns. Some of the ways in which Chinese car consumption and use differs from the American system of automobility is in how people spend their time.

There is the time that people now spend stuck in traffic jams, but there are other ways that people choose to spend their time more pleasurably. Below I will explore aspects of this: attending auto shows, decorating a new car, going drag racing and going on auto club trips. Important to understanding the pleasure in these activities is the status that cars convey.

Leisure time and cars

In 2008, I lived in the southwestern Chinese city of Kunming, provincial capital of Yunnan province, which borders on Myanmar (Burma), Laos and Vietnam. I had previously studied in Kunming in the mid-1990s (when I biked everywhere) and had conducted research in Yunnan for my first book on the impact of ethno-tourism in the borderland town of Dali (Notar 2006). It was during this earlier research that I became aware of the growing number of traffic accidents, and became interested in studying China's new car culture (Notar 2006, 127–132).

Kunming is a 'smaller' city by Chinese standards with a metropolitan area of 6.43 million persons (Xinhua Net 2012). Despite this, the city of Kunming, like Beijing, has similarly built a new car-friendly city (Zhang 2006). Interestingly, Kunming has also had the second highest rate of car consumption in China, next only to China's south-eastern boomtown of Shenzhen (Xu 2002).

Four of the many people I interviewed in Kunming – 'Lonewolf', Prof. Li, 'John' and Mr Wang (all pseudonyms) – exemplify changes in how a new automobile culture shapes how people spend their time.

'Lonewolf': auto shows and dreaming of cars

I first met 'Lonewolf' – his self-chosen English name for himself – on a flight from Beijing to Kunming. I had just attended the Beijing International Automotive Exhibition, known as 'Auto China', and noticed that the young guy sitting next to me on the plane was looking at photographs of the exhibition on his laptop. We started talking about 'Auto China' and spent the entire rest of the flight looking at the dozens of photographs that he had taken.

Lonewolf, a skinny guy with spiky hair in his twenties, worked for an aeroplane parts company and had been attending another trade show in Beijing for a few days. When his work at his trade show was finished for the day, he would go over to 'Auto China' to look at the hundreds of cars on display.

The first auto expo in China was held in a series of bamboo sheds in Shanghai in 1921 (Campanella 2010, 223–225). However, during the Mao years there were no auto shows. After Mao died in 1976, auto shows returned to China as part of reform and opening. The first larger-scale auto expo in reform-era China was the Shanghai Auto Show, held in 1985 (Xinhua Net 2005).

The Beijing International Automotive Exhibition was first held in 1990 at the China International Exhibition Center. Approximately 100,000 people came to see the 216 cars shown (Auto 18, 2010). By the time I first attended the show in April 2008, over 800 vehicles were shown. By April 2012, over 800,000 people attended and over 1,100 vehicles were shown (Auto China 2016).[3] In its size and scale, the Beijing Auto Expo has come to rival some of the top auto expos in the world: Paris, Frankfurt, LA and Detroit.

Lonewolf had just started working and had not yet saved enough money to buy a car, even a low-end Chery (*Qirui*) QQ hatchback, which sells for less than US$5,000. But he spent much of his free time dreaming about which kind of car he might eventually buy.

Later, when I interviewed Lonewolf, I asked him what he did with all of the photos he had taken at the Auto Expo. He told me that he emailed them to friends and colleagues, and similarly, they would share their photographs with him. They would spend much time comparing photographs of and reactions to the different cars on display, as well as the beautiful young women models who posed with the cars.

Lonewolf's spending time looking at cars and dreaming of getting a new car (along with a beautiful girl) is similar to that of many young American men. As in the US (see Lutz 2010), auto shows in China are both a form of entertainment and marketing. In China in particular, auto shows are a way for auto manufacturers to reach potential future consumers like Lonewolf, who cannot yet afford to buy a car. While going to auto shows may be an activity that is similar to US consumers, some of the other ways in which people are spending their free time in China, as related to cars, differs markedly.

Prof. Li: 'auto nanny' and car decorating

Prof. Li is a short, lively woman in her fifties. I first met her through another professor friend of mine who told me that Prof. Li had just bought a new car, and suggested that she might be willing to talk with me.

Prof. Li not only agreed to let me interview her and showed me her new car, but she also accompanied me to the shop where she had bought the decorations for her car, and later, even went with me one night to a drag racing strip on the outskirts of town.

Prof. Li, who taught at one of the universities in Kunming along with her husband, had purchased a bronze, four-door Chery (*Qirui*) sedan. Like many new car consumers in China, the decoration inside the car was just as important to her as the car exterior (*The Economist* 2005, 26). Like most of the new car consumers I interviewed, she had purchased leather seats – 'they're more durable and easy to clean', she noted. In addition, she, like many others, had bought seat covers. Prof. Li's were made of real sheepskin, but there were many other kinds available. When Prof. Li took me to the large auto accessories store called 'Auto Nanny', I saw that it was also possible to order seat covers in woven bamboo, silk brocade or shag carpeting, in a variety of colours and patterns.

Curiously to me, Prof. Li, as well as most others I interviewed, had paid for black tinted film to be placed on the windows, ordered from the 'American Tint' company. Although it was advertised as 'American', I told Prof. Li that in the US very few people had tinted windows except for gangsters and politicians. Prof. Li said that she thought that the popularity of black window tints in China had to do with people modelling their cars on those of officials, who all had such window tints so that no one could see inside.

In addition, Prof. Li had bought a steering wheel cover, a tissue box cover for the box of tissues in the back seat and a dash pad upon which she would place her cell phone.

While Prof. Li's car interior decoration was elaborate by most American standards, I noticed at the 'Auto Nanny' store that much more elaborate decorations were available. For example, there were seat belt covers with pink Hello Kitty designs, gearshift covers with Snoopy or other designs, holders for cups and keys and CDs. One could buy various things to hang from the rear view mirror (like the proverbial fuzzy dice) – images of the Buddha, or more surprisingly, Chairman Mao as a kind of protector god to ward off evil, or Chinese characters for longevity. One could also buy many different kinds of bumper stickers or decals, some meant to replicate luxury cars. For example, one could buy a silver Ferrari logo to place on one's low-end Chery QQ hatchback.

Lonewolf, like many Americans, spends time dreaming of buying a new car, but few Americans spend as much time as Prof. Li and other new car consumers in China going shopping for and decorating their car interiors. It seems not only that people are modelling their cars on officials' cars, like Prof. Li explained with the window tints, but also that cars now have a generally higher status for the Chinese consumer than the US consumer. In the mid- to late-1980s when I first went to China, before a man asked a woman to marry him, he and his family ideally should have acquired a bicycle, a sewing machine and a watch. Now, 20 years later and 20 years into China's booming economy, ideally a man and his family should have acquired a house and a car. Since a car is second only to a house in status as a kind of 'strategic object', the care going into decorating a car is similar to that of interior house decoration. Moreover, as the name of the store 'Auto Nanny' indicates, for most Chinese urban families with only one child, the addition of a car is almost like adding a new member to the family.

Yet, even Prof. Li's car interior decorations and the decorations I saw at the 'Auto Nanny' store pale in comparison to those who are decorating their cars for a new form of car-related leisure activity in China: drag racing and drifting.

'John': drag racing and drifting

I first met 'John' – the English name he had given himself – when I struck up a conversation with him about his car – a silver sports coupe – that was parked outside my family's apartment. He was in his early thirties, and was dressed in business attire – a button-down shirt and tie, grey slacks, black leather shoes. What struck me about John's car was not only that it had different decals on it, but also that it had dynamic coloured stripes painted on it.

John and his car were my first introduction to the world of modified cars, drag racing and 'drifting' in China. Inspired by Japanese popular graphic novels (called *manga* in Japan) and animated movies (*anime*), such as *Initial D* and *Tokyo Drift*, young men in China had started to modify, drag race and 'drift' cars.

To modify a car is not only to decorate it, as Prof. Li did with her car interior. It usually involves some elaborate paintwork – to indicate to others that it is modified – as well as more substantial modifications such as new engines, exhaust systems and tyres.

Sometimes men – and it is overwhelmingly men who are engaged in this activity – will do the modifications themselves, and sometimes they will ask a mechanic to do it. In John's case, he hired a mechanic to install a 'turbo' engine, elaborate sound system and under-body violet lights that made the car appear to float above the pavement at night.

John had his car modified not simply to show it off on the streets of Kunming, but primarily to drag race it with friends. Drag racing involves two cars competing side by side to see who can get to a finish line first. In Kunming, John and his friends raced at night on a stretch of new road that was not yet in use. Two guys would line up their cars, and a third guy would stand in the middle and say 'one, two, three, drive!' Whoever got to the finish line first won.

Before, after, and during the races there was much revving of turbo engines, playing of loud music and flashing of lights. When the cars were not racing, or zipping back around to get in race position, they were parked at the side where they could be showed off and admired – who had the nicest paint job, the best lights or the most powerful engine.

Drag racing was prohibited in Kunming (as in the rest of China) but the drivers played a game of cat-and-mouse with the police. John told me that he and his friends would send out a text message to each other – when? Then they would all meet and race until the police showed up, whereupon they would scatter. One night, Prof. Li asked to go and see the drag racing with me. Since I did not have my own car, and since in the past I had ridden to the site with John and his girlfriend, Prof. Li's husband offered to drive us over. We were watching the racing when, suddenly, I began to see guys jump into their cars and speed away. Then I noticed a police cruiser driving up – yikes. I urged Prof. Li's husband to drive us away quickly, but he was not as fast as the other drivers. We were the only car stopped by the police that night. When Prof. Li's husband told the police officer that we were just there to watch – their car was clearly not a modified car – he let us off with a warning and told us not to return. I was mortified that I had almost gotten Prof. Li and her husband into trouble. However, Prof. Li (if not her husband) seemed to find it exciting.

In addition to drag racing, some of John's friends also engaged in 'drifting' (*piaoyi*). Drifting is a technique that was invented by young Japanese men on the mountainous roads around Tokyo. It involves sliding through sharp curves so that one appears to 'drift' around the curve. Drifting is dangerous because, if a driver does not do it skilfully, he can slide off the road (Roth, this volume). Since Kunming, like Tokyo, has mountainous roads nearby, drifting has caught on there.

In the US and Europe we normally associate car modification and drag racing as an activity that has been done by working class or more marginalised young men. In US communities in Texas and California, car modification and drag racing has been done primarily by Chicano or Latino men and more recently, Asian-American men, as a way to challenge and resist the strictures of a structurally racist and classist society (Best 2006; Bright 1995; Chappell 2010). In Norway and Sweden, working class youths have used cars to challenge the strictures of middle-class family and bourgeois societal norms (Garvey 2001; O'Dell 2001). In contemporary China, however, it is elite young men who can afford to purchase and modify their own cars. John, for example, had an excellent white-collar job working for a bank. When John found out that my husband's cousin in Tokyo had been part of the Mazda racing team in Japan, John asked my husband if his cousin could help him order a new engine to be shipped from Japan – a very expensive proposition. In contrast to the US case, John and his friends' modification, racing and drifting represents a flaunting of their elite status – even in front of the police – rather than any form of resistance.

Mr Wang: auto club tripping

In addition to drag racing, John and his friends would also go on road trips together, driving in a convoy to scenic towns north of Kunming. The phenomenon of the 'road trip' has caught on in China, but in one popular form it has differed from the classic American family or buddy road trip in that it is done in a convoy where each driver drives his or her own car. Called a 'self-drive tour' (*zijia you*), these trips have been organised by car dealers and car clubs (for descriptions of auto club trips see Conover 2016; Notar 2012).

I first met Mr Wang when a Chery (*Qirui*) car dealership in Kunming invited me to go along on a 'self-drive tour'. The dealership had organised the trip for new owners of Chery 'Tigo' SUVs. Since I did not have my own SUV, I took turns riding in different cars and chatting with different drivers throughout the day, one of them being Mr Wang.

The morning of the tour, Mr Wang and the other drivers met at a Sinopec gas station on one of Kunming's ring roads. Once there, the Chery dealer who was hosting the tour distributed flags, t-shirts and stickers to each of the drivers. Thus, bodies and SUVs adorned with the Chery brand logo, the drivers followed the dealer out of town and drove to the tobacco company town of Yuxi, about 50 miles south. After a multi-course banquet lunch, we drove to a parking lot by a park, where the dealer-host engaged Mr Wang and the other drivers in a series of competitions – tyre changing, tyre rolling and car decorating.

I realised that this auto club trip represented a kind of 'coming out' party for the new car owners, who, like debutantes, were debuting their new SUVs and their new skill as drivers before a larger public. The auto club trip, as well as the t-shirts and stickers, etc., also served to foster brand recognition and identification amongst the drivers like Mr Wang and their families.

Conclusion

A few weeks after the auto club trip, I bumped into Mr Wang on a pedestrian overpass over a ring road. He was pushing an old bicycle. 'Mr Wang,' I asked, surprised, 'what happened to your new SUV?'

'Oh,' he laughed, 'since my office is not too far from my home, and since traffic has gotten so bad, I just bike to work.'

Does Mr Wang's return to riding a bicycle signal a potential return of bicycle culture in China? It is unlikely. Despite the negative impacts of automobility – the destruction of old urban centres, increased smog and lung disease, obesity, and traffic fatalities – given the high status associated with driving one's own car, as well as the pleasure people find in doing car-related activities – going to auto shows, decorating their car interiors, going on car club trips and drag racing – China, like the US, seems to now be 'carjacked' (Lutz and Fernandez 2010). It is difficult to imagine that China will return to the days of streets dominated by millions of bicycles. Initially, planners sought to explicitly limit bicycle use (CAE 2003, 242), and bicycles have become more of a leisure item than a transportation item (see Gerth 2010, 33; Gerth 2016). Now, however, given car congestion, urban planners in cities such as Beijing, where only 46 per cent of the population takes public transit, bikes or walks, are imposing car restrictions and trying to re-encourage bicycle use, difficult now because of the smog (Du 2016). Not that it would be impossible to shift back to a bicycle society: countries like Denmark and the Netherlands have both committed to promoting a cycling culture. When I was in Copenhagen for the first time last summer for a faculty workshop on sustainability, it felt oddly familiar – the numbers of bicycle commuters reminded me of China from the 1980s to the mid-1990s.

Still, as one urban planner from the city of Chongqing told me in the summer of 2015: 'We have decided to follow the US model of car culture, but it is unsustainable for us. We need to find other solutions'.

Notes

1 Interestingly, since China practices patrilocality – that is a woman usually lives with her husband's family after marriage – women commuted more than men during the Mao years (see Gaubatz 1999, 31).

2 Zhang Yang poignantly depicts the demolition and displacement of an old Beijing neighbourhood in the 1999 film *Shower* (Xizao).
3 The famous Frankfurt International Motor Show, by comparison, in 2011, had 1,012 exhibitors and 928,000 visitors (IAA 2016).

References

Alcorn, Ted. 2011. Uncertainty Clouds China's Road Traffic Fatality Data. *The Lancet* 378 (9788): 305–306.

Anderson. G. E. 2012. *Designated Drivers: How China Plans to Dominate the Global Auto Industry.* Singapore: John Wiley & Sons Singapore.

Appadurai, Arjun, (ed.). 1990 [1986]. *The Social Life of Things.* Cambridge: Cambridge University Press.

Auto 18. 2010. Di jiyi Beijing chezhan jingxin choubei chenggong chuangban [The First Beijing Auto Show is Meticulously Prepared, Successfully Established]. *Zhongguo qiche jioyiwang*, 13 April, www.auto18.com/news/html/2010-04-13/news_20100413173589. html (accessed 15 January 2016).

Auto China. 2016. Exhibition Reviews. http://autochina.auto-fairs.com/general-information/exhibition-reviews/ (accessed 15 January 2016).

Baldwin, Peter C. 1999. *Domesticating the Street: The Reform of Public Space in Hartford, 1850–1930.* Columbus: Ohio State University Press.

Barmé, Geremie R. 2002. Engines of Revolution: Car Cultures in China. In *Autopia,* edited by Peter Wollen and Joe Kerr, 177–190. London: Reaktion Books.

Bekker, Henk. 2015. China and Worldwide German Luxury Car Sales. www.best-selling-cars.com/china/2015-q3-china-and-worldwide-german-luxury-car-sales/ (accessed 15 December 2015).

Best, Amy L. 2006. *Fast Cars, Cool Rides.* New York: New York University Press.

Bourdieu, Pierre. 1984. *Distinction.* London: Routledge and Kegan Paul.

Bright, Brenda Jo. 1995. Remappings: Los Angeles Low Riders. In *Looking High and Low,* edited by Brenda Jo Bright and Liza Bakewell, 89–123. Tucson: University of Arizona Press.

Brilliant, Ashleigh. 1989 (1964). *The Great Car Craze.* Santa Barbara: Woodbridge Press.

Bruno, Debra. 2012. In China, Obesity Becomes a Problem that's Foreign to Survivors of Its Great Famine. *The Washington Post,* 31 December, http://articles.washingtonpost.com/2012-12-31/national/36103804_1_chinese-waistlines-chinese-center-obesity (accessed 29 July 2013).

Buck, David D. 2000. Railway City and National Capital: Two Faces of the Modern in Changchun. In *Remaking the Chinese City,* edited by Joseph W. Esherick, 65–89. Honolulu: University of Hawai'i Press.

CAE. 2003. *Personal Cars and China.* Washington, DC: The National Academies Press.

Campanella, Thomas J. 2010 [2008]. *The Concrete Dragon: China's Urban Revolution and What it Means for the World.* Princeton: Princeton Architectural Press.

Chappell, Ben. 2010. Custom Contestations: Low Riders and Urban Space. *City & Society* 22 (1): 25–47.

China Daily. 2009. China Outpaces US in Monthly Auto Sales. 10 February, www.chinadaily.com.cn/China/2009-02/10/content_746215.htm (accessed 10 February 2009).

China Daily. 2011. Study: China Traffic Deaths Higher than Police Say. 7 January, www.chinadaily.com.cn/china/2011-01/07/content_11808453.htm (accessed 27 October 2011).

China Daily. 2013. China Continues as World's Top Automaker, Market. 11 January.

China Daily. 2014. Top Ten Best Selling Cars in Chinese Mainland. 26 March, www. chinadaily.com.cn/bizchina/motoring/2014-03/26/content_17376010.htm (accessed 15 December 2015).

China Daily. 2015. Top Ten Best Selling Cars in Chinese Mainland 2014. 20 January, www.chinadaily.com.cn/bizchina/2015-01/20/content_19352567.htm (accessed 15 December).

Chu, Wan-Wen. 2011. How the Chinese Government Promoted a Global Automotive Industry. *Industrial and Corporate Change* 5: 1–42.

Conover, Ted. 2006. Capitalist Roaders. *The New York Times Magazine*, 2 July, www. nytimes.com/2006/07/02/magazine/02china.html?pagewanted=all (accessed 12 December 2011).

Davis, Deborah. 2000. Introduction. In *The Consumer Revolution in Urban China*, edited by Deborah Davis, 1–22. Berkeley: University of California Press.

Dikötter, Frank. 2006. *Exotic Commodities: Modern Objects and Everyday Life in China*. New York: Columbia University Press.

Doig, Will. 2012 Carmeggedon is Coming! *Salon*, 23 August, www.salon.com/2012/08/23/ carmeggedon_is_coming (accessed 9 January 2013).

Dongfeng Motor Corporation. 2015. Corporate Profile. www.dfmc.com.cn/info/ introduce_en.aspx (accessed 15 December 2015).

Du Xiaoying. 2016. Beijing Takes Action to Ease its Thick Traffic Congestion. China Daily, 4 January, www.chinadaily.com.cn/business/motoring/2016-01/04/content_2292 0572.htm (accessed 3 May 2016).

Dunne, Michael J. 2011. *American Wheels Chinese Roads: The Story of General Motors in China*. Singapore: John Wiley & Sons.

The Economist. 2005. Dream Machines. 4 June.

Edelstein, Stephen. 2015. Chinese Electric Car Sales Booming, But Not Because Buyers Want Them. *Green Car Reports*, 31 August, www.greencarreports.com/news/1099806_ chinese-electric-car-sales-booming-but-not-because-buyers-want-them (accessed 15 December 2015).

FAW (First Auto Works). 2015. Profile. www.faw.com/aboutFaw/aboutFaw.jsp?pros= Profile.jsp&phight=580&about=Profile (accessed 15 December 2015).

Fortune. 2015. Global 500. http://fortune.com/global500/ (accessed 15 December 2015).

Garvey, Pauline. 2001. Driving, Drinking and Daring in Norway. In *Car Cultures*, edited by Daniel Miller, 133–152. Oxford: Berg.

Gaubatz, Piper Rae. 1999 (1995). Urban Transportation in post-Mao China: Impacts of the Reform-Era on China's Urban Form. In *Urban Spaces in Contemporary China*, edited by Deborah S. Davis, Richard Kraus, Barry Naughton and Elizabeth J. Perry, 28–60. Cambridge: Woodrow Wilson Center Press and Cambridge University Press.

Gerth, Karl. 2010. *As China Goes, So Goes the World: How Chinese Consumers Are Transforming Everything*. New York: Hill and Wang.

Gerth, Karl. 2016. Driven to Change: The Chinese State-Led Development of a Car Culture and Economy. In *Energy and Transport in Green Transition: Perspectives on Ecomodernity*, edited by Atle Midttun and Nina Witoszek, 130–151. New York: Routledge.

GM. 2015. Baojun 730. http://media.gmchina.com/media/cn/en/baojun/vehicles/730/ 2014.html (accessed 15 December 2015).

Harwitt, Eric. 1995. *China's Automobile Industry: Policies, Problems, and Prospects*. Armonk, NY: M. E. Sharpe.

Hessler, Peter. 2010. *Country Driving*. New York: Harper Collins.

IAA (Internationale Automobil-Ausstellung). 2016. IAA History. www.iaa.de/en/about-the-iaa/iaa-history/ (accessed 15 January 2016).

Kennedy, Bruce. 2014. China Breaks World Record for Car Sales in 2013. *CBS Moneywatch*, 31 January, www.cbsnews.com/news/china-breaks-world-record-for-car-sales-in-2013/ (accessed 14 May 2014).

Lee, Leo Ou-Fan. 1999. *Shanghai Modern*. Cambridge, MA: Harvard University Press.

Lemonnier, Pierre. 2012. *Mundane Objects*. Walnut Creek, CA: Left Coast Press.

Li, Anding. 2011. *Che Ji* [A Tale of Cars in China]. Beijing: Sanlian Shudian.

Li, Fangfang. 2011. Fast Forward: Lamborghini Sees China as No. 1 Market. *China Daily*, 16 September, www.chinadaily.com.cn/cndy/2011-09/16/content_13712056.htm (accessed 12 August 2013).

Lu, Hanchao.1999. *Beyond the Neon Lights*. Berkeley: University of California Press.

Lutz, Catherine. 2014. The U.S. Car Colossus and the Production of Inequality. *American Ethnologist* 41 (2): 232–245.

Lutz, Catherine and Anne Lutz Fernandez. 2010. *Carjacked*. New York: Palgrave Macmillan.

Mann, Jim. 1989. *Beijing Jeep: The Short, Unhappy Romance of American Business in China*. New York: Simon and Schuster.

Mufson, Steven. 2015. This Documentary Went Viral in China. Then it was Censored. It Won't be Forgotten. *Washington Post*, 16 March, www.washingtonpost.com/news/energy-environment/wp/2015/03/16/this-documentary-went-viral-in-china-then-it-was-censored-it-wont-be-forgotten/ (accessed 17 December 2015).

Nesbitt, Jimmy. 2014. Motorcycle Industry Asks to Switch Gears. *China Daily*, 1 October.

Notar, Beth E. 2006. *Displacing Desire: Travel and Popular Culture in China*. Honolulu: University of Hawai'i Press.

Notar, Beth E. 2012. 'Coming Out' to 'Hit the Road': Temporal, Spatial and Affective Mobilities of Taxi Drivers and Day Trippers in Kunming, China. *City and Society* 24 (3): 281–301.

Notar, Beth E. 2014. 'Let's Go F.B.!': Metaphors of Cars and Corruption in China. In *Vehicles: Cars, Canoes, and Other Metaphors of Moral Imagination*, edited by David Lipset and Richard Handler, 133–155. New York: Berghahn Press.

O'Dell, Tom. 2001. Raggare and the Panic of Mobility: Modernity and Everyday Life in Sweden. In *Car Cultures*, edited by Daniel Miller, 105–132. New York: Berg.

Posth, Martin. 2008. *1,000 Days in Shanghai: The Story of Volkswagen: The First Chinese-German Car Factory*. Singapore: John Wiley & Sons.

PRNewswire. 2015. China Used Car Market Report, 2015–2018. 22 September, www.prnewswire.com/news-releases/china-used-car-market-report-2015-2018-300147502.html (accessed 15 December 2015).

Rocks, David with Chen Wu. 2004. A Phoenix Named Flying Pigeon. *Bloomberg Businessweek News*, 19 September, www.businessweek.com/stories/2004-09-19/a-phoenix-named-flying-pigeon (accessed 19 July 2013).

Rohde, Robert A. and Richard A. Muller. Air Pollution in China: Mapping of Concentrations and Sources. *Berkeley Earth*, July, http://berkeleyearth.org/wp-content/uploads/2015/08/China-Air-Quality-Paper-July-2015.pdf (accessed 15 December 2015).

Sachs, Wolfgang. 1992 (1984). *For the Love of the Automobile*. Berkeley: University of California Press.

Seiler, Cotton. 2008. *Republic of Drivers*. Chicago: University of Chicago Press.

Sun Yat-sen. 1929 (1922). *The International Development of China*, 2nd ed. New York: The Knickerbocker Press.

Urry, John. 2004. The 'System' of Automobility. *Theory, Culture & Society* 21 (4/5): 25–39.

Vanderklippe, Nathan. 2014. Manufacturing; Redefining 'Made in China'. *The Globe and Mail*, 1 December.

Veblen, Thorstein. 1998 (1899). *The Theory of the Leisure Class*. New York: Prometheus Books.

Vidal, John and David Adams. 2007. China Overtakes U.S. as World's Biggest CO2 Emitter. *The Guardian*, 20 June.

Wong, Edward. 2013. Life in a Toxic Country. *The New York Times*, 3 August, www.nytimes.com/2013/08/04/sunday-review/life-in-a-toxiccountry.html?pagewanted=2&_r=0&hp&pagewanted=print (accessed 3 August 2013).

Xinhua Net. 2005. Di yijie Shanghai chezhan [The First Shanghai Auto Show]. http://news3.xinhuanet.com/auto/2005-04/21/content_2860274.htm; (accessed 15 January 2016).

Xinhua Net. 2012. Overview of Kunming. http://news.xinhuanet.com/english/special/2012-10/11/c_131900329.htm; (accessed 6 August 2013).

Xu, Tian. 2002. Mid-range Cars Pull Away in the Mainland Market. www.tdctrade.com/imn/02032203/auto06.htm (accessed 16 August 2007).

Young, Angela. 2015. Chinese Consumers Bought Nearly 300 per cent More Electric Cars This Year Compared to 2014. *International Business Times*, 13 December, www.ibtimes.com/chinese-consumers-bought-nearly-300-more-electric-cars-year-compared-2014-2222591 (accessed 15 December 2015).

Zhang, Jun. 2009. Driving Toward Modernity: An Ethnography of Automobiles in Contemporary China. PhD dissertation, Yale University.

Zhang, Leping. 1948. *Sanmao Liulang ji, diyi ji* [Sanmao the Vagabond, vol. 1]. Shanghai: Shanghai dagong bao guan.

Zhang, Li. 2006. Contesting Spatial Modernity in Late Socialist China. *Current Anthropology* 47 (3): 461–484.

10 The rise and fall of the 'people's car'

Middle-class aspirations, status and mobile symbolism in 'New India'

Kenneth Bo Nielsen and Harold Wilhite

In January 2008, Tata Motors – a leading Indian automobile company – launched its new Tata Nano at the Auto Expo in Delhi. Promoted as an Indian 'people's car', and priced at only 100,000 Indian Rupees (INR), the arrival of the Nano on the Indian scene generated widespread excitement with its promise of bringing car ownership within reach of even ordinary middle class families; and for demonstrating 'New India's unique capacity for innovation and engineering. Yet seven years after the launch, the Nano has, contrary to expectations, barely made an impact on the Indian car market, and is widely regarded as a failure.

Drawing on social theories of consumption, this article offers a detailed study of the rise and fall of the Nano. The purpose of doing so is twofold. First, we seek to explain why a car that was widely predicted to revolutionise automobility in India failed to do so in practice. Second, we seek to demonstrate how cars, as a particular consumer good, feed into historically constituted linkages between objects and social status displays in India, and how these linkages are mediated in new ways in a context of accelerated global economic integration and trade, an increasingly globalised media, and refashioned consumer aspirations. By embedding the story of the Indian 'people's car' from drawing room to showroom in a longer history of automobility and consumption in India, the article thus maps out the changing popular representations and symbolic imaginaries that attach to the car as a means to mobility and an object of identity and social status. To this end, we base our account primarily on public representations and discourse on the Nano, as found in the national and international media. Here, the voices of producers, dealers, prospective and actual consumers, marketing agencies, critics, and 'the motor press' have interfaced to provide a multifaceted picture of the Nano. Our narrative covers the period from around 2003, when Tata Motors first aired the idea of producing an inexpensive Indian 'people's car' (Freiberg *et al.* 2011, 29), and up to early 2015 when rumours started circulating that the company may shut down the Nano project unless sales improve (Kartikey 2015). We also rely on promotional material, including pamphlets, blog entries and videos, produced or promoted by Tata Motors.

We proceed to situate the story of the Nano with reference to the trajectory of the car in post-colonial India. We then turn to the narrative account of the rise and fall of the Nano. We argue that the Nano failed neither because it was a mediocre car, nor because it remained economically out of reach for most Indians. Rather, we suggest that its insertion into the lower ranks of a powerful status hierarchy of identity-defining objects precluded it from adequately tapping into new and hegemonic forms of middle class aspiration in 'New India'. The popular rejection of the Nano was thus not directed only at the object itself, but also at the image of 'the Indian middle class consumer subject' that the car conjures up. To substantiate this argument we engage with the growing literature (e.g. Fernandes 2006, 2009; Fernandes and Heller 2008; Brosius 2010; D'Costa 2010a; Saavala 2010; Donner 2011; Upadhya 2011; Kaur 2012, 2015; Kaur and Hansen 2015) on the link between consumption practices, social status, the formation of a so-called 'new middle class', and the public discourse of a 'New India' in which the nation is projected as rapidly entering into a new world of global possibilities.

The car in post-colonial India

Until well into the 1990s, the domestically produced Ambassador was the King of the Indian road. In 1949 the government of India had banned the import of completely built vehicles; and from 1953 it refused permission to Indian manufacturers to assemble imported vehicles without increasing local content. The result was the withdrawal from India of both General Motors and Ford, while domestic manufacturers such as Hindustan Motors – who produced the Ambassador – and Premier Automobiles consolidated their grip on production (D'Costa 2005, 82). These two domestic companies came to form a duopoly in the Indian car industry which would last until the 1970s.

Based on the Morris Oxford III model first produced in the UK in the 1950s, the sturdy, stocky Ambassador acquired a reputation as the quintessential Indian car, a symbol of Indian independence and modernity (Sardar 2002, 212). 'Fit for Indian conditions' – which usually meant potholed and poorly maintained roads – the Ambassador would witness few improvements or changes after production began in the late 1950s. As Rajan (cited in Corbridge *et al.* 2013, 128) has observed, over four decades of production the Ambassador came in only five different models 'and the sole difference between them seemed to be the headlights and the shape of the grill'.

Because the car industry was tightly regulated and cars treated as luxury products subject to price controls (D'Costa 2005), the Ambassador was never affordable for the vast majority of Indians. It was the car of ministers, politicians and distinguished civil servants, and of a small segment of the upper middle class. It was, in effect, a well-established marker of social status and distinction, something to which only the upper echelons of society could aspire (Wilhite 2008, 123).

In the 1970s Sanjay Gandhi – the son of then Prime Minister Indira Gandhi – promoted the idea of domestic production of an Indian 'people's car'. Sanjay Gandhi had served a brief apprenticeship with Rolls-Royce in the UK before he returned to India in 1971 to start a car manufacturing company of his own, Maruti Limited (Guha 2007, 469–470). Sanjay Gandhi had vowed, in the mid-1970s, that his company would soon produce a car that would 'out-corner either the Fiat or the Ambassador' (quoted in Guha 2007, 509); but when Sanjay Gandhi died in a plane crash in 1980, Maruti had still not produced a single vehicle (D'Costa 2005, 85).

In 1982 Maruti signed a joint venture with Japanese automaker Suzuki, a specialist in small car production. A year later the company released its 'Maruti 800' model, the first car within the affordable range for the Indian middle class. The Maruti 800 would not only move many Indian families from two to four wheels; it would be the vanguard of a new consumption-driven Indian political economy as envisioned and promoted by Rajiv Gandhi (Kurien 1994, 88–104), India's Prime Minister from 1984–1989. Rajiv Gandhi shifted the economic development emphasis from production to consumption and 'to the possibility of commodities that would tap into the tastes and consumption practices of the urban middle classes' (Fernandes 2000, 613). Of course, this economic shift and the emergence of new consumption practices in the middle class did not emerge over night, but were rather the long-term outputs of a process that D'Costa (2005, 2013) calls embourgeoisment, by which an emergent 'state-produced' middle class with increasing purchasing power created political and economic pressure on the state to deregulate the economy and facilitate market expansion. This embourgeoisment on the demand side would, from the 1980s, go hand in hand with the expansion and internationalisation of an increasingly mature auto industry on the supply side, as first materialised in the Maruti 800, an 'aesthetically pleasing and economically attractive' vehicle from the point of view of 'a consuming class accustomed to expensive and shoddy products' (D'Costa 2005, 91).

Nonetheless, in the 1980s there was still a lingering element of the long-standing social valuation of frugality in middle class consumption. Thus, in this early phase of the birth of the consumption economy, products were still designed to be practical, functional and durable. The thinking was that just as the unchanging design of the Ambassador had allowed 'every mechanic of any ilk, every taxi driver [to] take it apart and put it together again blindfolded' (Sardar 2002, 212), successive versions of the Maruti 800 would similarly remain fairly standardised and the parts would be interchangeable, allowing owners to harvest social approval by making their car last while keeping it in mint condition. The Maruti 800 would remain India's best-selling car for around two decades – yet it was still priced at such a level that it precluded the vast majority of Indians from aspiring for car ownership.

As Wilhite (2008, 123) reports from Kerala, in the 1980s the Ambassador and the Maruti 800 combined to constitute a fixed and stable social hierarchy: 'With some exceptions … the rich and elite drove Ambassadors, and most everyone else able to afford a car drove a Maruti'. Yet this began to change after 1991 and the opening of India to foreign models, manufacturers and investments. The liberalisation of the car industry had begun in the late 1970s and gathered speed during the 1980s until the passenger car segment was completely de-licensed in 1993 (D'Costa 2005, 103). Since then, the auto industry has rapidly internationalised, with more and more MNCs – including e.g. Honda, Toyota, Ford, GM and BMW (Mazumdar 2012, 74) – active in the market and offering a much greater variety of car models. This process has coincided with high rates of economic growth over the past two decades, and a concomitant expansion of the middle class (Fernandes 2006) so that more Indians than ever before – especially in metropolitan areas – now aspire to the expanding comforts of middle class life. This comfort expansion includes air conditioned homes, an increasing number of household electric appliances such as washing machines and microwave ovens, and a growth in home entertainment technologies such as televisions (with cable connections) and personal computers, as well as an explosion in the ownership and use of smart phones. Car ownership forms an important ingredient in this comfort regime, unambiguously replacing the motorcycle as *the* preferred means of middle class mobility (Wilhite 2008, 122). As Krishna and Bajpai (2015, 71) write, cars are 'totems' or 'marker assets' of upper middle class status.[1]

The availability of a multiplicity of cars and models played into a period in which frugality was waning (or rearticulated – see below) as a positive factor in social performance. While even well-to-do families had earlier felt that flaunting their assets was in bad taste, the rush for consumer goods such as cars, washing machines and television sets that followed in the period after liberalisation soon displaced this older ethos (Krishna and Bajpai 2015). Indeed, as Fernandes (2009) argues, the unfolding politics of state-led economic liberalisation and the formation of new, conspicuous or 'aspirational' (Mazzarella 2003) consumption practices among India's new middle class have been mutually constitutive and reinforcing. As new products and new models of household appliances and cars of differing price and quality became available, holding onto older commodities was gradually associated with an inability to keep up, either economically or socially. This was also reflected in, for instance, changing dowry practices in which the traditional commodities of land and gold began to be supplemented by household appliances and cars, both new and used.

As first theorised by Veblen (1899) in his landmark work on consumption in late nineteenth century Europe, people in socially stratified societies use commodities to emulate the consumption of the elite. In India of the 1980s, the vast difference in cost between the Ambassador and the Maruti made this form for emulation prohibitive for the vast majority of the middle class. However, the proliferation of models and prices in the 1990s changed this consumption landscape. Foreign cars, SUVs and other kinds of quasi-luxury cars were moved within reach if families borrowed money and stretched household economies. The car, highly visible in driveways and on the roads, became a perfect means to project a family's social identity. As Saavala (2010, 120, 192) argues, a family that now buys a car not simply does so for practical purposes, but above all to position themselves in relation to those who, for example, only have a motorbike. And for people wanting to make an impression in business circles, or through dowry exchanges, being seen as someone able to afford a car may even override the need to invest in a house.

As shown by Bourdieu's (1984) adaptation of Veblen's performance theory to late twentieth century European societies, where class distinctions were blurred and consumption choices vastly elaborated, consumption not only signals a move upward through social hierarchy, but rather through an articulated social space consisting of multiple identities. In the Indian context, Brosius (2010) has drawn on Bourdieu to show how the intangible and fuzzy nature of the middle class category makes the social performance of taste and preferences through consumption practices particularly important in the production of class distinctions. The proliferation of automobile models in India from 1991 created a vast new and dynamic consumption landscape in which new models, and thus new potential social identities, were being produced at a high rate.[2] Not only did this contribute to a rapid growth in car ownership at a projected rate of 2.3 million cars per year over the next decade (Ghate and Sundar 2013), it also led to a considerable reworking and refashioning of the earlier bi-polar Ambassador-Maruti social hierarchy in order to incorporate an ever greater variety of vehicles. This has increasingly rendered the Ambassador the car of 'Old India': a somewhat inelegant and old-fashioned product of the laggard state-led development of the Nehruvian socialism of the pre-reform era. The suspension of the production of the Ambassador in 2014, and the phase-out of the Maruti 800 from 2010, are indicative and even symptomatic of these changes. The Nano's prolonged planning, design and production process played out in this changing consumption landscape.

The making of the Nano

The idea of producing a genuinely inexpensive car for the *aam admi* – the common man – took shape in the head of the then Chairman of the Tata Group, Ratan Tata, in the early 2000s. According to Ratan Tata (quoted in Noronha 2008), he had always had a 'sort of unconscious urge' to do something for the people of India in the field of transportation. Having observed how mass transport in India is often not available or is of poor quality; and that two-wheelers, with the father driving, a child standing in front and the wife behind holding a baby, are an unsafe mode of transportation, he was motivated to create a safer alternative for Indian families. Ratan Tata ostensibly began to doodle, contemplating the feasibility of rebuilding cars around the scooter, even if, as he put it (quoted in Noronha 2008), 'nobody took the idea seriously' at the time.[3] Yet by 2003 the project of creating the car was well under way.

Tata's vision was broadly shared among industrialists and politicians. During his inaugural address at the 2004 Auto Expo in New Delhi, the then Deputy Prime Minister, L. K. Advani, had stressed the importance for the nation of exploring new ways to produce and promote affordable transportation for the great Indian multitude. Emphasising the need for 'cost effective products which fulfil the aspiration of a large chunk of our population', Advani had asked rhetorically: 'If only we had a people's car costing no more than INR 100,000, how many millions of people would be queuing up to buy it?' Advani challenged the captains of India's auto industry: 'bring down the cost of the vehicle and make them more affordable' (quoted in *The Economic Times* 2004).

While most auto manufacturers at the time doubted whether producing a car priced at only INR 100,000 was at all feasible, Ratan Tata responded to the Deputy Prime Minister's challenge by declaring that 'the one *lakh* car is under development' (quoted in rediff.com 2004). Yet such claims notwithstanding, Ratan Tata repeatedly had to reassure critics within the automotive industry – whose response to the idea of a 'one *lakh* car' ranged 'from the incredulous to the frankly dismissive' (Wells 2010, 445) – that his version of 'the people's car' would be a real car, not a simple four-wheeled auto rickshaw or 'a car with plastic curtains and no roof' (quoted in Tiwari 2009, 106).

Clouded in secrecy, the penultimate design of the car was arrived at in 2005, and by 2006 the design was 'frozen'. In May of the same year, Tata Motors announced that West Bengal would be the future home of the mother plant where the new car would be produced – and the fact that the car was kept behind a curtain of impenetrable security (Freiberg, Freiberg, and Dunston 2011, 205) added to the mystique and excitement. It only received the name 'Nano' when it was launched in January 2008.

Approaching the launch

In the years leading up to the launch, the Nano was the target of considerable public attention, for reasons both positive and negative. The establishment of the new Nano factory in West Bengal embroiled Tata Motors in perhaps the most talked-about controversy over land acquisition for industrialisation in recent years (Nielsen 2010). Yet when people spoke about the car itself, the public mood was more upbeat and excited – some even described it as 'the most awaited car in the world' (Hutton 2009). This brief report in *Forbes* is broadly representative of how the car was projected in leading media channels, both at home and abroad:

> If the yet-to-be-named car is a success when it goes on sale next year, it would herald the emergence of Tata Motors on the global auto scene, mark the advent of India as a global center for small-car production and represent a victory for those who advocate making cheap goods for potential customers at the 'bottom of the pyramid' in emerging markets. Most of all, it would give millions of people now relegated to lesser means of transportation the chance to drive cars ... it is a hugely ambitious project.
>
> (Meredith 2007)

Yet success was virtually guaranteed, not least because, as *The American* perceptively wrote, Tata Motors had a history of being 'adept at learning not just the needs but the hopes and desires of their customer base in this, "the most optimistic country in the world"' (Bennett 2008). *The American* believed that when Tata Motors had marketed its popular Tata Ace truck, launched in 2005 – just a year before the Nano's design was frozen – it had come to appreciate just how much pent-up desire there was among people to get off two- and three-wheeled vehicles: 'Indians are very status-conscious, and the move to a four-wheeled vehicle is considered a huge event … even a little US\$2,500 four-door can be a dream machine, a freedom machine', it wrote (Bennett 2008).

A similar enthusiastic anticipation would mark the reception of the Nano at the launch itself, during which the media and the public had its first view of the new vehicle. This is how one enthusiastic Indian blogger described the event:

> Cut to the 10th of January 2008, at the Pragati Maidan in New Delhi, the day Tata's vision would be thrown open to worldwide scrutiny. Virtually everyone knew it would be a historic event, but I can't imagine that anyone was willing to bet just how momentous it would really be. Before this highly anticipated launch, people envisioned a makeshift vehicle that would be little more than four wheels and a tin roof – if at all that. When the car was finally revealed to the battling crowds, there was almost a sense of disbelief in the room … What the Nano has done is provide that all important utility, but in a spectacular package considering its asking price – one that appeals on many levels, whether through its visual appeal and smiling face or accommodating and spacious interiors. Not to mention the fact that it's a ground breaking car the likes of which the world hasn't seen in recent times. But perhaps most important of all, it's the brainchild of an Indian automaker … it makes a very bold statement about the engineering capabilities of our country. On a more universal level, it also points to just what you can achieve if you dare to dream or innovate, and then have the conviction to turn those dreams into reality.[4]

As *Der Spiegel* later observed, the Nano 'grabbed more attention than anything shown at the North America International Auto Show in Detroit held the same month' (Rowley and Srivastava 2008).

Nano, nation, 'New India'

Had space permitted we could have provided countless similar enthusiastic accounts of the arrival of the Nano. These accounts, we argue, to varying degrees tap into several overlapping discursive domains that, in combination, constitute the idea of 'New India'. As Edensor (2004) has shown, automobility and national identity are deeply intertwined and are often mediated by so-called 'iconic vehicles' to the extent that certain cars can, like the Ambassador until the 1980s, signify national identity. They are, in other words, loaded with national significance (2004, 102–104). Manufacturers and advertisers often seek to encode their vehicles with these symbolic national significations, and the Nano was no exception. Not only was it promoted as *the* car of the Indian people; in 2011 a special and one-off version of the Nano, the Tata Nano Goldplus, went on a six-month tour, stopping at 29 Tata-owned Goldplus jewellery stores across the country. The Nano Goldplus was no ordinary Nano. It was covered in 80 kg of 22 carat gold, 15 kg of silver, and inlaid with 10,000 semi-precious stones and gems, including a jewel-encrusted peacock on the front bumper and gold-plated wheels; and its design combined different traditions of craftsmanship from different Indian regions. Originally presented as part of a celebration of '5,000 years of Indian jewellery' in Mumbai, this car worth an estimated US\$4.5 million not only exuded affluence; it celebrated a famous yet diverse national tradition of skilled craftsmanship, and tied the nation together by traversing its length and breadth for half a year. This advertising strategy resembles what Mazzarella (2003, 138–145) calls 'auto-orientalism', in which globally recognised signifiers of Indian 'tradition' – skilled craftsmanship in jewellery and gold; the symbolically loaded peacock that is also India's national bird – are invoked to facilitate the aspirational consumption of 'a culturally marked self' (Mazzarella 2003, 138). In a comparable vein, the Nano's official webpage features a section called 'Nano Diaries' where Nano owners relate their experiences with driving the Nano, often on longer journeys traversing various corners of the country, thus inscribing the Nano onto the nation's physical geography.[5]

Such representations of course beg the question: which nation is being signified? As indicated above, we argue that what is conveyed through the Nano more generally is the idea of 'New India'. 'New India' at one level is taken to refer to the socio-political and economic realities that characterise India today after more than two decades of liberalising economic reforms and the increasing consolidation of capitalist markets of commodity production and consumption (D'Costa 2010b, 2). There now exists a considerable scholarly literature that has carefully deconstructed the 'newness' of this 'New India' to bring to light not only the continuities with the 'Old India' of the past, but also the persistent socio-economic inequalities that 'the Wall Street version' (D'Costa 2010b, 7) of 'New India' glosses over (see for example D'Costa 2010a, Kohli 2012, Corbridge and Shah 2013). While one could thus legitimately dismiss 'New India' as little more than a hyperreal construct – an 'image that precedes the real' (Kaur 2012, 619) – we here draw inspiration from Kaur (2012) in examining the significance of 'New India' precisely at the representational level, that is, as an ideational and symbolic construct that mobilises particular identities, desires and aspirations.

In a recent article, Foulkes and Madsen (2014, 89) portray 'New India' as a 'world of allure and illusion … where all rice is basmati, all tea is Darjeeling, and where Bollywood is the last stop before heaven'. A less tongue-in-cheek way of conceptualising 'New India' would be to portray India as 'a new world of enterprise, techno-mobility, consumption and fresh market opportunities' (Kaur and Hansen 2015, 2) as embodied in its globally renown IT and ITES industry; its impressive rates of economic growth during the first decade of this millennium; its global soft power spearheaded by Bollywood and its film stars; its long strides towards attracting corporate praise and unprecedented levels of foreign investment; and not least its rapidly emerging consumer-oriented new middle class that has, to a large extent, been counted, measured and celebrated precisely on the basis of its capacity and desire for consumption (Fernandes 2009; Brosius 2010). Middle-class status in 'New India' is inseparable from visible consumption (Saavala 2010); and it is this new middle class that has increasingly 'come to define and represent the nation as a whole', as Upadhya (2011, 169–170) writes. 'New India', in other words, is an India that wants to be seen as rapidly divesting itself of its image as a developing country and emerging instead as an important actor on the global scene, both politically, economically, technologically and culturally. The Nano, we suggest, was promoted and represented to tap into, and become iconic of, the ideas, desires and aspirations of 'New India' in a fourfold manner.

First, the Nano was represented as a triumph of the determined, individual entrepreneurial spirit of Ratan Tata who had dared to 'dream and innovate', and who had not budged in the face of ridicule. Not only had this made the Nano materialise; it had also seemingly already earned it its rightful parking place in the global history of automobility, alongside the legendary 'people's cars' of yesteryear: The American Ford T, the German Beetle and the British Mini. Thus, when presenting the Nano Ratan Tata took special pride in the fact that 'a car once thought impossible by the world is now a reality' (quoted in Tiwari 2009, 165). In addition, Ratan Tata's personal success placed him alongside other new business 'icons' (particularly within the IT industry) who have garnered 'immense symbolic power for the aspiring middle classes' (Upadhya 2011, 190). They have acquired this symbolic power because they embody what an individual can, in theory, achieve not through inherited or ascribed social status – as critics would argue was the case in 'Old India' – but through personal vision, acquired merit and hard work.

Second, the Nano firmly placed 'New India' on the global map as an assertive and innovative nation capable of spectacular engineering feats. Just how spectacular this 'feat' was can be deduced if one compares the price of India's 'people's car' to those other legendary 'people's cars' produced in advanced industrialised nations: Adjusting prices to 2009 US$, Ford's Model T would have cost US$21,000 and the Volkswagen Beetle US$11,000 when they were introduced. The Nano was, by then, priced at only US$2,100 (Freiberg et al. 2011, 214). This feat could, moreover, be rearticulated with the traditional Indian valuation of frugality, albeit in a very different form. Globally, the Nano was represented and hailed as the outcome of a particular Indian form of innovative 'Gandhian' or 'frugal' engineering in which the aim is to 'get more from less'. This style of innovative, low-cost engineering has in turn been subsumed under the Hindi word *jugaad*, a term initially used to describe jury-rigged, self-repaired bricolage vehicles. Over the past years, however, the term has been rearticulated with global business and marketing jargon to denote a special kind of shrewd, entrepreneurial, improvisational Indian savoir-faire, a sense of Indian genius that makes the most out of limited resources (Birtchnell 2011; Jeffrey and Young 2014).[6]

Third, the Nano was represented as imbued with emancipatory qualities. As the statement by Deputy Prime Minister Advani cited earlier shows, it was simultaneously assigned a key role in national development *and* held out the promise of democratising automobility by making a new and affordable form of personalised transportation available to the *aam admi*. Euphemistically referred to as 'the bottom of the pyramid' in the report from *Forbes* cited above, the *aam admi* had, when the Nano was launched, emerged as a discursive focal point in Indian politics.[7] The then-incumbent national government, led by the Congress Party, had won the 2004 elections by promising to curb the worst excesses of India's neoliberal economic policies, dedicating themselves instead to working for the betterment of the *aam admi*. In this context it is significant that the Tata Group has a carefully crafted public image as a business conglomerate imbued with a larger social purpose. The Tata Group shuns morally dubious businesses such as alcohol and tobacco and is known for its avowed nation-building ethos and philanthropy. The popular rhetoric surrounding the Nano thus resonated strongly with dominant tropes of national development and upliftment, and with the Tata Group's historical contribution to these, within the broader political landscape.

Last, and most importantly from the point of view of attracting customers, the Nano was represented as appealing directly to middle-class aspirations and desires for personal mobility and social status that we discussed above. From the vantage point of the Indian middle class, the car of course has obvious *practical* advantages compared to other forms of mobility, apart from the safety factor that Ratan Tata stressed. The choice of when, why and for how long to travel is, with a car, no longer subject to the vagaries of often crowded and uncomfortable public transportation; one is spared unpleasant situations of close, physical proximity with society's lower orders on crowded busses (Saavala 2010, 117–118); one is less impeded by the heavy monsoon that makes travel by bicycle or motorbike difficult at certain times of year; and one is sheltered from the air pollution and high rates of suspended particulate matter that haunt all major Indian cities, and of which cars are, paradoxically, the main producer. But as Ananya Roy (2011, 267) has argued, the crucial strength of the Nano was its symbolic ability to emerge as a 'phantasmagoria of middle-class consumption', an elusive and malleable object believed to embody a complex assemblage of shifting desires and aspirations for both physical and social mobility, status, comfort and affluence among 'New India's new middle class.

In this fourfold way, then, public representations that iconised the Nano powerfully synthesised key characteristics associated with 'New India' at the level of the nation, the family and the individual: Personal achievement through individual merit and determination; the realisation of middle-class consumerist desires for social and spatial mobility; national development; and a global reputation for creative innovation. Yet in practice, and for reasons we outline below, this synthesis would be difficult to sustain.

Hitting the road

After the official launch in January 2008 it would be another 18 months before the first Nano hit the road. So great was the initial demand that Tata Motors decided to institute a lottery – a computerised random selection procedure – to decide the owners of the first 100,000 cars among more than 200,000 orders. One report even suggested that buyers were willing to pay up to 30 per cent more than the original price for second hand models, just to get their hands on the car as soon as possible.

By most accounts, the Nano turned out to be an efficient, manoeuvrable and reliable car. Powered by a 624 cc, twin cylinder engine with a 35 HP output, the small car measuring just over three metres in length could easily accommodate four passengers. And with a maximum speed at around 100 kilometres per hour, it had no difficulties keeping up with larger vehicles. Most independent expert test drives reviewed the Nano more or less favourably, underlining its affordability, fuel efficiency and utility in India's cramped urban traffic. The UK-based *Autocar*, for instance, described it as 'an amazing car' and a truly Indian contribution to 'the new world of motoring'. The Germans, it claimed, would have put in 'too much stuff', raising the cost of the Nano to that of a Mini; and the Americans would cunningly have set the price just under that of the competition – this would disenfranchise all those people on motorcycles, who were projected as the most likely customers.[8]

However, the initial flurry of interest in the Nano soon subsided, at least partly due to engineering problems. A number of Nanos spontaneously combusted soon after they left the showroom. Several of them had faulty electrical switches that caused smoke and melted plastic components. There were a number of other reports of production problems, delays and technical snags. These contributed to plunging Nano sales and the assessment that 'two-and-a-half years after its glitzy launch, a car that was meant to revolutionize personal transport in India – and perhaps all of Asia – remain[ed] stuck in first gear' (Dhume 2011). In spite of a production capacity (and projected sales rate) of more than 20,000 vehicles per month, Nano sales for a long time generally hovered between 3,000 and 8,000 per month and only very rarely exceeded 10,000. In contrast, there have been several lows: In November 2010 when only 509 units were sold; throughout the first half of 2013 when sales hovered around 1,500 per month; and in fiscal year 2014–2015, when only 16,901 units were sold. This was the equivalent of less than one month's production at full capacity. For a car that wild estimates suggested would expand the Indian car market by upwards of 65 per cent (Tiwari 2009, 107) these are very modest sales figures.

According to Carl-Peter Forster (interviewed in *The Economist* 2011), the former boss of General Motors Europe who took over as head of Tata Motors in February 2010, there were, however, several additional explanations for the Nano's poor performance. When the car was launched there was no real national distribution scheme, very little marketing and advertising, and no effective system of consumer finance. The irony was that many rural Indians never got to hear about or have the opportunity to see the car that was supposed to help transform their lives. The Nano's marketing problems began, in fact, with its product positioning. The ex-showroom price including taxes etc. soon crept up to around INR 140,000, putting it out of reach of first-time buyers with no regular employment or payslips to back an application for credit. In an ironic way, the Nano's status as iconic of 'New India' was refracted through the prism of 'Old India' in which 'technical snags' in production; poorly targeted marketing and advertising; lacklustre infrastructure; inefficient distribution; the lack of dealers in small towns and rural areas; and a lack of institutional credit facilities prevented 'the people's car' from actually reaching 'the people'. Yet these technological and logistical challenges notwithstanding, the shifting consumption landscape which we described above also crucially shaped the public reception of the Nano.

The semantics of price: affordability versus cheapness

> Those climbing into India's middle class want cheap cars, but they don't want cars that seem cheap – and are willing to pay more than Tata reckoned for a vehicle that has a more upmarket image.
>
> (McLain 2013)

As argued earlier, people use cars to make statements about themselves and their families (Wilhite 2008, 127). As mobile symbols, the car 'materialises personality' (Sheller 2004, 225) and projects to the public how we like to see ourselves, and how we would like others to see us. As Hansen (2014) argues, cars convey and connote images of status, wealth and social standing in public spaces in a manner in which perhaps no other commodity can. In this context, there is a fine balance between frugality and cupidity; between moderation and excess; and not least between affordability and cheapness.

The Nano could only be made affordable by keeping production costs low. While keeping the price low was a potential source of pride and achievement insofar as it necessitated unprecedented innovation skills on the part of designers and subcontractors, from the point of view of consumers it meant doing away with the potential to symbolise something more than the owner barely managing the economics of a move to four wheels. In short, there was nothing to brag about. As one reviewer noted, the base Nano was pure minimalism: It had a manual gearbox with four speeds; no power steering; no ABS nor a vacuum booster for the four-wheel drum brakes; only one windshield wiper and one side mirror; the central speedometer with inset fuel gauge was the only gauge; there were no dash switches, no heater and no ventilation system (Hutton 2009); and only thinly padded nonadjustable seats. In material terms the car, in other words, exuded frugality and simplicity – the small boot, for example, could only be accessed by folding the rear seat forward. These values, however, had increasingly reseeded from the broader register of social performance among the new middle class, among whom bigger vehicles and a comfortable and lush interior design were much more important (Tetzlaff 2013).[9]

Ratan Tata had evidently been well aware of the delicate balance between cutting costs to ensure affordability, and the risk of projecting an image of 'cheapness'. Reflecting on the design process, he admitted that designing the Nano had involved 'saving money on every single bit of the car'. Yet his company had consistently been conscious that there should be no quality stigma attached to the Nano, even if it lacked some of the niceties of its fancier cousins: 'One thing we were clear about: This was never going to be a half-car. Nobody wants a car that is less than everybody else's car', he said (quoted in Noronha 2008).

Yet the stigma of being a car that was somehow 'less than everybody else's car' soon attached itself to the Nano. As Hormazd Sorabjee, the editor of *Autocar India*, put it: 'In communications, it's gone out as the world's cheapest car ... there's a kind of stigma attached to it, as though you can't afford anything else' (quoted in Dhume 2011). This sentiment was brought out by the prospective Nano owner Rajesh Malhotra who, when interviewed by *Der Spiegel* (Rowley and Srivastava 2008) in 2008, had been contemplating exchanging his US$1,400 motorbike for a Nano. While he had never been in a position to purchase a Maruti Suzuki 800 – which at the time cost nearly twice as much as the Nano – he was now having second thoughts about the Nano. Once taxes and insurance costs were added, the price of the entry-level Nano would rise to just over US$3,000. For an extra US$500, Malhotra claimed he could buy a decent used car with a more powerful engine and air conditioning, something which the Nano lacked. Thus, while he had been forced by his wife to save for the Nano, he was personally inclined to 'wait and see what others think'. More generally, the stigma attached to the Nano alienated several categories of potential buyers. As Tata Managing Director Karl Slym said (quoted in Philip 2013) in 2013, scooter drivers were not attracted because others 'don't think I'm buying a car, they think I'm buying something between a two-wheeler and a car'. And people who already had a car would not want to buy a Nano either, because 'it was supposed to be a two-wheeler replacement' (ibid.).

Evidently, not only comfort and engine power mattered to potential buyers; so too did public opinion and taste embedded in the broader consumption landscape. As we have argued, this landscape is fluid and the commercialised cultural markers that are used to define class status may change very frequently. Yet several studies have shown how, within this fluid landscape, a particular 'dominant fraction' within the new Indian middle class exerts a greater influence in terms of defining the standards against which the aspirations of other fractions of the same class and within the same landscape are measured (Fernandes and Heller 2008; Brosius 2010). To Fernandes and Heller (2008, 150), the dominant fraction of the middle class is engaged in a hegemonic project rooted in a politics of consumption that simultaneously holds out 'the promise of inclusion to other aspiring social segments even as it reconstitutes the subtle hierarchies and exclusions that anchor its class position'. The actual pursuit of this consumption-based 'promise of inclusion' by social groups aspiring to middle class status has been likened to a 'new sanskritisation' (Krishna and Bajpai 2015,

74) where the emulation of elite practices reaffirm and reproduce hierarchy and distinction, even as these are transformed. Cars and car ownership, we argue, figure crucially in these subtle processes of reconstructing distinction and exclusion. And here, the Nano has ended up at the lower rungs – not as 'the people's car', but as the car of that segment of the middle class who 'can't afford anything else', as Hormazd Sorabjee put it (quoted in Dhume 2011). Nano ownership has thus become indexical of an incomplete or adverse inclusion into the new Indian middle class; and 'Nano rejection' conversely a rejection of the status of an 'incomplete' Indian middle class consumer subject that the car conjures up. It may also plausibly be interpreted as a revolt on the part of Indian consumers against being assigned to an inferior position at the 'bottom of the pyramid' (following *Forbes*) in a global consumption hierarchy, where even a 'cheap' and simple car is expected to fulfil basic consumer aspirations – as Kaur (2015, 6, emphasis added) argues, 'the real prestige good in "New India" is … mastery of *global* culture and *full* membership in the *global* elite'. Owning a cheap and distinctly *Indian* car could evidently be no indicator of 'full membership'.

This rejection of the basic Nano – with all its connotations – is brought out not simply by how most early Nano-owners preferred to buy the more expensive 'CX' or 'LX' models (Wells 2010, 448) with extra features and conveniences (such as air conditioning; bottle holders; dual glove boxes; integrated music system; etc.); but also by how Tata Motors have recently worked hard to rub out the stigma attached to the Nano by rebranding it in new ways. This rebranding exercise provides an interesting window through which to examine how the company has, through advertising campaigns, sought to manipulate brand desire by establishing a different kind of aspirational resonance with a new category of consumers. In the next section we take a brief look at these recent marketing manoeuvres.

From the people's car to the cool people's car: the Nano refashioned

By mid-2015 the 'basic' Nano was no longer featured on the Tata Nano webpage, where only the three latest versions are promoted.[10] One is the compressed natural gas (CNG) powered Nano emax (with switch-on-the-go bi-fuel facility) which boasts the best-in-class CNG mileage at 36 km/kg. Launched in October 2013 and projected as environmentally friendly, the emax is promoted as a smart, intelligent and green choice for knowledgeable consumers who are conscious about their ecological footprint. It is priced from approximately INR 2.5 *lakh*.

The second new Nano that figures prominently on the webpage is the Nano Twist, launched in January 2014. Described as a 'new smart city car' with 'cool, young and trendy features', the Nano Twist was, in the words of Ranjit Yadav, the President of Tata Motors' Passenger Vehicle Business Unit, created to cater 'to the dynamic desires of our growing customer base of young, trendy urbanites' (Tata Motors Media Centre 2014). The Nano Twist has received a face-lift; is available in a range of 'trendy' colours; comes with a stereo and AC, as well as hubcaps and chrome trim. Prices start from around INR 2.35 *lakh*. The third new Nano, launched in May 2015, is the GenX Nano, a 'compact hatch' with automatic transmission, power steering, new technology to facilitate bumper to bumper driving in dense urban traffic, and a boot hatch that opens. Prices range from INR 2 to 3 *lakh*.

That the Nano is now promoted as 'the cool people's car' rather than simply 'the people's car' is equally evident in the many promotional videos of the Nano Twist that are available online. The videos celebrate the 'awesomeness, young-ness, kickassness, zigzagness, cityness and magicness' of the Nano. They exclu-sively portray young, trendy urbanites having a good time; and they highlight the Nano's ability to manoeuvre effectively in urban traffic, as well as the ease of parking because of the car's compactness. Increasingly, then, the Nano has been rebranded and redesigned to appeal to younger buyers who want a car that is 'a little more aspirational' (McLain 2013) than the basic Nano. It has also been rebranded as an ideal second or third car – a car for the 'youngster in the house' – for those families who can afford more than one car. These new marketing and branding strategies, and the different consumer subjectivities they appeal to – environmentally conscious; trendy urbanite; affluent family man; etc. – are undoubtedly more attuned to the real social location of the hegemonic sections of the middle class that claim to speak for 'New India' as a whole, and to their desired place in a global consumption landscape. But given the considerable increase in purchasing price that this rebranding necessitates, the Nano's claim to being a 'people's car' in the conventional sense is progressively undermined. The new key consumer group is far removed from the poor family of four cramped onto a two-wheeler that originally inspired Ratan Tata to build the car.

Conclusion

Our account of the rise and fall of the Tata Nano has covered a period of well over a decade during which important yet gradual shifts have occurred in India's increasingly globalised consumption landscape. This landscape is defined by an increasingly consolidated social dynamic in which commodities are seen as positive social identifiers, and where visible, aspirational consumption has become a key signifier of middle class status. Here, the car is one of the most important objects for projecting and conveying images of status, wealth and social standing among India's new middle class. Whether it be parked in front of the house or transporting its owner and family through urban geographies, the car has become the perfect vehicle for and symbol of the 'new' Indian middle class family (Saavala 2010) within a broader and increasingly complex and shifting landscape of commodities and associated social identities.

Prior to the launch, the massive hype surrounding the Nano indicated that the small car was expected to bring car ownership within the immediate reach of more Indian consumers than ever before; and by extension, to facilitate – and demonstrate to India and the world – the massive transition of Indian society towards a truly middle class consumerist society. In other words, it was expected to both tap into the tastes and desires of the 'New India' *and* to contribute to 'New India's realisation, growth and expansion. As we have argued, 'New India' as idea, image or brand (Kaur 2012, 2015) sees the nation as an emerging actor on the global stage, 'eager to make its presence felt in the global community' (Kaur 2015, 14). Politically, it claims the status as the world's largest democracy; economically, it has acquired a position as one of the most rapidly growing economies in the world; culturally, it boasts considerable soft power resources; and technologically, a (limited) number of its leading and increasingly mature industries have the ability to engineer and produce advanced technologies – including automotive technologies – for both domestic and foreign markets at better quality and more affordable prices than manufacturers in other countries. The Nano aimed to both capitalise on and fortify this image of innovative, world-class engineering and thereby appeal to a thrifty and consumerist new Indian middle class, hoping to outcompete more expensive and luxurious foreign and domestic models. But as plunging Nano sales show, it has so far failed. A key explanation is that in conception, design and partly also in marketing, it largely appealed to an older ethos of frugality and simplicity as positive social signifiers, an ethos which had, however, increasingly lost its positive connotations. Tata's design and innovation discourse did not engage with the shift in the possession and social positioning of consumer goods such as household electrical appliances and cars – the frugal Nano was, in other words, incompatible with the consumerist desires of 'New India's new middle class.

In addition, the widespread rejection of the Nano by Indian consumers needs to be understood with reference to the internal processes of differentiation and distinction within the middle class. To the extent that an upper segment of this class plays a disproportionate or hegemonic role in setting the consumption standards against which the aspirations of other fractions of the same class are measured, subtle consumption hierarchies and forms of exclusion are continuously reconstituted. This reconstitution is increasingly mediated by accelerated global economic integration, trade and advertising, and an increasingly globalised media, thus rendering a mastery of global consumer tastes, aspirations and practices a precondition for 'full' middle class status. Having landed on the lower rungs of this hierarchy of identity-defining material objects, the Nano has come to acquire a dual set of negative identity connotations. First, it has come to signify an adverse or incomplete inclusion into the new middle class; and second, it has come to signify a consumer identity whose desires and aspirations can be fulfilled even by a simple, cheap vehicle. While the first identity position is shaped within the Indian consumption landscape itself, the second is defined by a globalised landscape insofar as it locates the 'Indian middle class consumer' at the bottom of a global consumption hierarchy, where tastes are simple or even unsophisticated, and consumption capacity very limited. The widespread rejection of the Nano is thus not merely about a refusal to purchase the car itself, but also a refusal on the part of consumers to occupy ascribed identity positions within national and global consumption hierarchies that the car connotes.

Acknowledgements

Some of the ideas presented here were first aired in more rudimentary form by Nielsen at the 'Indian Phantasm Conference' at the Museum of Cultural History in Oslo, Norway, 10–11 December 2012. A preliminary draft was later presented by Nielsen at a workshop organised by the Research School at the Centre for Development and the Environment at the University of Oslo, Norway, in September 2014. We are grateful to the participants for their constructive comments. Thanks also to Arve Hansen, Stig Toft Madsen and Stefan Tetzlaff for their careful reading of earlier drafts. The comments by the two anonymous referees were gratefully received.

Notes

1 India's current level of car ownership is still only 13 cars per 1,000 people (Ghate and Sundar 2013), but a greater variety of models, both domestic and foreign, are now available from more outlets, ranging from small Marutis to large SUVs to imported top-end vehicles.

2 By this we do not mean to deny India's longer history of using commodities and consumption in socio-political displays or performances. We merely suggest that the process of embourgeoisment (D'Costa 2005), the emergence of new forms of aspirational consumption (Mazzarella 2003), multiplex processes of globalisation – including of the auto industry – and economic restructuring in combination provide the grounds for a dynamic consumption landscape that is different from that of the past.

3 For a more detailed account of the inspiration for and making of the Nano as told from Tata's point of view, see Freiberg *et al.* (2011).

4 Quoted from an anonymous blog entry at http://automobilenano.blogspot.no/.

5 See www.tatanano.com/worldofawesomeness/nano-diaries-submit/.

6 For a laudatory version of this argument, see for example Freiberg *et al.*'s (2011) book *Nanovation*.

7 In 2012 a political party called the 'Aam Admi Party' was formally launched. In 2015 it won the Delhi legislative assembly elections.

8 A video of the test drive is available at www.youtube.com/watch?v=3sZitve3SUw.

9 The most popular cars in India today are the so-called 'compact sedans' that are larger than the Nano yet still conform to the maximum length limit of 4 metres that qualifies for a lower excise duty category than normal-size sedans. The Tata Zest is Tata Motor's attempt at tapping into this market segment, where most models cost from INR four to eight *lakh*.

10 See www.tatanano.com.

References

Bennett, Ralph Kinney. 2008. The $2,500 Car. *The American*, 11 January. www.aei.org/publication/the-2500-car/.

Birtchnell, Thomas. 2011. Jugaad as Systemic Risk and Disruptive Innovation in India. *Contemporary South Asia* 19 (4): 357–372.

Bourdieu, Pierre. 1984. *Distinction: A Social Critique of the Judgement of Taste*. London: Routledge and Kegan Paul.

Brosius, Christiane. 2010. *India's Middle Class: New Forms of Urban Leisure, Consumption and Prosperity*. New Delhi: Routledge.

Corbridge, S., J. Harriss and C. Jeffrey. 2013. *India Today: Economy, Politics & Society*. Cambridge: Polity.

Corbridge, Stuart and Alpa Shah. 2013. Introduction: The Underbelly of the Indian Boom. *Economy and Society* 42 (3): 335–347.

D'Costa, Anthony P. 2005. *The Long March to Capitalism: Embourgeoisment, Internationalization, and Industrial Transformation in India*. New York: Palgrave Macmillan.

D'Costa, Anthony P., (ed.). 2010a. *A New India? Critical Reflections in the Long Twentieth Century*. London: Anthem Press.

D'Costa, Anthony P. 2010b. What is this 'New' India? An Introduction. In *A New India? Critical Reflections in the Long Twentieth Century*, edited by Anthony P. D'Costa, 1–22. London: Anthem Press.

Dhume, Sadanand. 2011. Unloved at Any Speed. *Foreign Policy*, 7 October. www.foreignpolicy.com/articles/2011/10/07/tata_nano_unloved_at_any_speed.

Donner, Henrike, (ed.). 2011. *Being Middle-class in India: A Way of Life*. London: Routledge.

Edensor, Tim. 2004. Automobility and National Identity: Representation, Geography and Driving Practice. *Theory, Culture & Society* 21 (4/5): 101–120.

Fernandes, Leela. 2000. Nationalizing 'The Global': Media Images, Cultural Politics and the Middle Class in India. *Media, Culture and Society* 22 (5): 611–628.

Fernandes, Leela. 2006. *India's New Middle Class: Democratic Politics in an Era of Economic Reform*. Minneapolis: University of Minnesota Press.

Fernandes, Leela. 2009. The Political Economy of Lifestyle: Consumption, India's New Middle Class and State-led Development. In *The New Middle Classes: Globalizing Lifestyles, Consumerism and Environmental Concern*, edited by Hellmuth Lange and Lars Meier, 219–236. Dordrecht: Springer Netherlands.

Fernandes, Leela and Patrik Heller. 2008. Hegemonic Aspirations: New Middle Class Politics and India's Democracy in Comparative Perspective. In *Whatever Happened to Class? Reflections from South Asia*, edited by Ronald J. Herring and Rina Agarwala, 146–165. Delhi: Daanish Books.

Foulkes, Nicol and Stig Toft Madsen. 2014. Showtime and Exposures in New India: The Revelations of Lucky Farmhouse. In *Women, Gender and Everyday Social Transformation in India*, edited by Kenneth Bo Nielsen and Anne Waldrop, 89–102. London: Anthem Press.

Freiberg, Kevin, Jackie Freiberg and Dain Dunston. 2011. *Nanovation: How a Little Car Can Teach the World to Think Big & Act Bold*. Nashville: Thomas Nelson.

Ghate, Akshima T. and S. Sundar. 2013. Can We Reduce the Rate of Growth of Car Ownership? *Economic and Political Weekly* 48 (23): 32–40.

Guha, Ramchandra. 2007. *India After Gandhi: The History of the World's Largest Democracy*. London: Picador.

Hansen, Arve. 2014. Transportation and Integration: *Doi Moi* and Everyday Life in the Streets of Hanoi. Paper presented at the conference on 'Intra-Asian Connections: Interactions, Flows, Landscapes', the 6th international conference of the Asian Dynamics Initiative, University of Copenhagen, Denmark, 22–24 October.

Hutton, Ray. 2009. Tata Nano: Second Drive. *Car and Driver*, June. www.caranddriver.com/reviews/2009-tata-nano-second-drive.

Jeffrey, Craig and Stephen Young. 2014. Jugād: Youth and Enterprise in India. *Annals of the Association of American Geographers* 104 (1): 182–195.

Kartikey, Kumar. 2015. Is it the End of the Road for Tata Nano? *Zeenews*, 29 January. http://zeenews.india.com/business/automobiles/auto-news/is-it-the-end-of-the-road-for-tata-nano_117389.html.

Kaur, Ravinder. 2012. Nation's Two Bodies: Rethinking the Idea of 'New' India and Its Other. *Third World Quarterly* 33 (4): 603–621.

Kaur, Ravinder. 2015. Post-exotic India: On Remixed Histories and Smart Images. *Identities: Global Studies in Culture and Power*. Doi: 10.1080/1070289X.2015.1034134.

Kaur, Ravinder and Thomas Blom Hansen. 2015. Aesthetics of Arrival: Spectacle, Capital, Novelty in Post-reform India. *Identities: Global Studies in Culture and Power*. Doi: 10.1080/1070289X.2015.1034135.

Kohli, Atul. 2012. *Poverty Amid Plenty in the New India*. Cambridge: Cambridge University Press.

Krishna, Anirudh and Devendra Bajpai. 2015. Layers in Globalising Society and the New Middle Class in India. *Economic and Political Weekly* 50 (5): 69–77.

Kurien, C. T. 1994. *Global Capitalism and the Indian Economy*. New Delhi: Orient Longman.

Mazzarella, William. 2003. *Shovelling Smoke: Advertising and Globalization in Contemporary India*. Durham: Duke University Press.

Mazumdar, Surajit. 2012. Big Business and Economic Nationalism in India. In *Globalization and Economic Nationalism in Asia*, edited by Anthony P. D'Costa, 59–83. Oxford: Oxford University Press.

McLain, Sean. 2013. Why the World's Cheapest Car Flopped. *The Wall Street Journal*, 14 October. http://online.wsj.com/news/articles/SB10001424052702304520704579125312679104596.

Meredith, Robyn. 2007. The Next People's Car. *Forbes*, 16 April. www.forbes.com/free_forbes/2007/0416/070.html.

Nielsen, Kenneth Bo. 2010. Contesting India's Development? Industrialisation, Land Acquisition and Protest in West Bengal. *Forum for Development Studies* 37 (2): 145–170.

Noronha, Christabelle. 2008. The Making of the Nano. www.tata.com/aboutus/articles-inside/Sd75BUBmzSM=/TLYVr3YPkMU.

Philip, Siddharth. 2013. Tata's Nano, the World's Cheapest Car, Is Sputtering. *Businessweek*, 11 April. www.businessweek.com/articles/2013-04-11/tatas-nano-the-worlds-cheapest-car-is-sputtering.

Rediff.com. 2004. Rs 1-Lakh Car Under Development: Tata. 15 January. www.rediff.com/money/2004/jan/15auto2.htm.

Rowley, Ian and Mehul Srivastava. 2008. World's Cheapest Car gets More Expensive: The Nano Becomes a Costly Compromise for Carmaker Tata. *Der Spiegel*, 29 July. www.spiegel.de/international/business/world-s-cheapest-car-gets-more-expensive-the-nano-becomes-a-costly-promise-for-carmaker-tata-a-568688.html.

Roy, Ananya. 2011. The Blockade of a World-Class City: Dialectical Images of Indian Urbanism. In *Worlding Cities: Asian Experiments and the Art of Being Global*, edited by Ananya Roy and Aihwa Ong, 259–278. Basingstoke: Blackwell.

Saavala, Minna. 2010. *Middle-Class Moralities: Everyday Struggles over Belonging and Prestige in India*. Delhi: Orient Blackswan.

Sardar, Ziauddin. 2002. The Ambassador from India. In *Autopia: Cars and Culture*, edited by Joe Kerr and Peter Wollen, 209–218. London: Reaktion Books.

Sheller, Mimi. 2004. Automotive Emotions: Feeling the Car. *Theory, Culture & Society* 21 (4/5): 221–242.

Tata Motors Media Centre. 2014. Tata Motors launches the New Nano Twist. http://mediacentre.tatamotors.com/PressReleaseDetails.aspx?pid=822&val=2014%20-%20.VE9cTXbKyfC#.VE-E_HbKyfA.

Tetzlaff, Stefan. 2013. Motorisierung: Geschichte, Gegenwart und Zukunft Indiens [India on Wheels: Past, Present, and Future]. *Masala: Newsletter Virtual Library South Asia* 3.

The Economic Times. 2004. Advani Asks Auto Industry to Produce sub-Rs-1-Lakh Car. 15 January. http://articles.economictimes.indiatimes.com/2004-01-15/news/27401271_1_lakh-car-minister-l-k-advani-auto-expo.

The Economist. 2011. Stuck in Low Gear. 20 August. www.economist.com/node/21526374.

Tiwari, Prateeksha M. 2009. *Pride of the Nation: Ratan Tata*. New Delhi: Diamond Books.

Upadhya, Carol. 2011. Software and the 'New' Middle Class in the 'New India'. In *Elite and Everyman: The Cultural Politics of the Indian Middle Classes*, edited by Amita Baviskar and Raka Ray, 167–193. New Delhi: Routledge.

Veblen, Thorstein. 1899. *The Theory of the Leisure Class: An Economic Study of Institutions*. New York: Macmillan.

Wells, Peter. 2010. The Tata Nano, the Global 'Value' Segment and the Implications for the Traditional Automotive Industry Regions. *Cambridge Journal of Regions, Economy and Society* 3 (3): 443–457.

Wilhite, Harold. 2008. *Consumption and the Transformation of Everyday Life: A View from South India*. Hampshire: Palgrave Macmillan.

Index

Page numbers in *italics* denote tables, those in **bold** denote figures.

Taylor & Francis eBooks

Helping you to choose the right eBooks for your Library

Add Routledge titles to your library's digital collection today. Taylor and Francis ebooks contains over 50,000 titles in the Humanities, Social Sciences, Behavioural Sciences, Built Environment and Law.

Choose from a range of subject packages or create your own!

Benefits for you

» Free MARC records
» COUNTER-compliant usage statistics
» Flexible purchase and pricing options
» All titles DRM-free.

Benefits for your user

» Off-site, anytime access via Athens or referring URL
» Print or copy pages or chapters
» Full content search
» Bookmark, highlight and annotate text
» Access to thousands of pages of quality research at the click of a button.

REQUEST YOUR **FREE** INSTITUTIONAL TRIAL TODAY

Free Trials Available
We offer free trials to qualifying academic, corporate and government customers.

eCollections – Choose from over 30 subject eCollections, including:

Archaeology	Language Learning
Architecture	Law
Asian Studies	Literature
Business & Management	Media & Communication
Classical Studies	Middle East Studies
Construction	Music
Creative & Media Arts	Philosophy
Criminology & Criminal Justice	Planning
Economics	Politics
Education	Psychology & Mental Health
Energy	Religion
Engineering	Security
English Language & Linguistics	Social Work
Environment & Sustainability	Sociology
Geography	Sport
Health Studies	Theatre & Performance
History	Tourism, Hospitality & Events

For more information, pricing enquiries or to order a free trial, please contact your local sales team:
www.tandfebooks.com/page/sales

Routledge
Taylor & Francis Group

The home of
Routledge books

www.tandfebooks.com